THE VISION OF MORMONISM

THE VISION OF MORMONISM

PRESSING THE BOUNDARIES OF CHRISTIANITY

Robert L. Millet

PARAGON HOUSE
St. Paul, Minnesota

VISIONS OF REALITY
A Series on Religions as Worldviews

Series Editor: Roger Corless, Duke University, Emeritus

A common assumption behind many surveys of religions is that there is something called "religion" which is a uniquely classifiable phenomenon and which may be dealt with and written about according to recognized and agreed upon subdivisions. Systems identified as religions are then fitted into a prescribed format without considering whether the format is suited to the particular system under consideration.

This series is motivated by the awareness that, rather than there being something called "religion," there are many *religions,* and the more they are studied, the more each one manifests itself as equally profound, nontrivial, and adequate unto itself. Each volume will be an attempt to take each religion on its own terms. Comparison may be made with other religious traditions, but there will be no attempt to impose a single methodology in order to reduce the plurality to one basic scheme.

Published Volumes in the Visions of Reality Series:

THE VISION OF BUDDHISM
Roger Corless

THE VISION OF ISLAM
Sachiko Murata and William Chittick

THE VISION OF JUDAISM
Dan Cohn-Sherbok

THE VISION OF MORMONISM
Robert Millet

Truth is "Mormonism," God is the author of it. He is our shield. It is by Him we received our birth. It was by His voice that we were called to a dispensation of His Gospel in the beginning of the fullness of times. It was by Him we received the Book of Mormon; and it is by Him that we remain unto this day; and by Him we shall remain.... And in His Almighty name we are determined to endure tribulation as good soldiers unto the end.

—*Joseph Smith*

I see a wonderful future in a very uncertain world. If we will cling to our values, if we will build on our inheritance, if we will walk in obedience before the Lord, if we will simply live the gospel, we will be blessed in a magnificent and wonderful way. We will be looked upon as a peculiar people who have found the key to a peculiar happiness.

—*Gordon B. Hinckley*

Published in the United States by

Paragon House

1925 Oakcrest Avenue

St. Paul, MN 55113

Cover image by Gordon L. Anderson

Library of Congress Cataloging-in-Publication Data

Millet, Robert L.
  The vision of Mormonism : pressing the boundaries of Christianity / by
Robert L. Millet.
     p. cm. -- (Visions of reality)
  Summary: "Introduces the core beliefs and practices of the twenty-first
century Church of Jesus Christ of Latter-day Saints church and its
adherents, the Mormons"--Provided by publisher.
  Includes bibliographical references.
  ISBN 978-1-55778-868-9 (pbk. : alk. paper)
  1. Church of Jesus Christ of Latter-day Saints--Doctrines. 2. Mormon
Church--Doctrines. I. Title.
  BX8635.3.M558 2007
  289.3'32--dc22
                          2007028382

Manufactured in the United States of America

The paper used in this publication meets the minimum requirements of American
National Standard for Information Sciences—Permanence of Paper for Printed Library
Materials, ANSIZ39.48-1984.

10 9 8 7 6 5 4 3 2 1

For current information about all releases from Paragon House,
visit the web site at http://www.paragonhouse.com

CONTENTS

FOREWORD

WHAT HAPPENS TO A Latter-day Saint when he engages in deep, candid discussions with committed, open, friendly Christians, when he takes seriously the criticisms and misunderstandings others have of the LDS faith? This book answers that question. For years Bob Millet has been meeting with religious scholars and ministers to explore the similarities and differences between their faith and ours. What began as an effort at bridge-building, aimed at greater tolerance and understanding, ended up in Millet reexamining—and appreciating—Mormonism from a new perspective.

The same thing can happen when any of us encounter people from another culture or move into a new environment. We discover things in our religion we had not noticed before. We see new depths and learn to value doctrines we had overlooked. A large part of gospel learning consists in this discovery of new meanings and applications coming out of new experiences.

Millet describes his reexamination of his faith as a personal journey of discovery. He gives us the gospel but from his perspective after his intensive exchanges with persons of other faiths. We hear words not normally used in Mormon talk, words like "grace" and "transformation" and "the cross" and "saved." The overall effect is to reinforce trends in the Church evident for a number of decades. The doctrine of grace, for example, has been undergoing rehabilitation in recent years, and here Millet gives a thorough airing to its meaning for him. A chapter entitled "A Wretch Like Me" discusses a doctrine Latter-day Saints certainly believe in but don't often highlight. Bob tells us what it means to him.

Overall the book reinforces the claim, contested by many but obvious to Latter-day Saints, that we are Christian—not traditional

Christian, not Nicene Christian, but Christian nonetheless. Christ is at the center of our theology and everyday conduct.

Bob Millet tells us exactly what this means in one man's life.

Richard Lyman Bushman
Gouverneur Morris Professor of History Emeritus
Columbia University

Introduction

Mere Followers of Christ

I can still recall vividly the first dance I attended at the Catholic Youth Organization (CYO) with my friend Bill when we were both about thirteen years of age. The dance was held in a large gymnasium adjacent to the Sacred Heart Church in Baton Rouge, Louisiana. I really do not remember how many people were in attendance, but at the time it seemed like tens of thousands. What I do remember is that the "record hop," as they called it then, was open to the public and that you could drink all the Cokes you wanted. I seemed to realize that just about everyone there was a Roman Catholic, and I found myself thinking how different it would be if I were a Catholic among so many other people who felt about life basically as I did. In other words, it would have been different to be in the majority.

When I was a junior in high school, my friend Don invited me to a church social that was sponsored by the Istrouma Baptist Church in Baton Rouge. There I saw some of the best athletes in the city as well as some of the most attractive girls in the area. All the folks there seemed to be having a great time and, once again, I wondered what it would be like to be a Baptist and to know for the most part that everyone there held religious beliefs in common with me. I realized too just what a minority I was when I thought about the fact that at my own smaller high school, Baker High School, the Baptist influence was so strong in the town at the time that we were forbidden from holding school dances on the campus; our senior prom, for example, was held in a large assembly hall some miles from our town.

Only a few years ago, one of my dear friends, a Baptist pastor, encountered a bit of a difficulty with his daughter Indiana in her elementary school in a small town in Utah. A surprising number of children in her class (most all of whom were Latter-day Saints) had come to her at one time or another, pointed to her cross necklace, and indicated their displeasure. "That cross is bad," one of the children had said. Another remarked: "My mom and dad said that people shouldn't wear crosses." Having received the necklace from a loved one, Indiana felt a desire to wear the cross for two reasons—as an expression of appreciation for a lovely gift and as a sign that she was a Christian, a follower of Jesus. Because the barbs and criticisms continued over time, my friend Greg found it necessary to speak with the principal at the school, who invited him to prepare a small message for their local school newsletter. Greg then wrote a brief message about the importance of teaching our children to appreciate differences, to be tolerant of those not quite like us, and to treat other people as we would want to be treated. Now frankly, as a Latter-day Saint, I'm blown away by this last episode, especially since I cannot imagine any sane or balanced LDS parent teaching their child that there's something wrong with wearing a cross. But the occurrence did help me to see the other side of the story: What happens when one is in the majority? How do we treat people who speak or believe or act differently? Am I a different person when I am with my own kind than I am with persons of other religious persuasions? If so, why?

In spite of all we try to do to build the moral character and personal confidence of our children and grandchildren, what people think about them and say about them are impactful. Nobody likes to be the target of persecution. Of attacks. Of criticism. Or of exclusion. I think I have a pretty decent set of values and am fairly well adjusted socially; for the most part, my feelings of self-confidence are such that I am able to take criticism without much trauma. But I would be a liar if I expressed anything other than the fact that I like to be liked; I would prefer to be on people's "accepted" list rather than on their "rejected" or "snubbed" list.

Although the passing of years tends to result in the passing away of many things I once experienced, my memories of the past, especially religious memories, are fairly intact. I have many happy memories, but I also have a few that are not so happy. In the fall of 1957, my family and I moved to a town in southern Louisiana that had a very high concentration of Roman Catholics. Perhaps one quick episode will give you a feeling for how high that concentration was. My sixth-grade teacher, a Mrs. Templet, began the class period on the first day by asking, "Now, is there anyone in this room who is not a Roman Catholic?" There was a slight pause, and then she asked with a little more force: "Now I need to know this for sure. Answer me. Is there anyone here who is not Catholic?" It's hard now to put into words what I felt at that moment. I was a Mormon, a Latter-day Saint, a member of a religious group that was known by precious few people in Louisiana. I wanted to keep my hand down, to let this moment pass, to pretend that I was just like everyone else in class. But I couldn't. I remember feeling as though God would be utterly displeased with me, that I was forsaking the faith, that I was some sort of junior traitor to the cause if I should remain quiet. More time passed.

Across the room I saw a young man with blond hair but with a rather pale complexion raise his hand ever so timidly. Mrs. Templet responded strongly: "What are you?" He stuttered an answer: "I'm ... a Baptist." Now the pressure was really on. I had no reason to remain quiet, inasmuch as some other kid had broken the silence, broken the curse, and showed his courage as a member of a minority. I had to do something. My hand gradually went up, Mrs. Templet stared at me sternly (or so it seemed), and she inquired: "And you, what are you?" Just at the last second, just at the point at which I was planning to be heroic and noble and bold, my faith failed and I uttered: "Uh ... I'm a Baptist, too." Now don't get me wrong: I have hundreds of wonderful Baptist friends and feel a great sense of love and admiration for them. But I wasn't really a Baptist and I knew it. That's a lot of pressure for an eleven-year-old, at least enough to cause me to cave in. Truly there's nothing wrong with stating that you're a Baptist, unless of course you happen to be a Latter-day Saint.

I felt ashamed, deflated, defeated, and downright embarrassed before God. Mormons are a missionary-minded lot, and I had fumbled the ball in a major way. My little gospel light was not shining! I take the time to relate this story not just because it serves some cathartic purpose (although it does, to a certain extent) but to demonstrate that it's not easy to stand alone, especially when it comes to religious beliefs and values. While I grew up in the LDS faith and as the years passed, I gained a deeper commitment to my unusual way of life, but that doesn't mean that the pressure and the feelings of loneliness went away. I remember as a high schooler that our family was asked to leave our nice large ward (a local congregation) in Baton Rouge and attend a small branch (too few members to constitute an actual ward) in order to help strengthen that small gathering. We had no church building and at the time the general church in Salt Lake City required that we raise a certain percentage of the money to erect a chapel. Consequently, the only place we were able to acquire as a meeting house was the girls' gymnasium at the local high school.

Now by this point in time a few people here and there knew what Mormons were, and I really didn't have many people insulting me or making unkind remarks about my faith very often. What I did have, unfortunately, were a number of people asking me where our church building was. I always gulped and spoke in soft tones when I answered, "We meet in the girls' gym." They would inevitably respond "You meet where?" And I would repeat it: "We meet in the girls' gym." Then there would follow a rather consistent but mystified look and a shocking sound of "Oh."

Don't get me wrong: I wasn't always the good guy, the persecuted one, for I had my share of pointing the finger at others. There was a young woman in our class who was a very devout Jehovah's Witness. She was an extremely friendly and lovely person and happened also to be one of the very brightest young people in our class. But because she did not choose to stand and cite the Pledge of Allegiance with our class each morning, my friends and I would often make snide remarks or send offending notes to the effect that she was un-American, that she needed to move back to Russia. She was a very strong young woman who took her faith very seriously, but I can imagine that such un-Christian actions by us proved to be extremely painful. I have asked God many times to forgive me for such things. Now more than ever I sense how thoroughly inappropriate and how patently unbecoming for a professing Christian such behavior was. I am ashamed for being guilty of being a religious bigot, one who didn't have enough decency to allow someone to believe differently.

One would think that with the proliferation of Christian faiths in the last forty years, there would be a larger outpouring of love and acceptance and collegiality, even toward those who believe somewhat differently. Well, to be sure, a spirit of pluralism has gripped our land to the extent that tolerance has become the overriding virtue in life: For some it seems that to be intolerant is far more grievous a crime than to be guilty of murder. In other words, pluralism run amok can lead to what we see in our present world only so clearly—a form of moral and ethical relativism that refuses to speak of absolutes or to agree on time-honored values and principles. What matters is not what is, but what you feel or what you think. I suppose in the midst of this pluralism we should not be surprised that certain religious groups should feel an overpowering need to stand up, speak out, and draw lines in the sand to prevent further doctrinal and behavioral drift. Likewise, it is not surprising that in the midst of a greater proliferation of Christian faiths there has grown up a stronger sense of exclusion—a greater stress on creedal formulations, precise theology, specific wording—all in an effort to separate true believers from the heretics. Now I applaud any and all efforts to contend earnestly for the faith, but I'm saddened with how often strict doctrinal statements and pronouncements or a proliferation of creeds have proven to serve as badges of belonging and as devices that divide.

As I mentioned above, by the time I reached high school I had very few religious discussions with my friends and cannot even remember anyone openly attacking the Mormon faith. And of course during the 1960s it didn't much matter who you were or what you believed, for all things were relative since "all you need is love." It was not until I had been on a full-time mission to the Eastern states in the late 1960s that I first encountered what might be called anti-Mormon propaganda. My missionary companion and I had begun to tract in an area (to knock on each door and request an audience with the members of the family) in New Jersey and discovered that the local ministers, who must have heard that we were coming into the area, prepared the members of their congregations by distributing thousands of anti-Mormon pamphlets.

My first reaction to the pamphlets was one of total shock: I couldn't understand why anybody would want to take the time or spend the money to prepare thousands of tracts that would attempt to put down my religion. I knew there were some things about our own belief that were not particularly complimentary of other's beliefs (see my discussion of "only true church" in chapter 20), but I knew that the LDS Church was not in the business of producing anti-Catholic, anti-Jewish, or anti-Protestant materials to point up the errors or inadequacies of those particular faiths. After spending many hours with my companion attempting to provide answers for our critics, the second reaction I had was one of stark surprise that those doing the criticizing were not really interested in our response to the criticism. In other words, it didn't seem to matter that we really could answer most of their questions.

Having been a Latter-day Saint all my life and having been an employee of The Church of Jesus Christ of Latter-day Saints for over thirty years, I can honestly say that the mantra of "Mormons aren't Christian" is a relatively recent phenomenon. Yes, we have had critics since Joseph Smith announced his first vision and since the publication of the Book of Mormon in late March 1830. But I really did not encounter the notion that Latter-day Saints are not Christian until about two decades ago. Again, my initial reaction was one of shock and total surprise; while having had many religious conversations through the years and thus many differences with friends, no one had been so bold or hurtful to suggest that I wasn't even a Christian. A later reaction toward that particular mantra was one of "that's their problem," a kind of "if they don't believe I'm a true follower of Jesus, they're the ones that are messed up, not me."

To some extent, I maintained this rather cool and unfazed attitude toward the "Mormons aren't Christian" claim until fairly recently. During the last decade, and as I've spent a great deal of my time working closely with persons of other faiths and intimately involved in interfaith dialogue, I have become more and more concerned that the idea that "Mormons aren't Christians" is far more problematic than I had earlier supposed. I'm not too worried about what the academic or Church leaders may mean by the slogan; I presume they mean that Latter-day Saints are not within the line of historic Christian churches, are neither

Protestant nor Catholic, do not accept the traditional doctrine of the Trinity and the decisions of post–New Testament church councils, and that our belief in additional scripture excludes us from the traditional category of Christian.

What worries me, however, is what the man on the street or the woman in the pew understands (or misunderstands) when they hear that Latter-day Saints are not Christian. Does the layman believe that Latter-day Saints do not believe in the divinity of Jesus Christ, in his reality, his divine birth, or his miraculous dealings with humanity? Do people wonder whether Latter-day Saints believe and trust in Christ's substitutionary atonement and in his suffering and death for humankind? Do people wonder whether Mormons believe in the literal bodily resurrection of Jesus of Nazareth or whether we think he will come again in glory, to reign as King of kings and Lord of lords? In other words, if a person indicates to me that I'm not a Christian because I do not fit certain predetermined criteria that they have established, then I understand where they are coming from, even if I tend to disagree. If, on the other hand, to state that "Mormons are not Christian" is to say that we are not believers in the Christ of the New Testament, the Messiah prophesied by the ancients, and the Redeemer declared by the apostles, then I am extremely unsettled, for such is both a misunderstanding and a misrepresentation.

It was Jesus himself who counseled (or even commanded) that true followers were to "judge not" (Matthew 7:1). Now I'm fully aware that this passage of scripture has taken on all kinds of meanings in a world that suffers from the shifting sands of secularity. Of course we are to make judgments, every day of our lives. We must decide if one course is more important than another, if our association with this person is either beneficial or degrading, and whether this particular proposition is true or false. In short, we are to judge righteous judgment in that we are to use our heads and our hearts and the inspiration of the Holy Spirit to make intermediate judgments, choices, decisions, and discriminations that we face day by day. It seems to me that what Jesus counsels against is making final judgments—stating firmly and forthrightly that this or that person will go to hell (or to heaven), that this man or woman is forevermore lost (or saved), for such statements are beyond our capacity to make, inasmuch as we are lacking in data and detail. We cannot read another person's mind or fully discern another person's heart. We really cannot know by appearance alone whether one has received Jesus Christ as Lord and Savior, whether one has given his or her life to Him, whether one has submitted and surrendered their lives to the cause of Christianity.

It was J. B. Phillips who wrote: "The Roman Catholic who asserts positively that ordination in the Anglican Church is 'invalid,' and that no 'grace' is receivable through the Anglican sacraments, is plainly worshipping a God who is a Roman Catholic, and who operates reluctantly if at all, through non-Roman channels. The ultra-low churchman on the other hand must admit, if he is honest, that the god whom he worships disapproves most strongly of vestments, incense, and candles on the altar. The tragedy of these examples, which could be reproduced *ad nauseam* any day of the week, is not difference of opinion, which will probably be with us until the Day of Judgment, but the outrageous folly and damnable sin of trying to regard God as the Party Leader of a particular point of view." Phillips added: "No denomination has a monopoly on God's grace, and none has an exclusive recipe for producing Christian character."[1]

Forgive my naivete, but a Christian is, from my perspective, one who acknowledges their fallen state and their need for redemption; one who recognizes that the only source of that redemption is through the person and power of Jesus of Nazareth, the Messiah, the Savior; one who receives the proffered gift of atonement by covenant with Christ, seeks for, and obtains a remission of sins and a new heart; and one who has devoted themselves to evidencing their love and overwhelming appreciation for His magnificent sacrificial gift through demonstrating Christian discipleship, particularly in the way that we treat one another. John Stackhouse has written that "authentic Christianity entails a personal—we could now say 'experiential'—experience and appropriation of the Christian faith. More than this,… Christians fundamentally are not to be identified as those who practice the Christian religion per se but as those who have spiritually met Jesus Christ and have gratefully entered into a covenant of love with him."[2]

People of our day may debate whether Jesus of Nazareth was

divinely born, whether He performed miracles, whether He suffered and bled and died for our sins, or whether He rose from the dead. No one seems to doubt one aspect of Jesus' ministry—namely, Jesus loved people. He was more than willing to be inconvenienced. Over and over again we see His eagerness to bless, to lift, to lighten, and to liberate. Over and over we see His compassion manifest in the way He treated people, particularly those who were more unpopular. I am haunted by the words of Philip Yancey. He noted that "the more unsavory the characters, the more at ease they seem to feel around Jesus. People like these found Jesus appealing: a Samaritan social outcast, a military officer of the tyrant Herod, a quisling tax collector, a recent hostess to seven demons.

"In contrast, Jesus got a chilly response from more respectable types. Pious Pharisees thought him uncouth and worldly. A rich young ruler walked away shaking his head, and even the open-minded Nicodemus sought a meeting under the cover of darkness.

"Somehow we have created a community of respectability in the church," Yancey warned. "The down-and-out, who flocked to Jesus when he lived on earth, no longer feel welcome. How did Jesus, the only perfect person in history, manage to attract the notoriously imperfect? And what keeps us from following in his steps today?"[3]

No one loves and cherishes the study of doctrine more than I do. I have spent my professional life reading scripture, digesting secondary literature, attending conferences, and writing articles and books about doctrine. I believe wholeheartedly in the power of the word and thus in the power of doctrine. As one Latter-day Saint Church leader pointed out, "True doctrine, understood, changes attitudes and behaviors. The study of the doctrines of the gospel will improve behavior quicker than a study of behavior will improve behavior."[4] And yet it seems patently clear to me that whether one's doctrine was correct or one's theological leanings were proper were matters that were at least secondary to the man we call Jesus Christ. Jesus was deeply offended by self-righteousness, put off by pomposity, and verbally condemned those who focused more on externals than on the "weightier matters of the law," on things that really mattered. To be sure, Jesus loved and cherished the truth and taught it; he could do no other, for he *was* the

Truth (John 14:6). And yet he tended not to exclude but rather to draw his circle of inclusion far larger than the religious establishment of his day chose to do.

While Christians of various sorts must do their best to keep the doctrine of Christ pure and to hold tenaciously to the standards and foundational principles of Christianity, the cause of faith is hardly served by drawing more and darker lines of division, setting up more stakes of separation, or anxiously anathamatizing those who are different in some way. It was Richard John Neuhaus, a prominent Roman Catholic figure, who wisely observed that surely no person possessed of the Spirit of Christ would find delight or perverse pleasure in condemning or consigning another to hell. He added that while he supposed he had to believe in hell (a scriptural concept), we could always hope that hell would be empty![5] The archbishop of Canterbury, Rowan Williams, has observed that "Conversation may or may not lead to conversion in the sense of one party adopting the viewpoint of the other, and if we only conversed when that was our aim, we should experience nothing but very tense and polarized communication in this world." The fact is, "conversation assumes that I shall in some degree change because of the other—not by becoming the same, but simply by entering a larger world."[6]

"If it has been demonstrated that I have been willing to die for a 'Mormon,'" Joseph Smith taught, "I am bold to declare before Heaven that I am just as ready to die in defending the rights of a Presbyterian, a Baptist, or a good man of any other denomination; for the same principle which would trample upon the rights of the Latter-day Saints would trample upon the rights of the Roman Catholics, or of any other denomination who may be unpopular and too weak to defend themselves."[7] "If I esteem mankind to be in error," Joseph explained, "shall I bear them down? No. I will lift them up, and in their own way, too, if I cannot persuade them my way is better; and I will not seek to compel any man to believe as I do, only by the force of reasoning, for truth will cut its own way. Do you believe in Jesus Christ and the Gospel of salvation which he revealed? So do I. Christians should cease wrangling and contending with each other, and cultivate the principles of union and friendship in their midst."[8]

I am fully persuaded that there is no such thing (at least among us mortals) as a completely objective perspective and that no person can write from that lofty literary pedestal we refer to as an objective point of view. We are who we are and we see things, not necessarily as they are, but rather as *we are*. Now I'm not arguing here for a rabid relativism but rather am acknowledging that I am who I am and thus see things and write things accordingly. This book is about Mormonism, about some fundamental beliefs and practices of The Church of Jesus Christ of Latter-day Saints. I am a Mormon. I am a practicing Mormon, a believing Latter-day Saint. While I grew up in a part of the country where Mormons were few and far between, I nevertheless grew up in the LDS faith. I have been employed for over thirty years as a religious educator, for the last quarter century at the Church's flagship academic institution, Brigham Young University. All of this is to say that I bring some things to the writing of this book that a person of another faith would be unable to bring. There are some things that can be understood and explained only from within.

When I read books by Avery Cardinal Dulles or Father Richard John Neuhaus, I presume that theirs will be a Roman Catholic perspective, in fact, a believing Catholic perspective. When I read Eli Wiesel or Chaim Potok or Jacob Neusner, I expect to receive insights that have been processed through a thoroughly Jewish mind. And when I read John Stott or J. I. Packer or Philip Yancey or Billy Graham, I am neither surprised nor bothered by the fact that the data put forward and the conclusions drawn come from Evangelical Christian souls. And so, again, I am a Latter-day Saint reflecting on Latter-day Saint topics—more specifically, an LDS slant on religious (usually Christian) topics. At the same time, my intent as a writer is to clarify, to fill in the gaps, and, where necessary, to disabuse readers of misconceptions. If it seems at times as if I am being rather forceful in making my point, then just excuse my poor effort to explain; I have no desire to proselytize or convert, rather to inform and, where necessary, set the record straight.

I have read C. S. Lewis's master work *Mere Christianity* many times. In preparation for the writing of this book, I re-read it and focused on what Lewis believed to be "mere" Christianity. In its purest sense, *mere* means undiluted, finished, sole, sheer, and only what it is said to be. Lewis never claimed to be a theologian, something that many trained theologians are quick to point out. But he did deal with profound theological concepts in such a way that the man on the street could understand and apply them to daily living. In 1998 a colleague and I attended a theological conference at Wheaton College on the life and work of C. S. Lewis. The conference was most enjoyable, but what I appreciated most was the title of the conference, a phrase that aptly described the work of Lewis himself: Returning Theology to the Masses. In that sense I noted with much interest as I read his work what Lewis did not spend time upon, what academic jargon he did not employ, and what fine doctrinal distinctions he did not draw. Being Christian was not a complicated matter to Lewis, nor is it to me. The doctrinal foundation of Christianity was not something that needed to be erected by academicians alone but rather something that could and should be accessible as well to the unschooled and the untutored.

While Mormonism has been around since only 1830, the doctrines and teachings and practices have grown remarkably, such that it becomes difficult to capsulize it all in one volume. But that's what I would like to try to do in this book: to set forth clearly and understandably what Latter-day Saints really believe and what they do not. This is not an academic exercise per se, although I confess to being an academician. Rather, I would like where possible to keep the tone of the book light and conversational, willing to address hard issues but to do so in a nondefensive, simple, and plain manner. As is true with any religious organization, there is much about the faith that is rumor, urban legend, or apocryphal. The reader may disagree here and there, but that's part of the learning process; we can disagree, but let's at least disagree on the right stuff. Archbishop Fulton Sheen once wrote: "There are not over a hundred people in the United States who hate the Roman Catholic Church; there are millions, however, who hate what they wrongly believe to be the Catholic Church."[9] And so it is with the Mormon faith. My intent is not to convert or even persuade but to inform—to correct misunderstandings where they exist, to shed a bit of light where darkness or uncertainty prevail, and to open the door a little wider for mutual understanding and meaningful conversation.

ENDNOTES

1. Phillips, *Your God Is Too Small*, 38–39.

2. Stackhouse, *Evangelical Landscapes: Facing Critical Issues of the Day* (Grand Rapids, MI: Baker Books, 2002), 105–106.

3. Yancey, *The Jesus I Never Knew*, 147–48.

4. Boyd K. Packer, Conference Report, October 1986, 20; cited hereafter as CR.

5. Neuhaus, *Death on a Friday Afternoon*, 61, 143.

6. Williams, *Christ on Trial*, 64–65.

7. *Teachings of the Prophet Joseph Smith*, sel. Joseph Fielding Smith (Salt Lake City: Deseret Book, 1976), 313; cited hereafter as *TPJS*.

8. *TPJS,* 313–14.

9. Cited in Scott and Kimberly Hahn, *Rome Sweet Home*, xi.

ONE

Eternal Being

WHERE DID I COME from? Why am I here? Where am I going? All three questions deal with meaning, with purpose in life. How we choose to answer or ignore them will determine largely how we live our lives. Latter-day Saints do not claim to have all the answers to life's puzzles, but they do claim to have some. This chapter will focus on the LDS view of life before. Subsequent chapters will address the other two questions.

There's a very real sense in which Mormonism may be described as an outworking of what might be called "Joseph Smith's Eternalism." Eternalism is a concept, a system of belief, a plan whereby finite, mortal men and women seek to engage matters that are infinite and eternal. As you know, there is a real challenge associated with speaking of and comprehending "forever language." While the followers of Jesus claim that the immortality of the soul comes through His death and resurrection, Christians are not the only ones who believe that life will continue, will go on long after we breathe our last breath on earth. In other words, life doesn't cease when our bodily organs stop functioning; something within us—call it a soul or a spirit, if you will—continues to think and feel and interact and be. Forever.

Joseph Smith stepped forward and suggested that this eternal thing works in both directions,[1] that life as we know it did not originate with our mortal birth, that at the time of our conception or our first breath life did not suddenly spring into existence. Further, while Joseph believed in and taught of God's infinity and of his omnipo-

1

tence, he boldly declared that God did not "create" that spirit in the sense of bringing it into existence *ex nihilo*, out of nothing. Rather, it has always lived. For that matter, the Mormon Prophet declared that when it came to the creation of this earth, God drew upon element and matter and "organized" chaotic disorder into order.

Others outside the LDS faith have sensed that there is more to life than living and dying, more to what we do here than meets the physical eye. Many have perceived that this stage of our journey is but a part of a larger drama. William Wordsworth penned the following:

> Our birth is but a sleep and a forgetting:
> The Soul that rises with us, our life's Star,
> Hath had elsewhere its setting,
> And cometh from afar:
> Not in entire forgetfulness,
> And not in utter nakedness,
> But trailing clouds of glory do we come
> From God, who is our home:
> Heaven lies about us in our infancy![2]

Marcel Proust, the influential French novelist, wrote: "Everything in our life happens as though we entered upon it with a load of obligations contracted in a previous existence... obligations whose sanction is not of this present life, [that] seem to belong to a different world, founded on kindness, scruples, sacrifice, a world entirely different from this one, a world whence we emerge to be born on this earth, before returning thither."[3]

Mormons believe that men and women are literally the spirit sons and daughters of God, that we lived in a premortal existence before birth, that we grew and expanded in that "first estate" (Jude 1:6), all in preparation for this "second estate." In that world men and women were separate and distinct spirit personages, had consciousness, volition, maleness and femaleness, and moral agency. They developed and matured according to their adherence to God's eternal law, and in spite of the fact that they walked and talked with God, it was necessary for them to exercise faith in God's plan for the ultimate salvation of his children. The Latter-day Saints believe God is literally the Father of their spirits (see Numbers 16:22; 27:16; Hebrews 12:9), that they inherit from him the seeds of divine capacities and attributes, albeit in embryonic form.

An official LDS doctrinal proclamation affirms: "The Church of Jesus Christ of Latter-day Saints, basing its belief on divine revelation, ancient and modern, proclaims man to be the direct and lineal off-spring of Deity.... By His almighty power He organized the earth, and all that it contains, from spirit and element, which exist co-eternally with Himself.... Man is the child of God, formed in the divine image and endowed with divine attributes." Further: "The doctrine of the pre-existence—revealed so plainly, particularly in latter days, pours a wonderful flood of light upon the otherwise mysterious problem of man's origin.... It teaches that all men existed in the spirit before any man existed in the flesh, and that all who have inhabited the earth since Adam have taken bodies and become souls in like manner."[4]

In the long expanse of time before we were born into mortality, the spirit sons and daughters of God developed talents, strengths, and capacities. In a sense, no two persons remained alike.[5] Mormons teach that the greatest in the family of God was Jehovah, who eventually took a body and became Jesus of Nazareth, the Redeemer of human-kind. Jehovah was the firstborn of the Father, meaning the firstborn spirit child, the heir, the one entitled to the divine birthright. Jehovah was the advocate for God the Father's plan of salvation, the one who volunteered in that premortal existence to put into effect the terms and conditions of that divine plan and, more specifically, to suffer and die and rise again as Savior. Another spirit child of God offered to save mankind by an alternative plan. Lucifer stepped forward and said: "Behold, here am I, send me, I will be thy son, and I will redeem all mankind, that one soul shall not be lost, and surely I will do it; where-fore give me thine honor."

"But, behold, my Beloved Son, which was my Beloved and Chosen from the beginning, said unto me—Father, thy will be done, and the glory be thine forever.

"Wherefore, because that Satan rebelled against me, and sought to destroy the agency of man, which I, the Lord God, had given him, and also, that I should give unto him mine own power; by the power of mine Only Begotten, I caused that he should be cast down;

"And he became Satan, yea, even the devil, the father of all lies, to deceive and to blind men, and to lead them captive at his own will, even as many as would not hearken unto my voice" (Moses 4:1–4).

"The contention in heaven was," Joseph Smith explained—"Jesus said there would be certain souls that would not be saved; and the devil said he could save them all, and laid his plans before the grand council, who gave their vote in favor of Jesus Christ. So the devil rose up in rebellion against God, and was cast down, with all who put up their heads for him."[6] The Latter-day Saints believe that the fall of Lucifer and his followers—one-third of the spirit children of the Father (Revelation 12:4; D&C 29:36), allusions to which are found in the Bible (Isaiah 14:12–15; Luke 10:18; Revelation 12:7–9)—signaled the perpetuation of evil on earth. Lucifer or Satan, with his minions, became the enemies of God and of all righteousness and to this day seek to destroy the souls of men and women.

It is not uncommon for me to stand before a group of questioners and hear the following: "Bob, isn't it true that you folks believe Jesus and Lucifer are brothers?" This is a tough question to respond to on the spur of the moment, one that requires that I take the time to explain about the LDS concept of a premortal life, about Lucifer as a child of God who turned sour and thereafter rebelled against God, and about Jesus who, though he was the firstborn spirit son of God, also became God. John 1:1–2 speaks of the Word being in the beginning, being with God, and being God. This we believe wholeheartedly. Let's be clear: Jesus was God before he came to earth, and there was never a time when he and Lucifer enjoyed the same spiritual standing.

Truth was taught in that premortal sphere. The gospel was declared. The sons and daughters of God came to understand and appreciate the goodness and powers of Deity. They recognized that God the Father, the Supreme Being, was possessed of a physical, resurrected, immortal, and glorified body. They came to know that the fullness of eternal joy was to be had through becoming as God is; through coming to earth, taking a physical body, growing and maturing in their ability to overcome temptations and deal with the stresses of this world; and through qualifying, by accepting the gospel of Jesus Christ and incorporating the Lord's divine nature into their own, to return to the presence of God as living souls, spirits and bodies having been inseparably joined together through the resurrection, never again to be divided.

Before coming to earth, the sons and daughters of God were told that as mortals they would be required to walk by faith, to operate in this second estate without full knowledge of what they did and who they were in the life before. A veil of forgetfulness would be placed over their minds, causing them to "see through a glass, darkly" (1 Corinthians 13:12). One early Church leader, John Taylor, suggested what might have been said before we left our first estate: "Remember you go [to earth] on this condition, that is, you are to forget all things you ever saw, or knew to be transacted in the spirit world; …you must go and become one of the most helpless of all beings that I have created, while in your infancy, subject to sickness, pain, tears, mourning, sorrow and death. But when truth shall touch the cords of your heart they will vibrate; then intelligence shall illuminate your mind, and shed its lustre in your soul, and you shall begin to understand the things you once knew, but which had gone from you; you shall then begin to understand and know the object of your creation."[7]

Boyd K. Packer, a modern LDS Church leader, offered the following parable to illustrate the value of a knowledge of man and woman's eternality and specifically an understanding of our existence in an earlier sphere:

> Imagine that you are attending a football game. The teams seem evenly matched. One team has been trained to follow the rules; the other, to do just the opposite. They are committed to cheat and disobey every rule of sportsmanlike conduct.
>
> While the game ends in a tie, it is determined that it must continue until one side wins decisively.
>
> Soon the field is a quagmire.
>
> Players on both sides are being ground into the mud. The cheating of the opposing team turns to brutality.
>
> Players are carried off the field. Some have been injured critically; others, it is whispered, fatally. It ceases to be a game and becomes a battle.

You become very frustrated and upset. "Why let this go on? Neither team can win. It must be stopped."

Imagine that you confront the sponsor of the game and demand that he stop this useless, futile battle. You say it is senseless and without purpose. Has he no regard for the players?

He calmly replies that he will not call the game. You are mistaken. There is a great purpose in it. You have not understood.

He tells you that this is not a spectator sport—it is for the participants. It is for their sake that he permits the game to continue. Great benefit may come to them because of the challenges they face.

He points to players sitting on the bench, suited up, eager to enter the game. "When each one of them has been in, when each has met the day for which he has prepared so long and trained so hard, then, and only then, will I call the game."

Until then, it may not matter which team seems to be ahead. The present score is really not crucial. There are games within games, you know. Whatever is happening to the team, each player will have his day.

Those players on the team that keeps the rules will not be eternally disadvantaged because they keep the rules. They may be cornered or misused, even defeated for a time. But individual players on that team, regardless of what appears on the scoreboard, may already be victorious.

Each player will have a test sufficient to his needs; how each responds is the test.

When the game is finally over, you and they will see purpose in it all, may even express gratitude for having been on the field during the darkest part of the contest.

Then, in providing a bit of interpretation for this fascinating story, Elder Packer added: "I do not think the Lord is quite so hopeless about what's going on in the world as we are. He could put a stop to all of it any moment. But He will not! Not until every player has a chance to meet the test for which we were preparing before the world was, before we came into mortality."

Elder Packer also observed: "This doctrine of premortal life was known to ancient Christians. For nearly five hundred years the doctrine was taught, but it was then rejected as a heresy.... Once they rejected this doctrine, the doctrine of premortal life...they could never unravel the mystery of life."[8]

Who, then, is God? There are many beliefs about God that we share with our friends of other faiths, while there are some tenets with which others would disagree. We believe, for example, that

- God is the Almighty, the Creator, the Father of Lights.

- God has all power, is all-knowing, and is, by means of his Spirit, everywhere present.

- God is the ultimate object of our worship and adoration.

- God is the possessor of every perfection, virtue, divine attribute, and heavenly quality.

- God was God before the world was created and the same God after it was created.

- God is an independent being. While he is pleased to receive our respect, love, reverence, and worship, his godhood does not require it.

- God is an exalted, glorified Man of Holiness. He is more than a force or a great First Cause; he is our Father in heaven, the Father of our spirits.

- God the Father has a glorified, physical body, and we are created in his image and likeness.

- God is a being or person of perfected passions and is, as is his Son Jesus Christ, touched with the feeling of our infirmities (Hebrews 4:15). Our prayers to him, especially our petitions, are heard and responded to. His infinity does not preclude either his immediacy or his intimacy.

That God has a physical body (D&C 130:22) is inextricably tied to such doctrines as the immortality of the soul, the literal resurrection, eternal marriage, and the continuation of the family unit into eternity, all of which we will address in subsequent chapters of this book. The Father's physical body does not limit his capacity or detract one wit from his infinite holiness, any more than Christ's resurrected body did so (see Luke 24; John 20–21). The risen Lord said of himself: "All power is given unto me in heaven and in earth" (Matthew 28:18). Interestingly enough, research by Professor David Paulsen of the BYU Philosophy Department indicates that the idea of God's corporeality was taught in the early Christian Church into the fourth and fifth centuries, before being lost to the knowledge of the people.[9]

Scholars of other faiths have commented on the possibility of God's corporeality. James L. Kugel, professor of Hebrew literature at Harvard, has written that some of scholars' "most basic assumptions about God," including the idea "that he has no body but exists everywhere simultaneously," are not "articulated in the most ancient parts of the Bible.... We like to think that what our religions say nowadays about God is what people have always believed." Further, "biblical narratives did not like to speak of God actually appearing to human beings directly and conversing with them face-to-face. The reason was not that God in those days was thought to be invisible, as certainly not that He was (as later philosophers and theologians were to claim) altogether spiritual and therefore had no body to be seen. Rather, God in the Bible is not usually seen by human beings for an entirely different reason; especially in the earliest parts: catching sight of Him was believed to be extremely dangerous." Kugel later observes that "the same God who buttonholes the patriarchs and speaks to Moses face-to-face is perceived in later times as a huge, cosmic deity—not necessarily invisible or lacking a body, but so huge as to surpass our own capacities of apprehension, almost our imagination." In time the God who spoke to Moses directly "became an embarrassment to later theologians. It is, they said, really the great, universal God" who is "omniscient and omnipresent and utterly unphysical." He asks, "Indeed, does not the eventual emergence of Christianity—in particular Nicene Christianity, with its doctrine of the Trinity—likewise represent in its own way an attempt to fill the gap left by the God of Old?"[10]

An Evangelical Christian scholar, Clark Pinnock, has written that if we "are to take biblical metaphors seriously, is God in some way embodied? Critics will be quick to say that, although there are expressions of this idea in the Bible, they are not to be taken literally. However, the idea is not as foreign to the Bible's view of God as we have assumed. In tradition, God is thought to function primarily as a disembodied spirit but this is scarcely a biblical idea. For example, Israel is called to hear God's word and gaze on his glory and beauty. Human beings are said to be embodied creatures created in the image of God. Is there perhaps something in God that corresponds with embodiment? Having a body is certainly not a negative thing because it makes it possible for us to be agents. Perhaps God's agency would be easier to envisage if he were in some way corporeal. Add to that the fact that in the theophanies of the Old Testament God encounters humans in the form of a man.... Add to that that God took on a body in the incarnation and Christ has taken that body with him into glory. It seems to me that the Bible does not think of God as formless."[11]

In what many people in the religious world consider to be one of the most controversial elements of LDS thought, Joseph Smith taught that "God himself was once as we are now, and is an exalted man, and sits enthroned in yonder heavens!... If the veil were rent today, and the great God who holds this world in its orbit, and who upholds all worlds and all things by his power, was to make himself visible—I say, if you were to see him today, you would see him like a man in form— like yourselves in all the person, image, and very form as a man."[12] It was in that same sermon, delivered on April 7, 1844, that the Mormon Prophet also taught that man could eventually, through the powers of the gospel of Jesus Christ, become as God is. We will postpone our discussion of the latter concept, the notion of human deification, until chapter 26.

As to the former idea—that God was once a man—let me comment briefly. First of all, Latter-day Saints do indeed believe that God is an exalted Man, and that men and women are created in his image in a very real way. Second, we believe that "there is a God in heaven, who is infinite and eternal, from everlasting to everlasting the same unchangeable God, the framer of heaven and earth, and all things which are in them" (D&C 20:17). Further that God sits enthroned "with glory, honor, majesty, might, dominion, truth, justice, judgment, mercy, and an infinity of fullness, from everlasting to everlasting" (D&C 109:77). In other words, based upon these and a host of other scriptural passages, I as a Latter-day Saint do not believe in what some have termed a "finite God." Third, this is a doctrine that we know precious little about. Gordon B. Hinckley, fifteenth president of the Church, speaking of this concept, said: "I don't know that we emphasize it. I haven't heard it discussed for a long time in public discourse. I don't know all the circumstances under which that statement was made. I understand the philosophical background behind it, but I don't know a lot about it, and I don't think others know a lot about it."[13] Consequently, God's status before he was God is not exactly what could be termed a central, saving teaching in Mormonism, one that is linked directly to redemption in Christ. For me it is a "shelf doctrine," something that I'm aware of but seldom if ever even reflect on, something that is a part of our history but not central to our doctrine. It would not be an issue brought up in Sabbath sermons or Sunday School lessons or even everyday conversations. Nor does acceptance or nonacceptance of it affect one's standing in the Church.

A friend and colleague, Truman G. Madsen, pointed out: "On the question of God's existence, most monotheistic traditions agree. God is a self-existing being. That is to say that nothing other than God accounts for the reality of God. He simply is. In the language of the scholastics, he has a-seity, self-existence. Unique in LDS thought…is a parallel thesis, namely, something in the human self is co-existent and co-eternal with God…. In contrast to [traditional religious or philosophical] views, in LDS thought, intelligence has ontological and eternal status. There is nothing contingent or ephemeral about it…. A God (or anything else) held to be directly or totally the cause of all that exists is indirectly the cause of all that occurs, including all human action and inaction. Genuine human choice and autonomy then appear inexplicable." But for Latter-day Saints, "Freedom is implicit in primal and premortal human nature, and continues through physical embodiment and maturation in this world. It is our inescapable 'response-ability.'"[14]

Latter-day Saints believe that a knowledge of the eternality of men and women as well as the corporeality and accessibility/approachability/knowability of the Almighty makes the phrase "the Fatherhood of God and the brotherhood of man" more than memorable metaphor. For example, a few years ago I found myself on a plane during the middle of an extremely busy month—more places to go, reading to catch up on, and writing deadlines to meet. The man who sat in the seat next to me kept trying to strike up a conversation, but I had important things to do. I sloughed off his friendly gestures again and again. He finally asked what I did for a living, I replied tersely that I was a professor of religion, and then he *really* wanted to chat. But I would have nothing to do with it. Finally he turned away in disappointment and read the newspaper.

It is not just that I was rude and unfriendly; I would feel guilty enough as a follower of Christ if that was all I regretted. Knowing what I know, believing what I believe, I am not prone to accept every chance meeting as just that—a chance meeting. The older I get and the more deeply I feel the love and direction of God in my life, the fewer interactions seem to be coincidental. What could have come from a congenial conversation with this man? Could such an encounter have lifted him, inspired me, or informed the both of us? Did I allow something of significance to pass? Will I perhaps never have the opportunity to engage this man, this person, this personality, this individual, this human soul again? Believing God is my Father, that He is in charge of things, and that this man is truly my brother, have I missed an opportunity that may never present itself again? I fear I have. Thus I find myself on subways, in train stations, in airports looking more carefully and ponderously at the long lines of humankind as they pass by me. Who are these people? They are the children of God. They are my brothers and sisters. My connection with them is far more than one of a coresident on this planet but also a coeternal member of the family of God.

And so it is that some things we see or hear or feel seem to have such a strange and vague sense of familiarity; they seem to be "spirit memories." "Our knowledge of persons and things before we came here," Joseph F. Smith, the sixth president of the LDS Church, wrote, "combined with the divinity awakened within our souls through obedience to the gospel, powerfully affects, in my opinion, all our likes and dislikes, and guides our preferences in the course of this life, provided we give careful heed to the admonitions of the Spirit. All those salient truths which come home so forcibly to the head and heart," he continued, "seem but the awakening of the memories of the spirit."[15] It was Joseph Smith himself who taught, only two months before his death, that "if men do not comprehend the character of God, they do not comprehend themselves."[16] Thus the quest for self-discovery, so prevalent in a world filled with angst and alienation and anomie, is inextricably tied with the quest to know God, which Jesus taught is indeed life eternal (John 17:3). And so Mormons affirm, as Professor Madsen explained many years ago, "One begins mortality with the veil drawn, but slowly he is moved to penetrate the veil within himself. He is, in time, led to seek the 'holy of holies' within the temple of his own being."[17]

ENDNOTES

1. My words, paraphrasing Joseph Smith in *TPJS*, 352–54.

2. Wordsworth, "Ode: Intimations of Immortality from Recollections of Early Childhood," in Noyes, ed., *English Romantic Poetry and Prose*, 327–28.

3. Proust, *Homo Viator*, 8.

4. In Clark, ed. *Messages of the First Presidency* 4:199–206.

5. See Bruce R. McConkie, *The Mortal Messiah*, 1:23.

6. *TPJS*, 357.

7. Taylor, "The Origin and Destiny of Women," in Lundwall, ed., *The Vision*, 146–47.

8. Packer, CR, October 1983, 21–22.

9. Paulsen, "The Doctrine of Divine Embodiment."

10. Kugel, *The God of Old*, xii, 5–6, 63, 195; see also 81, 104–6, 134–35.

11. Pinnock, *The Most Moved Mover*, 33–34.

12. Smith, *TPJS*, 345.

13. Hinckley, cited in Ostling and Ostling, *Mormon America*, 296.

14. Madsen, "The Latter-day Saint View of Human Nature," in Madsen, Freedman, and Kuhlken, eds., *On Human Nature*, 95–96.

15. Joseph F. Smith, *Gospel Doctrine*, 12–13.

16. *TPJS,* 343.

17. Madsen, *Eternal Man*, 20.

TWO

A Purpose to It All

LIFE IS GOOD, AND, to be sure, there are moments and seasons in life that make it all worthwhile, that whisper peace and assurance to our souls, that affirm in the language of the Book of Mormon that "men are that they might have joy" (2 Nephi 2:25). But there are times when our sense of wellness is shaken to the core, occasions when we bow our heads, weep, and cry out, "O God, where are you?" Indeed, when we think of the nightmare of the Holocaust, as well as the devilish and unnecessary loss of life under totalitarian regimes, we find ourselves saying, "This isn't the way things are supposed to be!"

One Evangelical scholar, Cornelius Plantinga, has observed: "In the film *Grand Canyon*, an immigration attorney breaks out of a traffic jam and attempts to bypass it. His route takes him along streets that seem progressively darker and more deserted. Then the predictable… nightmare: his expensive car stalls on one of those alarming streets whose teenage guardians favor expensive guns and sneakers. The attorney does manage to phone for a tow truck, but before it arrives, five young street toughs surround his disabled car and threaten him with considerable bodily harm. Then, just in time, the tow truck shows up and its driver—an earnest, genial man—begins to hook up the disabled car. The toughs protest: the truck driver is interrupting their meal. So the driver takes the leader of the group aside and attempts a five-sentence introduction to metaphysics: 'Man,' he says, 'the world ain't supposed to work like this. Maybe you don't know that, but this ain't the way it's supposed to be. I'm supposed to be able to do my job without askin' you if I can. And that dude is supposed to be able to wait with his car without you rippin' him off. Everything's supposed to be different than what it is here.'"[1]

No, things aren't the way they ought to be. And they haven't been since Adam and Eve left the Garden of Eden. This is a fallen world, and we are brought face-to-face on a regular basis with the fact that for this temporal time and season not all well-laid plans will come to fruition. Times change. Youth fades. Things break down. Bodies grow old and decay. In late June 2001, I was rushed to the hospital because of a serious heart attack. I walk a little slower now, don't have the stamina I once had, and in general feel like the old tabernacle is losing the battle against mortality.

Because there is pain, because there is sorrow, because there is tragedy, men and women ask: Where is God, especially when it hurts? In speaking to Brigham Young University students over half a century ago, Elder Spencer W. Kimball asked some tough questions about human suffering and tragedy, and, at the same time, provided a provocative and elevated perspective on God:

> Was it the Lord who directed the plane into the mountain to snuff out the lives of its occupants, or were there mechanical faults or human errors?
>
> Did our Father in Heaven cause the collision of the cars that took six people into eternity, or was it the error of the driver who ignored safety rules?
>
> Did God take the life of the young mother or prompt the child to toddle into the canal or guide the other child into the path of the oncoming car?...
>
> Did the Lord cause the man to suffer a heart attack? Was the death of the missionary untimely? Answer, if you can. I cannot, for though I know God has a major role in our lives, I do not know how much he causes to happen and how much he merely permits....
>
> Could the Lord have prevented these tragedies? The answer is, Yes. The Lord is omnipotent, with all power to control our lives, save us pain, prevent all accidents, drive all planes and cars, feed us,

protect us, save us from labor, effort, sickness, even from death, if he will. But he will not....

The basic gospel law is free agency and eternal development. To force us to be careful or righteous would be to nullify that fundamental law and make growth impossible.[2]

It is especially challenging for persons who view God solely as a dispenser of good gifts and happy times to fathom how and in what manner he is related, if at all, to earthly trauma. Having been brought up on a constant diet of "God is love" or "God is good," they inevitably equate such goodness with kindness. "By the goodness of God," C. S. Lewis pointed out, "we mean nowadays almost exclusively His lovingness; and in this we may be right. And by Love, in this context, most of us mean kindness—the desire to see others than the self happy; not happy in this way or in that, but just happy. What would really satisfy us would be a God who said of anything we happened to like doing, 'What does it matter so long as they are contented?' We want, in fact, not so much a Father in Heaven as a grandfather in heaven—a senile benevolence who, as they say, 'liked to see young people enjoying themselves,' and whose plan for the universe was simply that it might be truly said at the end of each day, 'a good time was had by all.'"[3]

The God Latter-day Saints have come to know is a divine being who indeed has all power, all knowledge, and who possesses every godly attribute in perfection. That same God has granted to each of us moral agency, the capacity to choose what we will do with our lives. Agency is paramount. We also know, in a very personal way, of the reality of evil and of the fact that Lucifer is bent upon our destruction and the overthrow of the Father's plan. He does everything in his power to pervert and corrupt the right way and to entice men and women to use their agency unwisely.

There are some things even more horrible to contemplate than the Holocaust, more unspeakable than millions of innocent people being put to death by crazed dictators, more frightening than terrorists hijacking planes and murdering thousands. Consider this thought: What if there was no agency? What if people did not have the right to choose? Agency, one of the greatest of all the gifts of a benevolent and generous

God, comes at a price. Allowing us to choose automatically opens the door to improper, unwise, immoral, and evil choices and thus to abuse and human tragedy.

One philosopher, Richard Swinburne, wrote: "A God who gives humans such free will necessarily brings about the possibility and puts outside his own control whether or not…evil occurs. It is not logically possible—that is, it would be self-contradictory to suppose—that God could give us such free will and yet ensure that we always use it in the right way….

"A world in which agents can benefit each other but not do each other harm is one where they have very limited responsibility for each other. If my responsibility for you is limited to whether or not to give you a camcorder, but I cannot cause you pain, stunt your growth, or limit your education, then I do not have a great deal of responsibility for you…. A good God, like a good father, will delegate responsibility. In order to allow creatures a share in creation, he will allow them the choice of hurting and maiming, of frustrating the divine plan."

Now note these perceptive insights: "I am fortunate if the natural possibility of my suffering if you choose to hurt me is the vehicle which makes your choice really matter. My vulnerability, my openness to suffering (which necessarily involves my actually suffering if you make the wrong choice), means that you are not just like a pilot in a simulator, where it does not matter if mistakes are made. That our choices matter tremendously, that we can make great differences to things for good or ill, is one of the greatest gifts a creator can give us. And if my suffering is the means by which he can give you that choice, I too am in this respect fortunate."[4]

Where is God when it hurts? He is in his heavens. He is aware. He knows. In ways that we cannot even comprehend, He knows. And he blesses and lifts and liberates and lightens the burdens of his children whenever he can. But he cannot remove us from the toils and tragedies and contradictions of life without robbing us of mortal experience. These things come with the turf. They are part of the test. So much depends on how we choose to look upon what most consider to be the unfairness and the senseless nature of temporal trauma. So much depends upon what we understand about God our Father, about his plan of salvation, and about how vital it is for us to move ahead, even when our burdens or the burdens of others seem unbearable. While a measure of joy and happiness and a sense of overcoming can be ours in this life, the fullness of joy is reserved for the next estate, when spirit and body are reunited in the resurrection (D&C 93:33). In other words, as someone has reminded us, we now participate in part two of a three-act play. The phrase "And they lived happily ever after" refers not to this act but rather the next one. "Wherefore, fear not even unto death," the Redeemer declared; "for in this world your joy is not full, but in me your joy is full" (D&C 101:36). As one Church leader observed, "When we tear ourselves free from the entanglements of the world, are we promised a religion of repose or an Eden of ease? No! We are promised tears and trials and toil! But we are also promised final triumph, the mere contemplation of which tingles the soul."

Every one of us will, at one time or another, face adversity, whether it be in the form of financial reversals, personal struggles, the loss of a loved one, or some type of profound disappointment. Adversity will come to us, one and all, whether we are prepared for it or not. Too often in tough times we yield ourselves to stress and distress, to despondency and discouragement, much more so than our forebears would have. Certainly life is more complex, the demands on our time are more intense, and the temptations of the devil are more sophisticated.

At the same time, it seems to me that there is a mind-set, characteristic of our day, that opens us to despair. That mind-set is one in which we assume, given all the pleasures and luxuries of our day and age, that all should be well with us, that we should be perpetually happy. Many of us have bought into and imbibed the jargon and the philosophy of our pop psychology world. The fact is, life can be tough. We are not guaranteed a stress-free existence, nor did the Lord promise us a mortal life void of challenge and difficulty. Now, lest you misunderstand my point, there is much in the world that is glorious and beautiful and uplifting and inspiring; many of the relationships we establish, for example, are elevating and enriching—they bring the deepest of joys into our lives. But we receive our joys alongside our sorrows. Both elements of the equation come with the turf, with earth. And we knew this before we came.

C. S. Lewis once observed that God has paid us the "intolerable compliment" of loving us, "in the deepest, most tragic, most inexorable sense." "We are," he continued, "not metaphorically but in very truth, a Divine work of art, something that God is making, and therefore something with which He will not be satisfied until it has a certain character."[5] Thus it is perfectly "natural for us to wish that God had designed for us a less glorious and less arduous destiny; but then we are wishing not for more love but for less."[6] "For whom the Lord loveth he chasteneth, and scourgeth every son whom he receiveth…. Now no chastening for the present seemeth to be joyous, but grievous: nevertheless afterward it yieldeth the peaceable fruit of righteousness unto them which are exercised [trained, disciplined] thereby" (Hebrews 12:6, 11).

In short, there are great lessons to be learned from life's struggles, lessons that can perhaps be acquired in no other way. Many of our afflictions we bring upon ourselves through our own impatience, short-sightedness, or sins. There are even lessons to be learned from our sins—not the least of which is the motivation to avoid in the future the pain associated with our misdeeds. There are, however, lessons that come to us from God through challenges and distresses and setbacks and failures. There is a purifying work of pain, a divine work that can transform the soul of the distressed one, *if* he or she approaches the difficulty with the proper attitude. It is not uncommon for persons who have lost a loved one, or who now must face the prospect of a terminal disease, or whose financial fortunes have been dramatically reversed, to ask: "Why? Why would God do this to me? Why is this happening?" These are of course natural reactions to trauma, especially when each one of us would be perfectly content to remain perfectly content! But that's not why we are here.

On more than one occasion I have suggested to the sufferers, as kindly and lovingly as I could, that "Why is this happening?" is not the proper question. Why *is* it happening? Because we are mortal, because things like this happen in a mortal world. No one of us is required by God to enjoy suffering or to anticipate with delight the next trial. I have an associate who said to me once: "You know, Bob, I learn so much from my trials that I find myself praying that the Lord will send more trials my way." I smiled, but I thought to myself: "No way! You wouldn't catch me dead praying for trials. They come without asking for them." On the other hand, it makes little sense for us to come to earth to be proven, and then to ask why we are being proven. The Father is the Husbandman, the Vinedresser. The Savior is the Vine, and we are the branches. The Vinedresser chooses the manner in which He will purge the branches. Why? "Every branch that beareth fruit," the Master stated, "he [the Father] purgeth it, that it may bring forth more fruit" (John 15:2).

A modern Church leader, Richard G. Scott, pointed out that "When you face adversity, you can be led to ask many questions. Some serve a useful purpose; others do not. To ask, Why does this have to happen to me? Why do I have to suffer this now? What have I done to cause this? will lead you into blind alleys.... Rather ask, What am I to do? What am I to learn from this experience? What am I to change? Whom am I to help? How can I remember my many blessings in times of trial?"[7]

In describing life within a prison camp, Victor Frankl has written that "we who lived in concentration camps can remember the men who walked through the huts comforting others, giving away their last piece of bread. They may have been few in number, but they offer sufficient proof that everything can be taken from a man but one thing: the last of...human freedoms—to choose one's attitude in any given set of circumstances, [and] to choose one's own way [of life]."[8]

As difficult as it is for me to acknowledge this, we must occasionally be willing to be "broken" if we really expect to gain that broken heart and contrite spirit about which the scriptures speak (Psalms 51:17; 3 Nephi 9:30; D&C 59:8). Inasmuch as our will is the only thing that we can, in the long run, really consecrate to God, the Lord needs to know of our willingness to be broken by him. That is, to what degree are we willing to submit, to surrender, to yield our hearts unto him? "What happens in the breaking of a horse?" Charles Stanley has asked. "Contrary to what many people believe, the horse's spirit isn't broken. A well-broken horse remains strong, eager, quick-witted, and aware, and he loves to gallop when given free rein. Rather, it is the horse's independence that is broken. The breaking of a horse results in the horse giving instant obedience to its rider.

"When a child of God is broken, God does not destroy his or her spirit. We don't lose our zest for living when we come to Christ. We don't lose the force of our personality. Rather, we lose our independence. Our will is brought into submission to the will of the Father so that we can give instant obedience to the one whom we call Savior and Lord....

"We can choose to respond to brokenness with anger, bitterness, and hate. We can rail against our circumstances. We can strike out against those whom we believe have caused us pain. Those options are available to us because we have free will. The way to blessing, however, lies in turning to God to heal us and make us whole. We decide whether we will yield to him and trust him."[9] Indeed, if we approach them properly, our trials can teach and sanctify us, can assist us to know the fellowship of Christ's suffering (Philippians 3:10). Francis Webster, one of those who suffered unspeakable pain as a member of the ill-fated Martin Handcart Company, a group who found themselves helpless in the depth of winter along the trek to the Great Salt Lake Valley, said: "Every one of us came through with the absolute knowledge that God lives for we became acquainted with him in our extremities."[10]

At a very difficult time for my wife Shauna and me—when we watched helplessly as loved ones chose painful and unproductive paths—we found ourselves, early in the process of dealing with the pain, at a crossroads. We sensed, at that early juncture, that our attitude toward what we were experiencing was everything. To be honest, both of us went through a period of weeks and months in which our days were filled with self-doubt, with personal recrimination, with loads of questions about what we had done wrong over the years. But as we prayed with intensity and read scriptures with new and searching eyes, there began to distill upon us the quiet but powerful realization that only we could determine how we would deal with our dilemma. Would we allow our problems to strangle our marriage and family? Would we permit these difficulties to drive us into seclusion? Or would we yield to doubt and cynicism, given that we had tried so hard through the years to do what we were asked?

I will be forevermore grateful that the two of us sensed that we must face this together and that the one thing we could not afford to have happen was for the trial to drive the two of us apart. Further, after a time of being wrung out emotionally and spiritually, we both sensed that God was our only hope for peace, our only means of extricating ourselves from dysfunctional living. It was then that our prayers and our yearnings began to change. It was then that we found ourselves shorn of self-concern and naked in our ineptitude; it was then that we acknowledged our nothingness and drew upon the strength and lifting power of our Divine Redeemer. Oh, we were still concerned, and we kept trying. But we were trying, as C. S. Lewis pointed out, "in a new way, a less worried way."[11]

We should not be unnerved by trials and challenges and even a bad day once in a while. And there are certainly times when a third party, be it a church leader, parent, dear friend, or even a professional counselor, can assist us to put things in place or in proper perspective. It may even be necessary in some instances for an individual to have medication prescribed by a competent physician. But we must never, ever, minimize the impact the Master can have in our lives, the calming and reassuring and healing balm that He can be to us, no matter the depth of our despair or the seriousness of our situation. "Whatever Jesus lays his hands upon lives," Elder Howard W. Hunter testified. "If Jesus lays his hands upon a marriage, it lives. If he is allowed to lay his hands upon the family, it lives."[12] The touch of the Master's hand is life and light and love. It calms. It soothes. It sanctifies. It empowers. It transcends anything earthly. Those who have been healed by that sacred and sensitive touch are they who can joyously proclaim, like Andrew, Simon Peter's brother, "We have found the Messiah" (John 1:41).

I do not wish in any way to minimize some of the tremendous challenges that many of our friends face. These are real and sobering. I am very much aware that there are many today who have been subjected to much pain and distress in their lives, to abuse, to neglect, to the agonies of wanting more than anything to live a normal life and to feel normal feelings, but who seem unable to do so. I would say, first of all, that each one of us, whoever we are, wrestles with something. Perhaps it's things like my weight or height or complexion or baldness or IQ. Perhaps it's stuff that passes in time like a phase. Perhaps it's the torture of watching helplessly as loved ones choose unwisely and thereby close doors of opportunity for themselves and foreclose future privileges. And then there are the terrible traumas in our life, those occasions when someone we love, despite our tender trust, deals a blow that strikes at the center of all we hold dear and all we value about ourselves.

I know that the day is coming when all the wrongs, the awful wrongs of this life, will be righted, when the God of justice will attend to all evil. Those things that are beyond our power to control will be corrected, either here or hereafter. Many of us may come to enjoy the lifting, liberating powers of the Atonement in this life and all our losses will be made up before we pass from this sphere of existence. Perhaps some of us will wrestle all our days with our traumas and our trials, for He who orchestrates the events of our lives will surely fix the time of our release. I have a conviction that when a person passes through the veil of death, all those impediments and challenges and crosses that were beyond his or her power to control—abuse, neglect, immoral environment, weighty traditions, etc.—will be torn away like a film, and perfect peace will prevail in our hearts.

In some cases our Lord and Master seems to ask of us the impossible—to forgive those who have hurt us so dreadfully. As Bruce and Marie Hafen have observed, "That picture somehow has a familiar look—we've seen all this before. Of course, because this picture depicts the sacrifice of Jesus Christ: He took upon himself undeserved and unbearable burdens, heaped upon him by people who often said, and often believed, that they loved him. And he assumed that load not for any need of his, but only to help them.

"So to forgive—not just for abuse victims, but for each of us—is to be a Christ figure, a transitional point in the war between good and evil, stopping the current of evil by absorbing it in every pore, thereby protecting the innocent next generation and helping to enable the repentance and healing of those whose failures sent the jolts into our own systems."[13]

And so we hold on, we press on, we move ahead, even though the road is not necessarily straight and the path is not necessarily clear. Lessons we are to learn through our suffering may or may not be obvious. The one lesson, perhaps overarching all the rest, is patience. Elder

Orson F. Whitney taught: "No pain that we suffer, no trial that we experience is wasted. It ministers to our education, to the development of such qualities as patience, faith, fortitude, and humility. All that we suffer and all that we endure, especially when we endure it patiently, builds up our characters, purifies our hearts, expands our souls, and makes us more tender and charitable, more worthy to be called the children of God."[14]

At the time my wife Shauna and I were going through some of our deepest sorrows and distresses, we could not have sensed what lessons for life were being chiseled into our souls. It all seemed during that season of stress so overwhelming, so awful, so terribly unfair. And as is true with most of us, it's tough to learn lessons while you're in the midst of the refiner's fire. Now while I would not wish to go through that experience again, at the same time I would not trade the lessons we learned for anything in this world or the next. They were timeless lessons, eternal and tender tutorials that have drawn us closer to the Good Shepherd and expanded our consciousness and empathy for his precious sheep. We learned some things about God during those years of trial, but we also learned some things about ourselves. Fortunately or unfortunately, the only way I can know to what extent I will serve God at all hazards is to have my mettle tested. In asking Abraham to offer his son Isaac, for example, Abraham needed to learn something about Abraham.

In some ways, then, facing our trials courageously and resolutely prepares us for fellowship with those who have passed the tests of mortality. Now, to be sure, The Church of Jesus Christ of Latter-day Saints does not subscribe to a doctrine of asceticism, nor do we teach that we should seek after either persecution or pain. But persecution and pain are the lot of the people of God in all ages, and each of us, saint and sinner alike, becomes acquainted with the Suffering Servant through our suffering. We have been taught, by those who know best, that "All these things shall give thee experience, and shall be for thy good. The Son of Man hath descended below them all. Art thou greater than he?" (D&C 122:7).

No, we are not greater than He, nor should we suppose that fellowship with Him who was well acquainted with grief will come through a life of ease. As the apostle Peter counseled us: "Beloved, think it not strange concerning the fiery trial which is to try you, as though some strange thing happened unto you: but rejoice, inasmuch as ye are partakers of Christ's sufferings; that, when his glory shall be revealed, ye may be glad also with exceeding joy" (1 Peter 4:12–13). As tough as it is, over time and through seasons of experience we come to glory in our trials, for only through times of weakness and distress do we eventually emerge into a day of strength and power (2 Corinthians 12:9–10).

There is a popular phrase among religious types these days: "God loves you and has a plan for your life." To be sure, our Heavenly Father loves us, one and all. He knows us by name, knows our pains and our traumas, our deepest needs. Things are not really chaotic; someone is in charge. Things are not hopeless; there is a Light at the end of the tunnel. Jesus Christ came to bring beauty for ashes (Isaiah 61:1–3)— to replace distress with comfort, worry with peace, turmoil with rest. The Good Shepherd came to earth on a search-and-rescue mission—to identify and gather in those who have strayed, to welcome the wanderer back home, with a robe, a ring, and a fatted calf. Our Precious Savior condescended—left his throne divine—to come down and be with his people, the sheep of his fold. He came to right all the terrible wrongs of this life, to fix the unfixable, to repair the irreparable. He came to heal us by his tender touch, to still the storms of our startled hearts.

Because things do not always turn out as we had expected, because today was not the day we bargained for, "Every one of us," Elder Jeffrey R. Holland pointed out, "has times when we need to know things will get better.... For emotional health and spiritual stamina, everyone needs to be able to look forward to some respite, to do something pleasant and renewing and hopeful, whether that blessing be near at hand or still some distance ahead....

"My declaration is that this is precisely what the gospel of Jesus Christ offers us, especially in times of need. There *is* help. There *is* happiness. There really *is* light at the end of the tunnel. It is the Light of the World.... I say: Hold on. Keep trying. God loves you. Things will improve. Christ comes to you in his 'more excellent ministry' with a future of 'better promises.'"[15]

ENDNOTES

1. Plantinga, *Not the Way It's Supposed to Be*, 7.
2. Kimball, "Tragedy or Destiny?" in *Faith Precedes the Miracle*, 96.
3. Lewis, *The Problem of Pain*, 35–36.
4. Swinburne, *Is There a God?*, 98–103.
5. Lewis, *The Problem of Pain* (New York: Touchstone, 1996), 37.
6. Ibid. 38.
7. Scott, CR, October 1995, 18.
8. Frankl, *Man's Search for Meaning*, 34.
9. Stanley, *The Blessings of Brokenness*, 47–48, 53.
10. Cited in Faust, *Finding Light in a Dark World*, 55.
11. Lewis, *Mere Christianity*, 147.
12. Hunter, CR, October 1979, 93.
13. Hafen and Hafen, *The Belonging Heart*, 122–23.
14. Whitney, cited in Kimball, *Faith Precedes the Miracle*, 98.
15. Holland, CR, October 1999, 45.

THREE

Old-Time Religion

SOME OF THE EARLIEST memories I have are linked with my religious life. I remember the older people in the Church, the seasoned veterans of the faith who represented stability and strength and were my link with the past. There was Sister Cavin who bore such a powerful witness in our monthly testimony meetings; Brother King Hunt who motivated us constantly to do genealogical research and become better acquainted with our forebears; Dr. Fife who always taught the young people: "The devil deals in kisses; to him it's just a bubble. He knows you'll both want more, and that's what leads to trouble"; and wonderful Sister Anderson who taught my Sunday School class when I was at such an impressionable age; as someone has said, we could warm our hands by the fire of her faith.

I remember being picked up at Cub Scout meetings on Thursday afternoons by my Primary teacher (Primary is the Church's organization for the teaching and training of children ages three through eleven). I remember dancing with people ten times my age at what were then called Gold 'n Green Balls, annual dances and socials held in the church cultural hall. I remember taking part in church basketball and volleyball tournaments as well as annual speech festivals. Life as a Latter-day Saint certainly entailed more than four walls and preaching; it impacted almost every phase of my life.

My grandfather, Anatole J. Millet, was born and raised in a French-speaking Cajun home in Reserve, Louisiana. In the early 1930s he was introduced to Mormonism and decided to leave his Roman Catholic heritage behind and become a Latter-day Saint. His family was incensed by that decision and asked him to leave home, which he did. He married my grandmother, Margaret Parker, a Mormon, and they raised their four sons in the LDS faith in the Baton Rouge area. Grandpa was not an educated man by this world's standards, having never graduated from high school, but he knew how to work and spent his mature years as an employee of what we called the Standard Oil Company, what later became known as Esso and then Exxon. He also knew how to read, and he put that gift into practice as he immersed himself in a study of the Bible, Book of Mormon, Doctrine and Covenants, and Pearl of Great Price. His knowledge of Mormonism and his personal witness of its truthfulness and relevance in today's world grew by leaps and bounds as time passed.

With Grandpa's depth of gospel understanding came a boldness and a confidence to speak out, even to search out opportunities to teach what he believed to be a distinctive saving message. He met regularly with Catholic priests and Protestant ministers and challenged the foundation of their faith; was called upon frequently to speak in church and at funerals; and even had a weekly gospel program on radio station WJBO for a number of years in which he played music from the Mormon Tabernacle Choir and delivered short sermons. As an aside, I find it a bit amusing and yet quite touching to get a feeling for how seriously he took his work as a lay leader within the Mormon Church; for one thing, it is not unusual to find the following in his handwriting at the front of several of his books (now in my own library): A. J. Millet, D.D. (I presume he meant "doctor of divinity").

Grandpa Millet was a powerful speaker, a man filled with the fire of enthusiasm for his message and with an evident gift for public speaking. I remember so well his sermons: systematically laid out, presented with great vigor and volume, and always accompanied with his pounding on the pulpit when it came time to make his point emphatically. He never needed a microphone when he spoke, for his voice would resound throughout the church house. Grandpa died at a young age, in his early fifties, having literally worn himself out riding his bicycle from one LDS home to another, singing and preaching, praying and confirming the Saints. It was not uncommon for him to ride his bike home from Standard Oil in the afternoons and then head directly to the church building site, there to spend many long hours working on the new chapel on Hiawatha Street.

My father, Albert L. Millet, was very much like his father; he loved the Lord, loved the gospel, and spent much of his life defending and propagating the faith. His sermons were very much like Grandpa's, and few people were asked to speak in church and offer consolation at funerals more than Dad. He also died at a young age (61), but he left me a legacy of faith and a host of memories that tie me back historically and experientially to a time when Mormons were little known, little appreciated, and seldom listened to. Whether I like it or not, I am tied by blood and by heritage to the "old-time religion" of my fathers and mothers. I am not a lineal descendant of early LDS pioneers who crossed the plains and gave all they had to settle the Great Basin, but I am a descendant of Mormon pioneers who gave all they had to lay the foundation for the faith I now enjoy, a faith I hope to transmit to my children and grandchildren.

In thinking back on my formative years, most everyone I knew was religious—at least they had strong and deep-seated beliefs and always attended church regularly. I can remember one friend, a Methodist boy, who was a fine young man, but his family was not much into religious stuff. I don't think I knew what an atheist or an agnostic was until I entered college. I know there are a ton of people who feel the "good ole days" of the 1950s weren't really so good, but I'm an old-fashioned traditionalist who thinks often of how nice it was to leave the keys in the car at night, leave the front door of the house unlocked, walk the streets at night without fear, and come together as families and extended families often. Yes, there were some matters in society, especially where I grew up, that were not so pleasant: My memories of "colored" and white drinking fountains and restrooms, of segregation and racial discrimination, and of Ku Klux Klan rallies are very much intact. Changes were slow in coming, but they did come. But, on the whole, morality and decency and civility were the order of the day, and I miss all of that.

Obviously this kind of yearning for the good ole days is not something that Latter-day Saints monopolize. Some of my friends of other faiths pine about the days before "seeker friendly" churches were the norm. I sat on a plane a few years ago with a man (probably 40–45 years of age) who was a Southern Baptist from Dallas, Texas, a member of what has come to be known as a "mega-church." I asked him to share with me his feelings about his church, and he indicated that while he loved being part of such a large and dynamic organization that was reaching out in all directions to offer salvation to the masses, there were some things he and his wife missed deeply. He said: "I personally miss sermons that are meaty, substantive, Bible-based, and longer than fifteen to twenty minutes."

He then pointed out that his wife was educated in music at a fine university, really missed choirs and beautiful classic Christian hymns, and found less satisfaction in praise songs and praise teams, music that certainly contained meaningful messages but which catered to a younger generation's tastes—a kind of pop rock spirituality. As an Evangelical associate of mine put it, the thing that's wrong with Christian contemporary music is the same thing wrong with pop music in general. "Except for the very best, it generally hits you hard with a shot of pleasure, and then it leaves you physically and emotionally stimulated but intellectually and spiritually malnourished. Most of it is junk food; you don't need teeth to eat it, and there is nothing to digest. The moronic 'Baby, Baby, love, love' of MTV gets baptized into 'Jesus, Jesus, love, love' with approximately the same effect: warm fuzzies."[1]

There's a more basic sense in which Mormons are eager to get back to the ole-time religion. Joseph Smith and the Latter-day Saints came into being in an era of the nineteenth century known as a time of primitivism or restorationism. People everywhere were seeking for a return of biblical (New Testament) Christianity, a return of the primitive Church, a return of the teachings and gifts enjoyed at the time of Jesus and the early apostles. A century earlier, Roger Williams, the man to whom we trace the beginnings of the Baptist movement, fled from the Massachusetts Bay Colony and settled in what we know now as Providence, Rhode Island. In speaking of Williams, Cotton Mather said, "Mr. Williams [finally] told [those who followed him] that being himself misled," he had unwittingly misled the people and "he was now satisfied that there was none upon earth that could administer baptism…[and therefore he advised them] "to forgo all …and wait for the coming of new apostles."[2] Likewise, Jonathan Edwards, the man believed by many today to be the father of modern Evangelicalism, remarked: "It seems to me a …unreasonable thing, to suppose that there should be a God …that has so much concern …and yet that he should never speak."[3]

This age in America's history was a time when men and women read the Bible, believed its story and message, and sought for a return to "the ancient order of things." Many longed for the reestablishment of primitive Christianity; others desired once more to enjoy the spiritual gifts and outpourings that had once graced the ancients. A classic illustration of one imbued with such desires was Alexander Campbell, the father of the Disciples of Christ, the Church of Christ, and the Christian Church. Campbell began one of many campaigns against creeds and a strict Calvinism. Alexander accepted the doctrine of believer's baptism by immersion, was baptized, and in 1811 accepted the pastorate at the Brush Run Baptist Church in what is now Bethany, West Virginia. Campbell's adherence to his restorationist beliefs proved a serious concern to the Baptists, and he was rejected by many Baptist colleagues in the ministry. Campbell's dissatisfaction with nominal Christianity is apparent in a statement from the first volume of his magazine, *Christian Baptist:* "We are convinced, fully convinced, that the whole head is sick, and the whole heart faint of modern fashionable Christianity."[4] In addition, Campbell the iconoclast "condemned all beliefs and practices that could not be validated by apostolic mandates. He proclaimed that missionary societies, tract societies, Bible societies, synods, associations, and theological seminaries were inconsistent with pure religion."[5]

Alexander Campbell's disillusionment with nineteenth-century religion was not an isolated perception. As late as 1838, Ralph Waldo Emerson stated in his famous "Divinity School Address" at Harvard that "the need was never greater of new revelation than now." Further, "the Church seems to totter to its fall, almost all life extinct." Continuing, "I look forward for the hour when the supreme Beauty, which ravished the souls of those Eastern men, and chiefly of those Hebrews, and through their lips spoke oracles to all time, shall speak in the west also."[6]

A number of early LDS Church leaders spoke of their own quest for truth and of the frustrations they felt before their encounter with Joseph Smith. Brigham Young stated: "My mind was opened to conviction, and I knew that the Christian world had not the religion that Jesus and the Apostles taught. I knew that there was not a Bible Christian on earth within my knowledge."[7] Wilford Woodruff, fourth president of the Church, said: "I did not join any church, believing that the Church of Christ in its true organization did not exist upon the earth."[8] Willard Richards, later a counselor to Brigham Young, became "convinced that the sects were all wrong, and that God had no church on earth, but that he would soon have a church on earth whose creed would be the truth."[9]

Mormons take this quest for "ole-time religion" a step farther. They believe that Christian doctrines have been taught and Christian ordinances (sacraments) administered by Christian prophets since the beginning of time. Adam and Eve were Christians. Noah warned the people in his day to repent, believe, and be baptized in the name of Jesus Christ. Abraham and Moses and Isaiah and Jeremiah and Ezekiel were Christian prophets. When Paul alluded to the fact that Abraham had the gospel (Galatians 3:8), we think he meant what he said. If all of this seems odd, anachronistic in the sense that there could obviously be no Christianity until the coming to earth of the Christ, Mormons believe otherwise. They believe and teach Christ's Eternal Gospel, the message that a gospel or plan of salvation was heard from the dawn of time.

In this sense, the Latter-day Saints do not accept a type of developmental or evolutionary approach to the New Testament. They do not accept the view that the antediluvians, for example, were primitives or that the so-called Christian era we generally associate with the birth or ministry of Jesus is in some way superior, on a higher plane, or more spiritually progressive than those of the Old Testament patriarchs or the prophets. It is true that the Mormons speak of the Christian era as "the meridian of time," but this has reference to the centrality of Christ's ministry, teachings, and atoning sacrifice more than to the uniqueness of the message delivered in the first century.

The Latter-day Saints believe that God has revealed himself and his plan of salvation during different periods of the earth's history called *dispensations*. The Adamic dispensation was the first. LDS scripture declares that Adam and Eve, after their expulsion from the Garden of Eden, called upon God in prayer and came to know the course in life they should pursue through God's voice, by the ministry of angels, and by revelation through the power of the Holy Spirit. This gospel was then taught to their children and their grandchildren, and thus the knowledge of God, of a coming Savior, and of a plan for the redemption and reclamation of wandering souls was in effect early on (see Moses 5:1–8). From the Pearl of Great Price comes the following counsel of God to Adam: "And he [God] called upon our father Adam by his own voice, saying: I am God; I made the world, and men before they were in the flesh. And he also said unto him: If thou wilt turn unto me, and hearken unto my voice, and believe, and repent of all thy transgressions, and be baptized, even in water, in the name of mine Only Begotten Son, who is full of grace and truth, which is Jesus Christ, the only name which shall be given under heaven, whereby salvation shall come unto the children of men, ye shall receive the gift of the Holy Ghost" (Moses 6:51–52). Adam was further instructed to teach his children of the necessity for spiritual rebirth, that "by transgression cometh the fall, which fall bringeth death, and inasmuch as ye were born into the world by water, and blood, and the spirit, which I have made, and so became of dust a living soul, even so ye must be born again into the kingdom of heaven, of water, and of the Spirit, and be cleansed by blood, even the blood of mine Only Begotten" (Moses 6:59).

Other dispensations followed, periods of time wherein the heavens were opened, prophets were called and empowered, and new truths and new authorities restored to the earth, usually following a time of falling away or apostasy. Thus the ministries and teachings of Enoch, Noah, Abraham, Moses, Jesus, and Joseph Smith introduced major dispensations, periods wherein God—his person and plan—was revealed anew. Lest there be misunderstanding at this point, I hasten to add that Jesus Christ is chief, preeminent, and supreme over all the prophets. Mormons would acknowledge Jesus as a prophet, a restorer, a revealer of God, but they stand firm in attesting to his divinity. While the prophets were called of God, he is God. He is the Son of God. He is God the Son. Under the Father, his is the power by which men and women are forgiven, redeemed, and born again unto a new spiritual life. Mormons teach that all the prophets from the beginning testified of Christ—that all of those called as spokesmen or mouthpieces for God were, first and foremost, witnesses of the Redeemer, inasmuch as "the testimony of Jesus is the spirit of prophecy" (Revelation 19:10). In the words of Peter, to Christ "give all the prophets witness" (Acts 10:43; see also 1 Peter 1:10–11).

The fullness of the gospel plan, the covenant between God and humankind, is thus known as the new and everlasting covenant. It is *new* in the sense that it is new to those to whom it is restored and revealed; it is *everlasting* in the sense that it has been around for a long, long time. For now, let us quote briefly from Joseph Smith on the eternal nature of the gospel covenant: "Perhaps our friends will say that the Gospel and its ordinances were not known till the days of John, the son of Zacharias, in the days of Herod, the king of Judea.

"But we will here look at this point: For our own part we cannot believe that the ancients in all ages were so ignorant of the system of heaven as many suppose, since all that were ever saved, *were saved through the power of this great plan of redemption,* as much before the coming of Christ as since; if not, God has had different plans in operation (if we may so express it), to bring men back to dwell with Himself; and this we cannot believe, since there has been no change in the constitution of man since he fell…. It will be noticed that, according to Paul (see Galatians 3:8) the Gospel was preached to Abraham. We would like to be informed in what name the Gospel was then preached, whether it was in the name of Christ or some other name. If in any other name, was it the Gospel? And if it was the Gospel, and that preached in the name of Christ, had it any ordinances [sacraments]? If not, was it the Gospel?"[10]

To say this another way, Latter-day Saints teach that the knowledge of a savior and the plan of salvation have been revealed throughout history, and not simply since the mortal ministry of Jesus of Nazareth. This may be one reason why so many elements common to Christianity, remnants of a primitive Christian message—a god becoming a man, a virgin birth, saving and ennobling truths, etc.—are to be found in cultures far and wide, even dating well before the birth of Jesus. As Joseph F. Smith, nephew of Joseph Smith and himself sixth president of the Church, explained: "When I read books that are scattered broad-cast through the world, throwing discredit upon words and teachings and doctrines of the Lord Jesus Christ, saying that some of the ideas Jesus uttered, truths that he promulgated, have been enunciated before by the ancient philosophers among the heathen nations of the world, I want to tell you that there is not a heathen philosopher that ever lived in all the world from the beginning, that had a truth or enunciated a principle of God's truth that did not receive it from the fountain head, from God himself." On another occasion he stated:

"Let it be remembered that Christ was with the Father from the beginning, that the gospel of truth and light existed from the begin-ning, and is from everlasting to everlasting. The Father, Son, and Holy Ghost, as one God, are the fountain of truth. From this fountain all the ancient learned philosophers have received their inspiration and wisdom—from it they have received all their knowledge. If we find truth in broken fragments through the ages, it may be set down as an incontrovertible fact that it originated at the fountain, and was given to philosophers, inventors, patriots, reformers, and prophets by the inspi-ration of God. It came from him through his Son Jesus Christ and the Holy Ghost, in the first place, and from no other source. It is eternal.

"Christ, therefore, being the fountain of truth, is no imitator. He taught the truth first; it was his before it was given to man. When he came to the earth he not only proclaimed new thought, but repeated some of the everlasting principles which had been heretofore only part-ly understood and enunciated by the wisest of men. And in so doing he enlarged in every instance upon the wisdom which they had originally received from him, because of his superior abilities and wisdom, and his association with the Father and the Holy Ghost. He did not imitate men. They made known in their imperfect way what the inspiration of Jesus Christ had taught them, for they obtained their enlightenment first from him."[11]

There is no indication that Joseph Smith ever read Jonathan Edwards. It is of some interest to me, however, that the idea of an eternal gospel, or the concept that vital truths trickled down through the generations in cultures throughout the world, was also taught by Edwards. I am indebted to my friend Gerald McDermott, who points out some of

Edwards's teachings on this matter. "Edwards used the *prisca theologia* tradition," a doctrine expounded by early Church fathers like Clement of Alexandria, Origen, Lactantius, and Eusebius, "to insist that most of the world has actually heard the basics of the gospel. Hence God has been more than just." Further, "Edwards was always quick to note that heathen religion and philosophy contained 'many absurdities.' But he learned from the *prisca theologia* that among the absurdities there were enough 'scraps of truth' to show the way to salvation."[12]

And so when I sing "Gimme that ole-time religion" as a Latter-day Saint, I am not just talking about the religion my Dad and Grand-dad enjoyed. I am not just pining for religious life in the 1950s or even in the 1850s. And, interestingly enough, I am not just wanting things to be like they were in the days of Jesus and Paul and John. From an LDS perspective, if the gospel was good enough for Adam and Enoch and Abraham and Moses, then it's good enough for me.

ENDNOTES

1. John G. Stackhouse, *Evangelical Landscapes*, 16.

2. Cotton Mather, *Magnolia Christi Americana* (Harford: Silas Andrus & Sons, 1853), 498; cited in Jeffrey R. Holland, CR, October 2004, 6.

3. Ibid.

4. D. S. Burnet, ed., *The Christian Baptist*, 1:33.

5. Milton V. Backman Jr., *American Religions and the Rise of Mormonism*, 241.

6. In Ahlstrom, ed., *Theology in America*, 315–16.

7. Young, *Journal of Discourses* 5:75; cited hereafter as *JD*.

8. Woodruff, *JD* 4:99.

9. Richards, in *History of the Church* 2:470.

10. *TPJS,* 59–60, emphasis added.

11. Smith, *Gospel Doctrine*, 395–99.

12. Cited in McDermott, *Jonathan Edwards Confronts the Gods*, 80, 96.

FOUR

A Wretch Like Me

MOST OF US DEAL WITH the harsh realities of physical deterioration quite well. What we are less eager to face up to is that we live in a fallen world and are subject to spiritual death. We have thoughts that are unclean, feelings that are un-Christian, desires that are unholy, attitudes that are divisive, inclinations that are disruptive to order and decency. We manifest pride and arrogance and too often filter our decisions through the lenses of ego. We are consumed with judgmentalism and tend to look more harshly upon the flaws and misdeeds of others than is wise or charitable. We complain and murmur when things do not go as we had hoped or when they go slower than we had anticipated. Even those who have come out of the world by covenant into the marvelous light of Christ (see 1 Peter 2:9) are subject to these temptations and spiritual distractions from the path of peace. "Search your hearts," Joseph Smith once counseled the Saints, "and see if you are like God. I have searched mine, and feel to repent of all my sins."[1]

What *is* the LDS perspective on the nature of men and women? Do Mormons believe that people are basically good, or do they, in harmony with their brothers and sisters of other Christian faiths, see humankind as flawed and depraved? This is not as easy to answer as one might suspect. As we pointed out in the previous chapter, Joseph Smith and his successors have taught that all people on earth are spirit sons and daughters of God the Eternal Father and that from him we inherit the seeds of goodness and divinity. In that sense, one might be prone to say that Latter-day Saints believe that humankind is basically good, inasmuch as we are related to the Greatest Good, God himself. But this is referring to *eternal* man, not man or woman that is spoken of so often in scripture, namely, *mortal* man or fallen woman.

I like the way John Stott speaks of the nature of humanity. He emphasizes that Christians believe in both the Creation and the Fall. Through the Creation there is planted upon and within humankind the image and likeness of God. Through the Fall, however, that image and likeness are marred, such that our ways of thinking, feeling, and acting are affected negatively. "So, then," Stott summarizes, "everything in us that is attributable to our creation in the image of God we gratefully affirm, while everything in us that is attributable to the Fall we must resolutely repudiate or deny. Thus we are called both to self-affirmation and to self-denial, and we need discernment to distinguish which is appropriate and when."[2]

While the Latter-day Saints believe in the reality, breadth, and depth of the Fall, at the same time our view of what took place in the Garden of Eden is remarkably optimistic when compared to that of traditional Christianity. To borrow the words of John Milton, Mormons believe in a "fortunate Fall." We believe the Fall was a part of God's divine plan and thus laid the foundation for the Atonement itself. In other words, if there had been no Fall, there would have been no Atonement. In the words of one Church leader, "The Fall had a twofold direction—downward, yet forward. It brought man into the world and set his feet upon progression's highway."[3] Or, in the language of the Book of Mormon, "Adam fell that men might be, and men are that they might have joy" (2 Nephi 2:25).

To illustrate that the LDS view of the Fall is not so terribly unusual, let me refer to the writings of other religious thinkers. C. S. Lewis did not hold to a traditional Christian view of human depravity. For one thing, Lewis concluded that if people are depraved, they cannot even decide between what is good and what is evil. "If God is wiser than we," he stated, "His judgment must differ from ours on many things, and not least on good and evil. What seems to us good may therefore not be good in His eyes, and what seems to us evil may not be evil. On the other hand, if God's moral judgment differs from ours so that our 'black' may be His 'white,' we can mean nothing by calling Him good."

This particular problem would affect our relationship to God, including our obedience to him. "If He is not (in our sense) 'good' we shall obey, if at all, only through fear—and should be equally ready to obey an omnipotent Fiend. The doctrine of Total Depravity—when the consequence is drawn that, since we are totally depraved, our idea of good is worth simply nothing—may thus turn Christianity into a form of devil-worship."[4] Lewis also observed: "I disbelieve that doctrine [total depravity], partly on the logical ground that if our depravity were total we should not know ourselves to be depraved, and partly because experience shows us much goodness in human nature."[5]

Lewis observed that the Fall offered "a deeper happiness and a fuller splendour" than if there had been no Fall. Because man has fallen, he pointed out, "for him God does the great deed." For man, the prodigal, "the eternal Lamb is killed." Thus "if ninety and nine righteous races inhabiting distant planets that circle distant suns, and needing no redemption on their own account, were made and glorified by the glory which had descended into our race"—namely Jesus Christ, the Lamb of God—then "redeemed humanity" would become "something more glorious than any unfallen race." "The greater the sin," he continued, "the greater the mercy: the deeper the death the brighter the rebirth. And this super-added glory will, with true vicariousness, exalt all creatures and those who have never fallen will thus bless Adam's fall."[6]

In a sermon delivered in 1782 entitled "God's Love to Fallen Man," the famous theologian/churchman John Wesley acknowledged that men and women are fallen and in a desperate condition without divine assistance. But because the Fall impels men and women to seek after such assistance, the Fall was, in the long run, a good thing. "May the Lover of men open the eyes of our understanding to perceive clearly that by the fall of Adam mankind in general have gained a capacity, first, for being more holy and happy on earth; and secondly, of being more happy in heaven, than otherwise they might have been." Quoting from the apostle John, Wesley stated that "'We love him, because he first loved us' [1 John 4:19], but this greatest instance of his love had never been given if Adam had not fallen." In other words, "God permitted [the Fall] (in order to a fuller manifestation) of his wisdom, justice and mercy, by bestowing on all who would receive it an infinitely

greater happiness than they possibly could have attained if Adam had
not fallen."[7]

Barbara Brown Taylor recently asked some interesting questions
about our first parents: "If God did not want them to eat from the tree,
then why did God put it there in the first place? ...If it was all a test
of the first couple's obedience, then why didn't God let them work up
to it a little?" Taylor went on to observe, "Some lovers of this story say
that Adam and Eve were destined to do what they did—not because
of original sin but because of God. God knew that they had to eat
the fruit. It was the only way for them to wake up, so that they could
make real choices from then on.... But nowhere in this story is the
word 'sin' mentioned, much less the phrase 'original sin.' That tagline
was assigned to the story much later—in the fourth century c.e.—by
Augustine of Hippo, who turned the tale of Adam and Eve into an
explanation for the human tendency to choose evil instead of good."[8]

Sometimes Latter-day Saints are a little nervous about teaching the
full effects of the Fall, concerned that perhaps we might be misunder-
stood as accepting a belief in universal human depravity. I guess it's the
word *depraved* that sends a chill down my spine, although I certainly
believe and am a witness of the reality and plight of fallen humanity.
When I think of someone being depraved, I find myself pondering on
someone who rapes and murders and plots the overthrow of a nation.
I'm told, however, by my Christian friends that "human depravity" is
sometimes rendered as "human inability," and if that's the case then I
have no problem with believing in human depravity; I'm a firm believer
in the fact that no man or woman—no matter their innate brilliance,
educational training, or personal self-control—can forgive their own
sins, change their own nature, or bring about happiness and fulfillment
here or glorified immortality hereafter.

As someone has observed, the widespread evidence of the Fall is
the greatest proof for the truthfulness of the Christian message. The
Fall does indeed take a toll on all humankind. It is real. Its effects cannot be ignored, nor can its pull on the human heart be mitigated by
enlightened conversation. A person's capacity to become Christlike is
one thing; his or her inclination to sin is quite another. Further, to
fail to teach the Fall effectively is to weaken our understanding of the

importance of the Atonement. Ezra Taft Benson, thirteenth president of the LDS Church, declared: "Just as man does not really desire food until he is hungry, so he does not desire the salvation of Christ until he knows why he needs Christ. No one adequately and properly knows why he needs Christ until he understands and accepts the doctrine of the Fall and its effect upon all mankind."[9] In other words, the Fall and the Atonement are a package deal: The one brings the other into existence. We do not appreciate and treasure the medicine until we appreciate the seriousness of the malady. We cannot look earnestly to the Redeemer if we do not sense the need for redemption. Jesus Christ came to earth to do more than offer sage advice. He is not merely a benevolent consultant or a spiritual adviser. He came to save us.

"All we, like sheep, have gone astray," Isaiah wrote; "we have turned everyone to his own way" (Isaiah 53:6). The Good Shepherd comes on a search-and-rescue mission after all of his lost sheep. He who never took a moral detour or a backward step reaches out and reaches down to lift us up. We are lost in that we do not know our way home without a guide, in that we are alienated from God and separated from things of righteousness. We are fallen in that we have chosen, like our Exemplar, to condescend to enter mortal life. Because our eternal spirit has taken its temporary abode in a physical body, we must be lifted up, quickened, and resuscitated spiritually if we are to return to the divine presence. As N. T. Wright observed, "Part of the Christian story…is that human beings have been so seriously damaged by evil that what they need isn't simply better self-knowledge, or better social conditions, but help, and indeed rescue, from outside themselves…. The need which the Christian faith answers is not so much that we are ignorant and need better information, but that we are lost and need someone to come and find us, stuck in the quicksand waiting to be rescued, dying and in need of new life."[10]

Latter-day Saints do not believe in the doctrine of original sin or that little children need to be baptized until they begin to become accountable before God (the LDS baptize children at eight years). Mormon scripture does teach, however, that men and women are "conceived in sin" (Moses 6:55). In one sense, to be conceived in sin is to be conceived into a world of sin, to come forth into a fallen sphere, a state in which sin predominates. In addition, conception becomes the vehicle, the means whereby a fallen nature—mortality, what the scriptures call the flesh—is transmitted to the posterity of Adam and Eve. In short, to say that we are not responsible for the fall of Adam and Eve is not to say that we are unaffected by it. To say that we do not inherit an original sin through the Fall is not to say that we do not inherit a fallen nature and thus the capacity to sin and suffer death. Fallenness and mortality are inherited. They come to us as a natural consequence of the second estate we call earth life.

Brigham Young observed that a critical and doubting disposition concerning the work of the Lord "arises from the power of evil that is so prevalent upon the face of the whole earth. It was given to you by your father and mother; it was mingled with your conception in the womb, and it has ripened in your flesh, in your blood, and in your bones, so that it has become riveted in your very nature."[11] On another occasion President Young explained: "There are no persons without evil passions to embitter their lives. Mankind are revengeful, passionate, hateful, and devilish in their dispositions. This we inherit through the Fall, and the grace of God is designed to enable us to overcome it."[12] We can grow in spiritual graces to the point wherein we have no more disposition to do evil but to do good continually (Mosiah 5:2) and wherein we cannot look upon sin save it be with abhorrence (Alma 13:12). We can delight in the things of the Lord, but as long as we dwell in the flesh we will be subject to the pulls of a fallen world.

Now again, Latter-day Saints fully accept the fact that we are the spirit sons and daughters of God and as such have unlimited potential for good and goodness. Joseph Smith taught these principles clearly. But this same Joseph Smith taught: "I have learned in my travels that man is treacherous and selfish, but few excepted."[13] "All are subjected to vanity while they travel through the crooked paths and difficulties which surround them. Where is the man that is free from vanity? None ever were perfect but Jesus."[14]

And, if the picture isn't bleak enough, there are the many good things we could do but do not choose to do—the sins of omission. "Therefore to him that knoweth to do good, and doeth it not, to him it is sin" (James 4:17). "Made for spirituality," Tom Wright reminds us, "we wallow in introspection. Made for joy, we settle for pleasure. Made for justice, we clamor for vengeance. Made for relationship, we insist on our own way. Made for beauty, we are satisfied with sentiment." And then, in a call for us to repent and mature, Wright affirms that the "new creation has already begun. The sun has begun to rise. Christians are called to leave behind, in the tomb of Jesus Christ, all that belongs to the brokenness and incompleteness of the present world. It is time, in the power of the Spirit, to take up our proper role, our fully human role, as agents, as heralds, and stewards of the new day that is dawning."[15]

In a sense, then, our lives are a study in contrast—carnality and unlimited divine possibility. A beloved Latter-day Saint children's hymn by Naomi W. Randall is entitled "I Am a Child of God."[16] Note the words carefully:

> I am a child of God,
> And he has sent me here,
> Has given me an earthly home,
> With parents kind and dear.

> *Chorus*
> Lead me, guide me, walk beside me.
> Help me find the way.
> Teach me all that I must do
> To live with him some day.

> I am a child of God,
> And so my needs are great;
> Help me to understand his words
> Before it grows too late.
> *Chorus*

> I am a child of God,
> Rich blessings are in store;
> If I but learn to do his will
> I'll live with him once more.
> *Chorus*

These words point our minds and hearts toward such matters as who we are, whose we are, where we came from, why we are here, and where we are going after death. But there's another side to the story. Two of my colleagues, Paul Sutorius and Curtis Wright, adapted the words of "I Am a Child of God" to give it a different emphasis:

> I am a child of God.
> That's only half the view:
> If I don't shed the natural man,
> I'm lost, and so are you.
>
> Lead me, guide me, reconcile me;
> Chasten me on earth:
> Help me overcome the Fall;
> Grant me second birth.
>
> I am a child of God,
> But that doesn't clear the slate:
> I'm carnal, sensual, devilish, too,
> In a lost and fallen state.
>
> Save me, change me, rearrange me,
> Gracious God above:
> Cleave unto my broken heart;
> Bestow redeeming love.
>
> I am a child of God.
> Yet I've become his child
> Through faith in his Beloved Son's
> Redemption undefiled.
>
> Lead me, guide me, justify me,
> Cleanse me, make me pure;
> Help me love as thou hast loved,
> Or I cannot endure.

One of the burdens of the Book of Mormon is the need for men and women to live in a constant state of gospel gladness, a condition of overwhelming thanksgiving for God's blessings, an attitude of divine indebtedness. Our relationship with the Almighty is not one of quid pro quo. Rather, there is never a time when our goodness, our personal righteousness, or our undying loyalty will place our Heavenly Father in our debt. Rather, no matter how hard we try to do what's right, how consistently we love and worship and serve, we will always be unprofitable servants (Mosiah 2:21; compare Luke 17:10), unworthy of unmerited blessings, but hopefully very much aware of his tender mercies and his constant watchcare.

Indeed, as millions upon millions have sung with great gratitude, it is an amazing grace, manifest by the Father through his Son, that would save a wretch like me. As Brigham Young explained, "It requires all the atonement of Christ, the mercy of the Father, the pity of angels, and the grace of the Lord Jesus Christ to be with us always, and then to do the very best we possibly can, to get rid of this sin within us, so that we may escape from this world into the celestial kingdom."[17]

ENDNOTES

1. Smith, *TPJS,* 372.

2. Stott, *Why I Am a Christian,* 78.

3. Orson F. Whitney, *Cowley and Whitney on Doctrine,* 287.

4. Lewis, *The Problem of Pain,* 33.

5. Ibid., 59.

6. Lewis, *Miracles,* 162.

7. In Outler and Heitzenrater, eds., *John Wesley's Sermons,* 477, 479, 483–84.

8. Taylor, *Speaking of Sin,* 46–47.

9. Benson, *A Witness and a Warning,* 33.

10. Wright, *Simply Christian,* 25, 92.

11. Young, *JD* 2:134.
12. Ibid., 8:160.
13. Smith, *TPJS,* 30.
14. Ibid., 187.
15. Wright, *Simply Christian,* 237.
16. *Hymns,* 1985, #301.
17. Young, *JD* 11:301.

FIVE

Justified and Reborn

ATTER-DAY SAINT scripture teaches that our hope and trust cannot be in ourselves, no matter how impressive our credentials or how stunning our achievements. People are mortal, and their imperfections and limitations are obvious. We cannot trust or hope in programs, procedures, lists, formulas, or laws of spiritual success. As Sheri Dew, a former member of the LDS general Relief Society presidency, pointed out, "The Savior isn't our last chance; He is our only chance. Our only chance to overcome self-doubt and catch a vision of who we may become. Our only chance to repent and have our sins washed clean. Our only chance to purify our hearts, subdue our weaknesses, and avoid the adversary. Our only chance to obtain redemption and exaltation. Our only chance to find peace and happiness in this life and eternal life in the world to come....

"The Lord knows the way because He *is* the way and is our only chance for successfully negotiating mortality. His Atonement makes available all of the power, peace, light, and strength that we need to deal with life's challenges—those ranging from our own mistakes and sins to trials over which we have no control but we still feel pain."[1]

Men and women come unto Christ not just to be taught but to be transformed. He is not only the Example or Prototype of a saved being but also the Change Agent and Benefactor. Jesus is not only a convenient resource; he is the vital and indispensable element in the quest for happiness here and eternal reward hereafter. There is no hope and no possibility of reconciliation with the Father except by and through the Savior.

One who chooses Christ chooses to be changed. The plan of salvation is not just a program bent on making bad men good and good men better, though it certainly does that; it is a system of salvation that seeks to renovate society and transform the whole of humankind. Those who are dead to the things of the Spirit must be quickened, made alive, or born again in order to enter the realm of divine experience. This is not optional but required. The new birth is the means by which "the dark veil of unbelief" is removed from the mind and by which the "light of the glory of God" infuses joy into the soul (Alma 19:6). It is the process by which persons "lay aside every sin, which easily doth beset [us], which doth bind [us] down to destruction" (Alma 7:15). It is the only way whereby we can receive the image of Christ in our countenances (Alma 5:14).

The renewal is a conversion from worldliness to saintliness, from being lured by the lurid to being enticed by holiness. That conversion comes by virtue of the cleansing blood of Jesus and through the medium of the Holy Spirit, who is the Sanctifier. Over time people are sanctified to the point that they begin to lose the desire for sin and instead find themselves drawn and enticed toward righteousness. One straying soul in the Book of Mormon underwent a dramatic conversion to Christ. He "stood up and began to speak unto [the people], bidding them to be of good comfort: for, said he, I have repented of my sins, and have been redeemed of the Lord; behold I am born of the Spirit. And the Lord said unto me: Marvel not that all mankind, yea, men and women, all nations, kindreds, tongues, and people, must be born again; yea, born of God, *changed from their carnal and fallen state, to a state of righteousness, being redeemed of God*, becoming his sons and daughters; *and thus they become new creatures*; and unless they do this, they can in nowise inherit the kingdom of God." (Mosiah 27:23–26, emphasis added.)

The Atonement provides the means not only for forgiveness of sins but also of reinstatement in the royal family. Again in the Book of Mormon, a prophet/king acknowledged this marvelous truth when he commended his people for their willingness to enter into the gospel covenant and come unto Christ. "And now, *because of the covenant which ye have made ye shall be called the children of Christ, his sons, and his daughters; for behold, this day he hath spiritually begotten you*; for ye say that your hearts are changed through faith on his name; therefore, *ye are born of him and have become his sons and his daughters*. And under this head ye are made free, and there is no other head whereby ye can be made free. There is no other name given whereby salvation cometh; therefore, I would that ye should take upon you the name of Christ, all you that have entered into the covenant with God that ye should be obedient unto the end of your lives." (Mosiah 5:7–8, emphasis added; compare 27:25.)

Just as the newborn in our mortal world automatically enters into a family relationship through birth, even so the new birth, the birth of the Spirit, becomes an avenue of life within the family of the Lord Jesus Christ. Christ is thus the Father of our awakening into newness of life, the Father of our resurrection, the Father of our salvation. As members of his family we know who we are and act accordingly—we take seriously our divine birthright as Christians. The Book of Mormon teaches that we are saved by merit, but not by our own merit. "*Since man had fallen*," one missionary declared, "*he could not merit anything of himself*, but the sufferings and death of Christ atone for their sins, through faith and repentance, and so forth" (Alma 22:14, emphasis added).

"Suppose we have the scriptures," Bruce McConkie asked, "the gospel, the priesthood, the Church, the ordinances, the organization, even the keys of the kingdom—everything that now is down to the last jot and tittle—and yet there is no atonement of Christ. What then? Can we be saved? Will all our good works save us? Will we be rewarded for all our righteousness?

"Most assuredly we will not. We are not saved by works alone, no matter how good; we are saved because God sent his Son to shed his blood in Gethsemane and on Calvary that all through him might ransomed be. We are saved by the blood of Christ.

'Salvation [does] not come by the church alone: and were it not for the atonement, given by the grace of God as a free gift, all men must unavoidably perish, and this notwithstanding the Church and all that appertains to it.'"[2]

Like the infant who grasps and clings to objects with selfish immaturity, we are so prone to be stingy with our lives, to insist on doing things our way, to chart a course that we want to pursue, to demand complete control. While we labor in the flesh we are subject to a kind of mortal myopia, a tragic shortsightedness in regard to eternal things. In our heart of hearts we know that God's ways are higher than ours and his thoughts and judgment so much grander than our own (Isaiah 55:8–9). The wise course is to allow the Captain of our Soul to have sway, to make us into new creatures far beyond anything we might bring about in our own limited and halting manner. In the words of Ezra Taft Benson, "Men and women who turn their lives over to God will discover that He can make a lot more out of their lives than they can. He will deepen their joys, expand their vision, quicken their minds, strengthen their muscles, lift their spirits, multiply their blessings, increase their opportunities, comfort their souls, raise up friends, and pour out peace."[3]

Those who have tasted of the heavenly gift and enjoyed the sweet fruits of gospel living want more than anything to be holy people. But we fall short. We make mistakes. We sin, and so we are not completely righteous. I am not, as a result of my own actions, a just man. Theoretically, there are two ways a person could be just—meaning declared or esteemed innocent, guiltless, free from the demands of divine justice. First, she could live her life perfectly, never taking a backward step, never deviating one inch from the straight and narrow path. In such a case, it could then be said of that man or woman that they were *justified by law or by works*. It would be a glorious thing to be in such a state, would it not? The problem here is that no person—not the greatest prophet or the mightiest apostle—has ever traversed life's paths without error or sin of some kind. It may be hypothetically possible, but it is practically impossible. This is what the prophets through the ages meant when they taught that "by the law no flesh is justified" (Romans 3:20; Galatians 2:16). Indeed, the Apostle Paul warned the Saints in his day about trying to establish one's own righteousness, even as the Jews had done through their strict observance of the Law of Moses (Romans 10:1–4; Philippians 3:8–9).

The second way that men and women become just is *by faith*. Faith is the complete trust, confidence in, and reliance upon the merits, mercy, and grace of Jesus Christ for salvation. It is a gift of the Spirit (1 Corinthians 12:9; Moroni 10:11), a divine endowment that affirms to the human heart the identity and redemptive mission of the Savior.

Men and women's good works, though acceptable to God, will always be insufficient to save them. In short, had there been no means of bridging the chasm between sinful humanity and a sinless God, nothing we could do would make up for the loss. Thus there is a need for some means to reconcile finite humanity with an infinite Deity, to repair the breech between earth and the heavens. Because "all have sinned and come short of the glory of God" (Romans 3:23), we cannot be justified by law or by works. Our only option is to be justified by faith, to lean upon One who did in fact keep the law of God perfectly. It is only through the name of Jesus Christ—meaning his power or authority, his atoning mission and work—that salvation comes to the children of men (Acts 4:12; Mosiah 3:17).

"I do not think there have been many good men on the earth since the days of Adam," Joseph Smith declared; "but there was one good man and his name was Jesus."[4] Also from Brother Joseph: "Who, among the Saints in these last days can consider himself as good as our Lord? Who is as perfect? Who is as pure? Who is as holy as He was? Are they to be found? He never transgressed or broke a commandment or law of heaven—no deceit was in His mouth, neither was guile found in His heart."[5] And finally: "Where is the man that is free from vanity? None ever were perfect but Jesus; and why was He perfect? Because He was the Son of God, and had the fullness of the Spirit, and greater power than any man."[6]

Justification is a legal term; being justified establishes my righteous *standing* before God. On the other hand, sanctification is an ongoing work of the Holy Spirit, one that deals with the gradual purification of my *state*. B. H. Roberts, one of the great Mormon thinkers, insightfully taught that the forgiven soul may still continue to "feel the force of sinful habits bearing heavily upon him. He who has been guilty of habitual untruthfulness, will at times find himself inclined, perhaps, to yield to that habit. He who has stolen may be sorely tempted, when opportunity arises, to steal again. While he who has indulged in licentious practices may again find himself disposed to give way to the seductive influence of the siren. So with drunkenness, malice, envy, covetousness, hatred, anger, and in short all the evil dispositions that flesh is heir to.

"There is an absolute necessity for some additional sanctifying grace that will strengthen the poor human nature, not only to enable it to resist temptation, but also to root out from the heart concupiscence—the blind tendency or inclination to evil. The heart must be purified, every passion, every propensity made submissive to the will, and the will of man brought into subjection to the will of God.

"Man's natural powers are unequal to this task; so, I believe, all will testify who have made the experiment. Mankind stand in some need of a strength superior to any they possess of themselves, to accomplish this work of rendering pure our fallen nature. Such strength, such power, such a sanctifying grace is conferred on man in being born of the Spirit—in receiving the Holy Ghost. Such, in the main, is its office, its work."[7]

Latter-day Saints believe that the process of cleansing and sanctifying through the baptisms of water and of the Spirit can be continued weekly as we partake of the Sacrament of the Lord's Supper. To be sure, the ordinance of baptism does not forgive sins or save a person, nor does partaking of the emblems of the Savior's broken body and spilt blood, for salvation is in Christ the Person; rather, baptism and the Sacrament of the Lord's Supper are channels that help to activate the power of God. A sacrament or ordinance is an outward manifestation of one's inward commitment to the Lord (his or her faith).

Some people have been led to describe the work of Atonement as essentially "the great exchange." Paul wrote: "For he [God the Father] hath made him [Christ the Son] to be sin for us, who knew no sin; that we might be made the righteousness of God in him" (2 Corinthians 5:21). "Christ hath redeemed us from the curse of the law, being made a curse for us" (Galatians 3:13). "But we see Jesus, who was made a little lower than the angels for the suffering of death, crowned with glory and honour; that he by the grace of God should taste death for every man" (Hebrews 2:9). What a deal! As we come unto Christ, there is imputed to us, placed on our spiritual account, if you will, the righteousness of Christ, and there is imputed to Christ the sinfulness of humanity.

We know that Jesus Christ came to earth to die for us. This truth is foundational to our faith. Equally important is that the Son of God desires to live in us. He does so through the power of his Holy Spirit.

Fundamental to the new life in Christ is being cleansed and forgiven. But also vital is being filled. The same Lord who purifies our souls fills our souls—he provides strength and energy and enabling power. As God's peculiar treasure, Christians are a purchased people; they are not their own. They have been bought back, purchased, redeemed by the precious blood of the Christ (1 Corinthians 6:19–20; 7:23; 1 Peter 1:18). And it is "the blood that maketh an atonement for the soul" (Leviticus 17:11).

ENDNOTES

1. Dew, CR, April 1999, 84–85.
2. McConkie, "What Think Ye of Salvation by Grace?", 48.
3. *Teachings of Ezra Taft Benson*, 361.
4. Smith, TPJS, 303.
5. Smith, TPJS, 67.
6. Smith, TPJS, 187–88.
7. Roberts, *The Gospel and Man's Relationship to Deity*, 170.

SIX

The Work of the Spirit

John wrote: "This then is the message which we have heard of [Christ], and declare unto you, that God is light, and in him is no darkness at all" (1 John 1:5). We do not travel far in our study of the Gospel of John before we read that Jesus Christ is "the true Light, which lighteth every man that cometh into the world" (John 1:9). Because Jehovah was the foreordained Redeemer and Savior, the Lamb slain from the foundation of the world (Revelation 5:6; 13:8; Moses 7:47), the Father's plan became his by adoption; the gospel of God (Romans 1:1–3) thus became known as the gospel of Jesus Christ. Likewise, because God the Father has invested his Beloved Son with his own attributes and powers, because the "Father of lights" (James 1:17) has ordained that Christ is to be the Light of lights, the Light of the world, those powers of life and light that we know as the power of God have come to be known as the Light of Christ or Spirit of Jesus Christ.

Though there is but passing reference to the Light of Christ in the New Testament, LDS scriptures abound in detail, assisting us immeasurably to understand how and in what manner the Light of Christ lights every man and woman born into mortality. We come to know, first of all, that light is a manifestation of the glory of God, a divine influence that fills the immensity of space, and the means whereby God, a corporeal being who can be in only one place at a time, is omnipresent. Bruce R. McConkie has written: "The light of Christ (also called the Spirit of Christ and the Spirit of the Lord) is a light, a power, and an influence that proceeds forth from the presence of God to fill the immensity of space.... It is the agency of God's power and the law by which all things are governed. It is also the agency used by the Holy Ghost to manifest truth and dispense spiritual gifts to many people at one and the same time. For instance, it is as though the Holy Ghost, who is a personage of spirit, was broadcasting all truth throughout the whole universe all the time, using the light of Christ as the agency by which the message is delivered. But only those who attune their souls to the Holy Spirit receive the available revelation. It is in this way that the person of the Holy Ghost makes his influence felt in the heart of every righteous person at one and the same time."[1]

By inheritance as well as by perfect obedience, Jesus Christ was entitled to a fullness of the Spirit. Jesus spoke often of his divine inheritance. "Therefore doth my Father love me," John recorded, "because I lay down my life, that I might take it again. No man taketh it from me, but I lay it down of myself. I have power to lay it down, and I have power to take it again. This commandment have I received of my Father" (John 10:17–18). Herein is the fundamental truth to be believed if we are to accept the divine Sonship of Christ. Jesus was the son of Mary, a mortal woman, and from her inherited mortality, including the capacity to die. Jesus was the son of God, and from him inherited the capacity to rise up from the dead in resurrected immortality.

Mormons teach that Jesus lived and moved and had his being in the Spirit of God, "for God giveth not the Spirit by measure unto him" (John 3:34). It was this fullness that enabled and empowered the lowly Nazarene to resist evil, dismiss Satan from his life, and enjoy constant communion with the Father. The Latter-day Saints teach, and the New Testament affirms, that the Beloved Son was in fact subordinate to his Father in mortality. Jesus came to carry out the will of the Father (John 4:34). He explained: "I seek not mine own will, but the will of the Father which hath sent me" (John 5:30; compare 6:38–40). In addition, the scriptures attest that God had power, knowledge, glory, and dominion that Jesus did not have at the time. Truly, "the Son can do nothing of himself, but what he seeth the Father do" (John 5:19). Even what the Son spoke was what the Father desired to be spoken. "For I have not spoken of myself; but the Father which sent me, he gave me a commandment, what I should say, and what I should speak. And I know that his commandment is life everlasting: whatsoever I speak therefore, even as the Father said unto me, so I speak" (John 12:49–50). Finally, "If ye loved me, ye would rejoice, because I said, I go unto the Father: for my Father is greater than I" (John 14:28).

On the other hand, the Father and the Son enjoyed much more than what we might call closeness; theirs was a divine indwelling relationship. Because he kept the law of God, Jesus was in the Father, and the Father was in Jesus (see John 14:10, 20; 17:21; 1 John 3:24). Though they were two separate and distinct persons, they were one—infinitely more one than separate. Their transcendent unity but epitomizes what ought to exist between God and all of his children. That is to say, we are under commission to seek the Spirit of God, to strive to be one with God, to be, as Joseph Smith explained, "agreed as one,"[2] to have, as Paul wrote, "the mind of Christ" (1 Corinthians 2:16). "Hereby know we that we dwell in him, and he in us, because he hath given us of his Spirit" (1 John 4:13). We thus gain the mind of Christ as Christ gained the mind of the Father—through the power of the Spirit.

The Holy Spirit, as the third member of the Godhead, is the minister of the Father and the Son. Christ sends the Comforter (John 15:26; 16:7). That Comforter is not an independent personage in the sense of speaking his own mind and delivering a completely original message. Jesus taught: "When he, the Spirit of truth, is come, he will guide you into all truth: for he shall not speak of himself; but whatsoever he shall hear [presumably, from the Father and/or the Son], that shall he speak: and he will shew you things to come. He shall glorify me: for he shall receive of mine, and shall shew it unto you" (John 16:13–14). The three separate members of the Godhead are one—they bear the same witness and teach the same truths (1 John 5:7).

John records that there came to Jesus by night a man named Nicodemus, a "ruler of the Jews," presumably a member of the Sanhedrin, a man who was "a master in Israel," meaning a master teacher or acknowledged scholar among the Jews. He and others had been impressed with the miracles of Jesus. He said: "Rabbi, we know that thou art a teacher come from God: for no man can do these miracles that thou doest, except God be with him." It was as though the Savior then desired to do two things: (1) to point out to Nicodemus that more was required of him than a verbal recognition of Jesus as a miracle worker; and (2) to anticipate the question that must have lurked in the shadows of Nicodemus's mind but that went unasked: "What must I do to inherit eternal life?" Jesus answered: "Except a man be born again, he cannot see the kingdom of God" (John 3:1–3.)

Jeremiah had spoken of a time when the Lord would again propose a covenant to his covenant people, when He would "put [his] law in their inward parts, and write it in their hearts," and that Jehovah would truly be their God and Israel would be his people (Jeremiah 31:31–34). Likewise, the Lord had spoken through Ezekiel: "Then will I sprinkle clean water upon you, and ye shall be clean: from all your filthiness, and from all your idols, will I cleanse you. A new heart also will I give you, and a new spirit will I put within you: and I will take away the stony heart out of your flesh, and I will give you an heart of flesh" (Ezekiel 36:25–26). Even in the Book of Jubilees, an apocryphal work, the concept of a new birth was to be found: "But after this they will return to me in all uprighteousness and with all of their heart and soul. And I shall cut off the foreskin of their heart and the foreskin of the heart of their descendants. And I shall create for them a holy spirit, and I shall purify them so that they will not turn away from following me from that day and forever. And their souls will cleave to me and to all my commandments. And they will do my commandments. And I shall be a father to them, and they will be sons to me" (Jubilees 1:23–25).

Nicodemus either did not understand what Jesus was teaching, or he sought to prolong an otherwise interesting discussion, for he asked: "How can a man be born when he is old? Can he enter the second time into his mother's womb, and be born?" (John 3:4.) Jesus continued: "Except a man be born of water and of the Spirit, he cannot enter into the kingdom of God" (John 3:5). The Christian world is divided over this matter of the new birth. A large segment of Christianity today believes that being born again consists of having a personal spiritual experience with Jesus. A large segment of Christianity believes that being born again consists of receiving the sacraments (ordinances) of the Church. And where are the Latter-day Saints? Where do we stand on this vital issue? Joseph Smith stated simply that "Being born again, comes by the Spirit of God through ordinances."[3] Brother Joseph explained on another occasion that it is one thing to *see* the kingdom of God and another to *enter* into that kingdom. One must have "a change of heart" to see the kingdom; that is, he or she must be awakened spiritually to recognize the truth, acknowledge one's sinfulness, and thus one's need for deliverance by a Savior. Further, the Mormon Prophet taught, a person must "subscribe [to] the articles of adoption"—faith, repentance, baptism, and the reception of the Holy Spirit, all of which are fruits of one's initial expression of trust—in order to enter into the kingdom.[4] True conversion includes acting upon the revealed witness and submitting to those divine statutes that make it possible for us to be born again and thereby adopted into the family of God.

Daniel Tyler heard the Prophet Joseph explain that the birth spoken of in John 3:3—the birth to see—"was not the gift of the Holy Ghost, which was promised after baptism, but was a portion of the Spirit, which attended the preaching of the gospel by the elders of the Church. The people wondered why they had not previously understood the plain declarations of scripture, as explained by the elder, as they had read them hundreds of times. When they read the Bible [now] it was a new book to them. This was being born again to see the kingdom of God. They were not in it, but could see it from the outside, which they could not do until the Spirit of the Lord took the veil from their eyes. It was a change of heart, but not of state; they were converted, but were yet in their sins. Although Cornelius [Acts 10] had seen an holy angel, and on the preaching of Peter the Holy Ghost was poured out upon him and his household, they were only born again to see the kingdom of God. Had they not been baptized afterwards they would not have been saved."[5]

The anointing or unction of the Holy Ghost that comes through the birth of the Spirit places us in a position to acquire new feelings, new insights, new perspectives that no mortal instructor could ever convey to us (1 John 2:20, 27). Those who are born of the Spirit begin to embody the "fruit of the Spirit," the patience, long-suffering, gentleness, kindness, meekness, joy, and pure love of Christ that characterize the true sons and daughters of Deity (Galatians 5:22–25; Moroni 7:47–48). Truly, "We know that we have passed from death unto life, because we love the brethren" (1 John 3:14). "Beloved, let us love one another," John wrote, "for love is of God; and every one that loveth is born of God, and knoweth God" (1 John 4:7).

"Whosoever is born of God," John the Beloved declared, "doth not commit sin; for his [Christ's] seed remaineth in him: and he cannot sin, because he is born of God" (1 John 3:9; see also verse 6; 1 John 5:18). This is a troublesome passage, perhaps because I have had the privilege of associating with wonderful people in my life, holy people, men and women of faith who have given their all to God and His work; but they are not perfect, at least they are not perfect in the sense that we generally think about the term—they are not free from sin. I feel no hesitation in affirming that I have been born of the Spirit, have tasted of the sweet fruits of rebirth, have had my mind and heart expanded by the powers of the Spirit, have had my witness of God's work deepened and solidified. But I painfully and honestly admit that I am not free from sin.

In his own translation of this passage, Joseph Smith rendered it as follows: "Whosoever is born of God *doth not continue in sin; for the Spirit of God remaineth in him; and he cannot continue in sin,* because he is born of God, having received that holy Spirit of promise." One who has walked in the light comes to treasure the light. Should he or she step into the darkness momentarily, they are repulsed by the darkness and yearn to return, as soon as possible, to the light. That is, those who have been born of the Spirit learn to repent quickly, to confess and forsake their misdeeds, to move on. Obviously serious sins require more time, but many of our transgressions may be faced head-on and dispensed with in no time at all.

It was in the Last Supper that the Savior delivered some of the most profound teachings of his ministry concerning the work of the Holy Ghost in leading souls to salvation. Jesus had been with his disciples for three years, had taught them, empowered them, and prepared them for what was to come. He had been their Tutor, their Comforter. "If ye love me," he taught his chosen followers, "keep my commandments. And I will pray the Father, and *he shall give you another Comforter,* that he may abide with you forever; even the Spirit of truth; whom the world cannot receive, because it seeth him not, neither knoweth him: but ye know him; for he dwelleth with you, and shall be in you" (John

14:15–17, emphasis added). As pointed out in the MacArthur Study Bible (Word Publishing, 1997), the word *another* literally implies "another of the same kind," that is "someone, like Jesus Himself who will take His place and do His work." The Greek word translated in the King James Version as Comforter is *paraclete*, literally "one called to stand along side of." Other meanings include "a friend, especially a legal friend." The word refers to "a counselor who supports a defendant at a trial. The Spirit, then, will be a great defender of the disciples." Thus other translations render the passage as "another Helper" (New King James Version), "another Counselor" (New International Version), and even "another Advocate" (New Revised Standard Version; see also the Revised English Bible). While ultimately Christ is our Advocate with the Father, the Savior has sent his Spirit to convict us of sin, convince us of the truth, and direct us toward righteousness (John 16:8–11). As the NIV Study Bible (Zondervan, 1985) clarifies, the Paraclete was "any person who helped someone in trouble with the law. The Spirit will always stand by Christ's people." The Holy Ghost, "one called alongside to help," would be that member of the Godhead who "encourages and exhorts" the Saints.

Truly, those who are "in Christ" become "new creatures" of the Spirit (2 Corinthians 5:17), and it is by the power of that Spirit that we come to know the Lord. "And this is life eternal," the Master explained just prior to departing the Upper Room for Gethsemane, "that they might know thee the only true God, and Jesus Christ, whom thou hast sent" (John 17:3). Note the following testimony of John: "We know that we are of God, and the whole world lieth in wickedness. And we know that the Son of God is come, and hath given us an understanding, that we may know him that is true, and we are in him that is true, even in his Son Jesus Christ. This is the true God, and eternal life" (1 John 5:19–20).

Clearly we owe everything to our Heavenly Father who created us. In addition, our everlasting gratitude must always be offered to our Lord and Savior who was sent to earth on a search-and-rescue mission—to retrieve the wandering sheep and redeem us from death and hell and endless torment. Had there been no Atonement, no amount of labor on our part could ever, worlds without end, compensate for the loss. Truly, as Jesus proclaimed at the Last Supper, without him we can do nothing (John 15:1–5). And finally, one of the priceless blessings extended to the Saints is the gift of the Holy Spirit, a sacred endowment of power, a supernal privilege of enjoying companionship with a member of the Eternal Godhead. Thanks be to God that that Spirit, about which the world knows precious little (John 14:17), is sent to quicken, inspire, teach, testify, reprove, sanctify, comfort, and seal. We cannot simply face the challenges of life and triumph over the flesh without divine assistance. And so we worship and we pray, we labor and we trust in the merits and mercy of the Holy Messiah. And we rejoice in the reality that the Holy Spirit is given to prepare us for association with God and holy beings hereafter.

ENDNOTES

1. McConkie, *A New Witness for the Articles of Faith*, 70.
2. Smith, *TPJS*, 372.
2. Smith, *TPJS*, 162.
3. Ibid., 328.
4. Tyler, "Recollections of the Prophet Joseph Smith," in Andrus and Andrus, comp., *They Knew the Prophet*, 50–51.

SEVEN

1+1+1 = ?

O N MORE THAN ONE occasion while speaking to groups of Christians about the doctrines of Mormonism, I have been informed that, as a Latter-day Saint, I am not really a Christian for several reasons: (1) My faith tradition does not trace its roots through historic Christianity, and thus (2) we are not Catholic, Orthodox, or Protestant; (3) we do not believe the Bible is the sole written revelation of God; and (4) we do not accept the trinitarian formulations growing out of the Church councils beginning in A.D. 325 with Nicea. I have usually responded by assuring my friends of other faiths that we believe in and worship Christ; gladly confess our sins, our weakness, our utter inability to be saved without divine assistance; that we recognize that the only hope for deliverance is through the name and power and Person of Jesus Christ; we accept his substitutionary atonement, seek to be washed and sanctified through his blood, and anticipate one day being raised from the dead, just as he was. In short, we worship the Christ of the New Testament.

Mormons teach that over the years that followed the death and resurrection of the Lord, Christians sought earnestly to "contend for the faith which was once delivered unto the saints" (Jude 1:3). The epistles of Paul, Peter, Jude, and John suggest and even illustrate the kinds of theological and ecclesiastical challenges facing the Christian Church by the close of the first century. With the deaths of the apostles and the loss of the priesthood or divine authority, the institutional power to perform saving ordinances (sacraments), obtain the mind of God for the larger Church, and interpret scripture was no longer on earth. To be sure, there were noble men and women throughout the earth during the centuries that followed, religious persons of goodwill, learned men who sought to hold the Church together and preserve holy writ. But we believe that these acted without apostolic or prophetic authority.

Two of the most difficult doctrinal issues to resolve within the first four centuries of Christianity was the status and relation of the members of the Godhead in general and the nature of Jesus Christ in particular. A belief in Father, Son, and Holy Spirit, as set forth in the New Testament, left the early Christians open to the accusation of the Jews that they were polytheistic and thus in violation of the Shema: "Hear, O Israel: The Lord our God is one Lord" (Deuteronomy 6:4). In an effort to satisfy the accusations of Jews who denounced the notion of three Gods and at the same time incorporate ancient but appealing Greek philosophical concepts of an all-powerful moving force in the universe, the Christian Church began to theologize and philosophize concerning the Father, Son, and Holy Spirit.

One classic work by Edwin Hatch, *The Influence of Greek Ideas on Christianity* (Harper & Row, 1957), describes the intersection of Christian theology and Greek philosophy: "It is impossible for any one, whether he be a student of history or no, to fail to notice a difference of both form and content between the Sermon on the Mount and the Nicene Creed.... The one belongs to a world of Syrian peasants, the other to a world of Greek philosophers.... The religion which our Lord preached ...took the Jewish conception of a Father in heaven, and gave it a new meaning." In short, "Greek Christianity of the fourth century was rooted in Hellenism. The Greek minds which had been ripening for Christianity had absorbed new ideas and new motives."[1] Some of the many views adopted and adapted from Greek thought include: a strict monotheism, a belief in only one God; an absolute distinction between mind and created things; God as utterly transcendent, existing outside time and space; the inferiority of created things; the incomprehensible and unknowable God; the incorporeality (nonphysicality) of God; and the notion that God is immutable, that he never changes. Centuries of debate on the nature of God, Christ, and the Holy Spirit took place at Nicea (325), Constantinople (381), Ephesus (431), and

Chalcedon (451), resulting in creedal statements that became the walk and talk of Christian doctrine.

The noted anti-Christian writer of the second century, Celsus, stated: "The Christians say that God has hands, a mouth, and a voice; they are always proclaiming that 'God said this' or 'God spoke.' 'The heavens declare the work of his hands,' they say. I can only comment that such a God is no God at all, for God has neither hands, mouth, nor voice, nor any characteristics of which we know. And they say that God made man in his own image, failing to realize that God is not at all like a man, nor vice versa; God resembles no form known to us.... [W]e know that God is without shape, without color. They say that God moved above the waters he created—but we know that it is contrary to the nature of God to move. Their absurd doctrines even contain reference to God walking about in the garden he created for man; and they speak of him being angry, jealous, moved to repentance, sorry, sleepy—in short, as being in every respect more a man than a God. They have not read Plato, who teaches us in the Republic that God (the Good) does not even participate in being."[2]

What was the result? One non-Latter-day Saint has observed that as "the classical theological tradition became misguided when under the influence of Hellenistic philosophy, it defined God's perfection in static, timeless terms. All change was considered an imperfection and thus not applicable to God."[3] Further, "since Plato, Western philosophy has been infatuated with the idea of an unchanging, timeless reality. Time and all change were considered less real and less good than the unchanging time-less realm.... This infatuation with the 'unchanging' unfortunately crept into the church early on and has colored the way Christians look at the world, read their Bibles, and develop their theology."[4]

Such Platonic concepts as the immutability (no change), impassibility (no feelings or passions), and timelessness of God made their way into Christian theology. As one group of Evangelical scholars has stated, "Many Christians experience an inconsistency between their beliefs about the nature of God and their religious practice. For example, people who believe that God cannot change his mind sometimes pray in ways that would require God to do exactly that. And Christians who make use of the free will defense for the problem of evil sometimes ask God to get them a job or a spouse, or keep them from being harmed, implying that God should override the free will of others in order to achieve these ends....

"These inharmonious elements are the result of the coupling of biblical ideas about God with notions of the divine nature drawn from Greek thought. The inevitable encounter between biblical and classical thought in the early church generated many significant insights and helped Christianity evangelize pagan thought and culture. Along with the good, however, came a certain theological virus that infected the Christian doctrine of God, making it ill and creating the sorts of problems mentioned above. The virus so permeates Christian theology that some have come to take the illness for granted, attributing it to divine mystery, while others remain unaware of the infection altogether."[5]

Latter-day Saints do not subscribe to the traditional doctrine of the Trinity because we believe it represents a superimposition of Hellenistic philosophy on the Bible, and that the simplest and clearest reading of the four Gospels sets forth a Godhead of three distinct beings and three Gods—not three coequal persons in one substance or essence. In addition, the doctrine of the Trinity is a mystery and in that sense is not really comprehensible. How, then, can a person be condemned (or rejected from the category of Christian) if he or she does not understand or accept it? It was Jesus himself who taught that it is life eternal to know God and to know Jesus Christ (John 17:3). As Millard Erickson has observed, "If God is infinite and we are finite, we will never be fully able to understand him. The fullness of what he is will exceed our powers to grasp. Thus, we cannot expect ever to resolve fully this great mystery."[6] Erickson goes on to acknowledge that while the Trinity is at the heart of most Christian theology, "This does not mean that complete and absolutely accurate understanding of the Trinity is essential for one to be a true Christian. We are saved by our trust in Jesus Christ and in the Triune God, not by our subscription to correct theology."[7] As Roman Catholic theologian Karl Rahner has pointed out, "We must be willing to admit that, should the doctrine of the Trinity have to be dropped as false, the major part of religious literature could well remain virtually unchanged." Further, "The Christian's idea of the incarnation would not have to change at all if there were no trinity."[8] In other words, what difference would it make in our worship or our daily walk with God if the doctrine of the Trinity were to cease to exist?

One scholar not of the LDS faith, Edward J. Fortman, observed: "There is no formal doctrine of the Trinity in the New Testament writers, if this means an explicit teaching that in one God there are three co-equal divine persons."[9] Further, *Harper's Bible Dictionary* states that "the word [Trinity] itself does not occur in the Bible. It is generally acknowledged that the church father Tertullian (ca. A.D. 145–220) either coined the term or was the first to use it with reference to God.... The formal doctrine of the Trinity as it was defined by the great church councils of the fourth and fifth centuries is not to be found in the New Testament."[10]

Again, for the Latter-day Saints, the plainest reading of the scriptures sets forth a Godhead of three distinct persons with separate and severable functions. In the Council of Nicea, the Greek word used to describe the oneness of the three members was *homoousios,* meaning "of one substance" or, as some have translated it, "of one essence." The Latin word was consubstantial. Thus Christians since then have come to speak of the ontological (pertaining to being) oneness of the Father, Son, and Holy Spirit. If the Nicene theologians meant to convey that the Father and Son are possessed of the "same substance" or "same essence" in the sense that they are both possessed of divinity, of a divine nature, then Latter-day Saints would agree. Jesus Christ is the Son of God. Jesus Christ is God the Son. He was fully human and fully divine. While the following scriptural references might be squeezed and adapted to convey that God and Christ are the same Being, the law of parsimony suggests to me that the New Testament is intended to be understood first by the man on the street, the woman in the pew, and then by the philosophers and theologians. In that light, consider scriptural passages that teach:[11]

1.   The will of the Son is somehow different from or subject to the will of the Father (see Matthew 26:39; Mark 14:36; Luke 22:42; John 4:34; 5:30; 6:38–40).

2.   The Father has power, knowledge, glory, and dominion that the Son does not have and to which the Son is in subjection

(see Matthew 24:36; Luke 18:18–19 ; 22:29; 23:34; John 5:19–27, 37; 8:42; 10:17–18; 11:41–42; 14:28; 15:9–10, 15; Acts 10:38, 40; 1 Corinthians 11:3; 15:28; Philippians 2:5–9; Hebrews 1:1–4). Why did Jesus need counsel from the Father if they are the same being?

3. Jesus needed help and a sustaining power from the Father to perform his mission on earth (Matthew 14:23; 26:37–44; 27:46; Luke 6:12).

4. Christ's doctrine is not his but the Father's (John 7:16–17). How could his doctrine not be his if he is the same being as the Father? Further, why does Paul consistently open his letters with a statement emphasizing the separateness of God the Father and his Son, Jesus Christ—particularly since all of these letters were written after the resurrection? (See Romans 1:1–3; 1 Corinthians 1:3; 2 Corinthians 1:2–3; Galatians 1:1–4; Ephesians 1:2–3; Philippians 1:1–2; Colossians 1:2–3; 1 Thessalonians 1:1; 2 Thessalonians 1:1–2; 1 Timothy 1:2; 2 Timothy 1:2; Titus 1:4; Philemon 1:3; and Hebrews 1:1–2, 5.)

5. The Holy Spirit is a being separate from the Father and Son. This is evidenced in Matthew 12:31–32 (here it seems that a certain type of sin against Christ is forgivable, but against the Holy Ghost is not); John 14:26 (cf. Luke 11:13; John 16:7); Acts 10:38 (if they are the same being, how can God anoint himself with himself?).

In short, Latter-day Saints believe that the simplest reading of the New Testament text produces the simplest conclusion—that the Father, the Son, and the Holy Spirit are separate and distinct personages, that they are one in purpose, one in mind, one in glory, but separate in person and being. I am persuaded that the sheer preponderance of references in the Bible would lead an uninformed reader—one unaffected by either the conclusions of the creeds (Protestant and Catholic positions) or insights from latter-day revelation (LDS position)—to the understanding that God the Father, Jesus Christ, and the Holy Ghost are separate beings. That is, one must look to the third- and fourth-century Christian Church, not to the New Testament itself, to make a strong case for the Trinity.

Well then, how do the Latter-day Saints view the relationship between the three members of the Godhead? Are the Mormons monotheistic, believers in one God? We believe the Father, Son, and Holy Spirit are one in that they constitute one Godhead. We believe they are one in that they possess all of the attributes of godliness in perfection. We believe they have the same mind, the same objective for humanity, the same purpose. We believe they are one in the sense that theirs is a covenantal relationship, a relationship established before the world was. Joseph Smith explained that "everlasting covenant was made between three personages before the organization of this earth, and relates to their dispensation of things to men on the earth; these personages…are called God the first, the Creator; God the second, the Redeemer; and God the third, the witness or Testator."[12] Finally, they are one in the scriptural sense that the love and unity among the three distinct personages is of such a magnitude that they are occasionally referred to simply as "God." Note the following from the Book of Mormon:

"And now, behold, my beloved brethren, this [the gospel] is the way; and there is none other way nor name given under heaven whereby man can be saved in the kingdom of God. And now, behold, this is the doctrine of Christ, and the only and true doctrine of the Father, and of the Son, and of the Holy Ghost, which is one God, without end" (2 Nephi 31:21).

In the resurrection, "Every thing shall be restored to its perfect frame, as it is now, or in the body, and shall be brought and be arraigned before the bar of Christ the Son, and God the Father, and the Holy Spirit, which is one Eternal God, to be judged according to their works, whether they be good or whether they be evil" (Alma 11:44).

"And after this manner shall ye baptize in my name; for behold, verily I say unto you, that the Father, and the Son, and the Holy Ghost are one; and I am in the Father, and the Father in me, and the Father and I are one" (3 Nephi 11:27; see also verse 36).

"And [Jesus] hath brought to pass the redemption of the world, whereby he that is found guiltless before him at the judgment day hath it given unto him to dwell in the presence of God in his kingdom, to sing ceaseless praises with the choirs above, unto the Father, and unto the Son, and unto the Holy Ghost, which are one God, in a state of happiness which hath no end" (Mormon 7:7).

"This unity is a type of completeness," James E. Talmage, a noted LDS writer and apostle, has written. "The mind of any one member of the Trinity is the mind of the others; seeing as each of them does with the eye of perfection, they see and understand alike. Under any given conditions each would act in the same way, guided by the same principles of unerring justice and equity. The one-ness of the Godhead, to which the scriptures so abundantly testify, implies no mystical union of substance, nor any unnatural and therefore impossible blending of personality. Father, Son, and Holy Ghost are as distinct in their persons and individualities as are any three personages in mortality. Yet their unity of purpose and operation is such as to make their edicts one, and their will the will of God."[13]

The Master desires that his followers be one—that there be no schisms, no factions, no divisions in the body of Christ. Indeed, the unity that exists in the Godhead is but a pattern of what ought to exist in every congregation, in every family, and in every heart that professes Jesus as the Christ. It would be difficult to argue the ontological oneness of the Father and the Son from John 17, the Savior's great High Priestly Intercessory Prayer. Jesus pleaded with the Father in behalf of those "which shall believe on me through their word: That they all may be one; as thou, Father, art in me, and I in thee, that they also may be one in us: that the world may believe that thou hast sent me" (John 17:20–21). Surely Jesus was not pleading for the Father to somehow make of the apostles one essence, one being, but rather that the apostles and those who hearkened to their words might be united in heart and mind by the power of the Spirit. "How marvelous it is," President Gordon B. Hinckley said, "that we can belong to a Church whose foundation lies in this great and significant doctrine, that God is our Father, that Jesus Christ is our Savior, and that the Holy Ghost is our companion. Think of it. Reflect on it. Pray about it. Live up to that great part of divinity that is within you."[14]

ENDNOTES

1. Hatch, *Influence of Greek Ideas on Christianity*, 1, 4–5.

2. Celsus, *On the True Doctrine*, 103; cited in Joseph F. McConkie, *Sons and Daughters of God*, 108–109.

3. Boyd, *God of the Possible*, 17.

4. Boyd, *God of the Possible*, 130; see also Pinnock, *Most Moved Mover*, 65–111.

5. Pinnock, Rice, Sanders, Hasker, and Basinger, *The Openness of God*, 8–9.

6. Erickson, *Making Sense of the Trinity*, 44.

7. Ibid., 46.

8. Rahner, *The Trinity*, 10–11.

9. Fortman, *The Triune God*, 32.

10. *Harper's Bible Dictionary*, s.v. "Trinity."

11. I am indebted to my colleague Thomas Sherry from the LDS Church Educational System for pointing out these verses and concepts.

12. Smith, *TPJS*, 190.

13. Talmage, *Articles of Faith*, 1975, 41.

14. Hinckley, member meeting, Madrid, Spain, 29 May 2004; cited in *Church News*, 3 December 2005, 2.

EIGHT

Who Needs a Church?

IT IS NOT UNCOMMON to witness Latter-day Saints standing and affirming, especially at the end of a lesson or a sermon, that "I know that this Church is true." To Mormons such an expression is perfectly logical and proper and right, but not infrequently such a statement of loyalty and devotion to the Church is seen, particularly by our Protestant friends, as odd and misplaced. A friend of mine who is now an ordained minister of a Protestant faith told me a little about his past. He indicated that his family had joined The Church of Jesus Christ of Latter-day Saints when he was a boy, and that he was extremely "active" in the Church and its programs for many years. He stated that an Evangelical friend of his had invited him to a summer Bible camp and that he accepted the invitation. There he came into contact with non-LDS people who had given their lives to Christ and who spoke of the Master and of his cleansing and redeeming power over and over during the week. According to my friend, these were things he had heard very little about in our Church.

He indicated to me that the Latter-day Saints in his local ward (congregation) were lovely people, caring men and women who tried really hard to live a moral and upright life. But, he said that while he had heard little of Christ, he had heard words like church and work and duties and commitment a great deal. He sensed a devotion to the Savior in his newfound Evangelical friends that he felt was missing among the Latter-day Saints. Consequently, he and other members of his family left our Church and became affiliated with a local Evangelical Christian church in the area. He rejoiced in the fact that he had "found Jesus." I listened to his story very intently. I sensed his sincerity. I said soberly: "I'm sorry." He replied: "Bob, you don't need to apologize." I came back: "Yes, I do need to apologize. I'm sorry that you didn't 'find Jesus' in our Church. I'm sorry that for whatever reason the Savior seemed to be difficult to find or hard to recognize. I'm sorry because I *have* found him, and you could have done the same."

I know there are those within the LDS faith who might suggest to my friend that perhaps he had been, to borrow the words of a popular song, "looking for Christ in all the wrong places." And some might even be prone, in more cynical moments, to propose that there must have been some standard of obedience, some Church requirement that the family simply didn't want to follow. And so they left. Well, to be honest, I'm in no position to judge another man or woman's heart or their motives, to know what they feel and sense and what they don't. What occurs to me now as I reflect on this story are two important points: (1) the message of Christ must be clear and obvious and certainly not difficult to perceive; and (2) the relationship of one's witness of Christ and his or her witness of the Church are not unrelated but perhaps not always understood.

For Latter-day Saints, the Church is vital. It not only represents what the scriptures call the body of Christ or the body of believers— the congregation of the faithful, the household of faith—but also is the means by which the powers and sacraments and message and worship and evangelization and association so central to the Christian life are made available to the people. Let there be no question about it: Salvation and eternal reward hereafter and peace and joy here are to be found first and foremost in Jesus Christ the Person. He is indeed the Way, the Truth, and the Life (John 14:6). He has, as the Apostle Paul wrote, "brought life and immortality to light through the gospel" (2 Timothy 1:10). Or, as one Book of Mormon prophet/king explained, "Salvation was, and is, and is to come, in and through the atoning blood of Christ, the Lord Omnipotent" (Mosiah 3:19). The Church proclaims and declares and spreads the gospel, the good news, the glad tidings that deliverance from sin and death and hell are available through the merciful plan of salvation, the center of which is Christ the Lord.

More than once I have sat in conversation with men and women who years before had chosen to be baptized into The Church of Jesus Christ of Latter-day Saints but had wandered off the path of Church affiliation or involvement. They might show up for church on Christmas or Easter, or they might be seen at a special activity, but seldom did they attend sacrament meeting, the main worship service. One man's comments are particularly memorable and may sound quite familiar to persons of other faiths as well. He said to me: "Bishop [the pastor or leader of a local congregation], I appreciate your interest and your concern for us, but we're doing just fine. Life is good. My wife and I both work long hours during the week, and so Saturday and Sunday are the only time we have to relax and get rested and renewed for the coming week. We usually drive down to our cabin and spend the weekend fishing, hunting, and boating." Then came the following: "You know, Bishop, you could do with a bit more relaxation yourself. I know you're a busy man, and there's just nothing quite like being out in nature to bring a person closer to God. It sure beats sitting cooped up in a room listening to boring talks among a bunch of stodgy, hypocritical people. Breathing fresh air, observing the beauties of the Almighty's creation—those are the things that build my faith in God."

Well, I suppose there's something to be said for the value, even the spiritual value, of spending more time under the oak tree or pondering upon the magnificence of the Lord's handiwork. But I responded to my friend, and I repeat it here, that one can do those kind of things and still worship regularly with the Saints, meaning with those who profess discipleship to Jesus. The Church serves many and varied functions, each of which contributes to the gradual sanctification of the soul. For Latter-day Saints, the Church is where we go to participate weekly in what the Christian world calls communion or the Eucharist, what we refer to as the Sacrament of the Lord's Supper, or more simply, the sacrament. Partaking of the emblems of our Lord's broken body and spilt blood (Mormons use bread and water); doing so in memory of Christ's life and teachings and love and suffering and death and Atonement and resurrection; cultivating the appropriate feelings of gratitude and thanksgiving to him and to our Heavenly Father for his sacrificial offering; meditating upon our own lives, including the covenant we have made to him and our need for his forgiveness of our sins; and renewing that covenant we made at the time of baptism by promising him that we will do all in our power to bring honor to his sacred name by keeping his commandments—these embody our poor effort to manifest a broken heart and a contrite spirit, our desire to have our souls cleansed of sin and our lives filled with God's enlivening and enriching Spirit. One cannot do that on the lake.

The Sacrament of the Lord's Supper as well as the other ordinances of salvation, must be performed by proper authority and done under the direction of the persons charged to oversee their performance. A baby is blessed, one is baptized by immersion and confirmed a member of the Church (and given the gift of the Holy Ghost), ordained to an office in the priesthood, all beneath the umbrella we call the Church. Men and women, boys and girls, come to know and love and depend upon the other members of the Church; the impact and sweet brotherhood and sisterhood that come through regular association with people who feel about the Lord as you do cannot be measured. Praying together, singing hymns as a congregation, listening to and applying the messages of scripture—all of these activities constitute that corporate worship that epitomizes the work of the Church. One cannot do that on the trail.

The work of the LDS Church is done through a lay ministry. Local Church leaders such as bishops and stake presidents (charged to preside over several congregations) serve for a limited period of time and do so without pay or earthly reward. To join The Church of Jesus Christ of Latter-day Saints is to enlist in an army of workers who have been called by their local church leaders to serve in a given capacity and devote the necessary time and energy and prayer to that calling. We are all called to minister to one another, to invite all to come unto Christ, to encourage and lift and strengthen those within the fold. We promise at the time of baptism to bear one another's burdens, to mourn with those who mourn, to comfort those who stand in need of comfort, and to "stand as witnesses of God at all times and in all things, and in all places that [we] may be in, even until death" (Mosiah 18:8–9). We visit and phone one another, see to one another's needs, seek to inspire one another, all in a systematic fashion within the overall organization of the local congregation. In other words, Church membership entails more than four walls and preaching. To be a practicing Mormon is to be involved throughout the week.

Attendance at church and active involvement is a great antidote to worldliness, not only because we are too worn out to sin but also because we receive thereby an added measure of spiritual strength. In August 1831, Joseph Smith recorded the following revelation: "Thou shalt thank the Lord thy God in all things. Thou shalt offer a sacrifice unto the Lord thy God in righteousness, even that of a broken heart and a contrite spirit. And that thou mayest more fully *keep thyself unspotted* from the world, thou shalt *go to the house of prayer* and offer up thy sacraments upon my holy day; for verily this is a day appointed unto you to rest from your labors, and to pay thy devotions unto the Most High; nevertheless thy vows shall be offered up in righteousness on all days and at all times; but remember that on this, the Lord's day, thou shalt offer thine oblations [offerings, either time, talents, or means] and thy sacraments unto the Most High, confessing thy sins unto thy brethren, and before the Lord" (D&C 59:7–12, emphasis added).

Latter-day Saints believe that Church callings and assignments—be it teaching Sunday School, working in the Relief Society (the women's organization), the Primary (the children's organization), as a financial clerk, or as the bishop—come by inspiration. Sometimes persons will be called to serve in organizations or do assignments in which they have little or no experience or even aptitude for the same. One does not seek out a calling, lobby for it, or send out résumés. As one Church leader pointed out many years ago, in this Church one assumes the position to which one is duly called, a position that the individual neither seeks nor declines. He went on to say that, in the Church, what matters is not *where* we serve, but *how*.[1]

I have been called a number of times over the years to serve as a teacher in my ward. Because of what I do for a living, it has been a comfortable fit for me, one that has brought me a great deal of satisfaction and enjoyment. By the time Shauna and I had been married for about ten years, I had taught just about everything a person could teach in the Church. When we moved to Utah in 1983 to assume our assignment at Brigham Young University, life took a different turn for me. I was not called to teach in Sunday School. I was not asked to serve in a major leadership capacity. Rather, the call came to serve as the assistant cubmaster. I accepted with a smile and indicated to the bishop that although I had never worked in such a capacity, I would give it my best shot. For the first few weeks I lived in a state of denial, going through the motions but just knowing that this calling was obviously a stopping-off point, an intermediate labor for one whose talents surely could be more appropriately utilized. I went to the pack meetings, politely did what I was asked to do, but no more. In looking back, I'm ashamed about the way I felt and acted; I was clearly caught up with myself and was tripping over my pride.

Providentially, my unhappiness with my calling (and, with the passing of time, the evidence that this would last a while), drove me to my knees. I knew, deep within my heart, that my attitude was all wrong, that my approach to service required a major overhaul. I pleaded with God for a period of weeks for the spirit of my calling, to see and feel what I needed to see and feel. As time went by, I looked more and more carefully at our cubmaster, Ray Owen. This saintly soul clearly loved these boys and was willing to do anything to help them. I marveled at the uncounted hours he spent preparing for pack meetings, attending leadership training, and simply hanging out with the young men. I was touched by the sincere devotion and commitment of the den mothers who willingly took time away from their own young families to serve the boys. In time, my hardened heart was softened and I managed to climb into the saddle of service and enjoy what the Lord had asked me to do. And, as so often is the case, I was released soon thereafter.

To be sure, I know how important Cub Scouting is for boys. That's simply not an issue with me. And I know how important it is for caring people to serve as leaders and workers in that program. In looking back on the episode, it seems clear to me that I wasn't in any way doubting the worth of the program or viewing it condescendingly. What I was doing was bristling at the suggestion that I do something different, something very different from what I had been called to do in the past. I was resisting change and fighting against the notion that I should leave my spiritual comfort zone. I was at ease teaching in the Church and serving in leadership roles; those things were clearly more suited to my experience and disposition. But Cub Scouting? I have come to know that the Lord does not really want me to be completely comfortable, at least if in doing so I coast, relax, and stop stretching and developing.

And that's what the kingdom of God is all about—men and women serving where they may or may not have specific training, aptitude, or strength. The Church is neither a factory nor a political organization where people forevermore fill a given role or politic for this or that job. We are led by farmers and plumbers and college presidents and art historians. We are taught by CPAs and lawyers and homemakers and custodians. We are called upon to bend and stretch and reach and try new things. We are called upon to climb higher, to move on.

"This church does not belong to its president," Gordon B. Hinckley, fifteenth president of the Church, stated. "Its head is the Lord Jesus Christ, whose name each of us has taken upon ourselves. We are all in this great endeavor together. We are here to assist our Father in His work and glory, 'to bring to pass the immortality and eternal life of man' (Moses 1:39). Your obligation is as serious in your sphere of responsibility as is my obligation in my sphere. No calling in this Church is small or of little consequence. All of us in the pursuit of our duty touch the lives of others...."

"You have as great an opportunity for satisfaction in the performance of your duty as I do in mine. The progress of this work will be determined by our joint efforts. Whatever your calling, it is as fraught with the same kind of opportunity to accomplish good as is mine. What is really important is that this is the work of the Master. Our work is to go about doing good as did He."[2]

Perhaps it would be well to mention one more purpose of the Church: to learn to live peaceably and work amiably with imperfect people, to make Christians out of us. One of the ways we know that we are growing up spiritually, maturing in the qualities of holiness and preparing ourselves to be with our Maker, is the extent to which we become more and more sensitive to people—to their plights, to their challenges, to their silent strugglings. For a number of years when I was a boy, my family was not active in the Church. We attended services only off and on, and my only continuing contact was a caring Primary teacher who picked me up every Thursday afternoon without fail. A small branch of the Church was begun in a city several miles from where I grew up, and my family was asked to attend there. I suppose my dad felt that it was time to get into gear spiritually and, maybe sensing that a new beginning would be the best thing, we started back to Church.

We came home from church and I overheard my father share some tender feelings with my mom. Dad explained that someone had come up to him at church and said: "Well, my goodness! What do we have here? You mean *you* decided to come to church? I think the walls *are* going to fall down!" Through his tears I heard my remarkable father utter these words, words that I will never forget, words that are emblazoned upon my soul: "This is my church, too. No man is going to run me out of my church." Dad was soon called to serve as a counselor in the presidency of the young men's organization, then a counselor in the branch presidency, and eventually as the first bishop of the ward. He was later called to serve as a counselor in the stake presidency in the newly created stake in that area.

Now, let's return to the typical Mormon testimony, "I know that this Church is true." What does that mean? (We will deal with the concept of "only true church" in chapter 22.) It does not mean that the Church saves, for it does not; Christ saves. It does not mean, for example, that because baptism is a required ordinance that it adds anything to the completed work of Jesus Christ or that it supplements his atoning sacrifice in any way. Baptism, as an ordinance, is an outward manifestation of my inward, personal covenant to come unto Christ, accept and rely upon the cleansing power of his blood, and make him truly the Lord of my life. In the truest sense, baptism does not forgive my sins, although the scriptures speak occasionally of baptism "washing away our sins" (Acts 22:16; D&C 39:10); Jesus Christ forgives my sins.

And thus the foundation of my faith, that around which all other elements of my testimony revolve, is my witness that God lives, that Jesus Christ is the Son of God, and that he was crucified for the sins of the world. To proclaim that "the Church is true" is to proclaim that the Church is an auxiliary, an aid, a divinely given means whereby one can come unto Christ, receive the covenants and ordinances of salvation at the hands of legal administrators, worship and praise the Almighty in sermon and song and service, and enjoy sweet fellowship with men and women who are just as fallible and spiritually needy as I am. As has been stated so well, the Church is less a sanctuary for the sanctified than it is a hospital for sinners. The Church is true in that it does what God intends for it to do. It is true in that it seeks to make of us true disciples of the Lord Jesus.

In writing to the saints at Ephesus, Paul explained that God had provided helps and governments to the Church through the appointment of officers—apostles, prophets, evangelists, pastors, teachers. Why? "For the perfecting of the saints, for the work of the ministry, for the edifying of the body of Christ; till we all come in the unity of the faith, and of the knowledge of the Son of God, unto a perfect man, unto the measure of the stature of the fullness of Christ: that we henceforth be no more children, tossed to and fro, and carried about with every wind of doctrine, by the sleight of men, and cunning craftiness, whereby they lie in wait to deceive; but speaking the truth in love, may grow up into him in all things, which is the head, even Christ" (Ephesians 4:12–15). The Church thus helps promote unity, orthodoxy, strength, and knowledge to withstand error, all in an effort to keep us from conforming to this world but rather being transformed by the Spirit, even to the renewing of our minds (Romans 12:2), leading eventually to that time when we all have "the mind of Christ" (1 Corinthians 2:16).

ENDNOTES

1. J. Reuben Clark, *Conference Report,* April 1951, 154.
2. Hinckley, CR, April 1995, 94.

NINE

Who is a Cult?

I FREQUENTLY LISTEN TO THE radio as I travel in my car, and much of the time I listen to religious (Christian) channels. Not only do I find the programs to be informative and often inspirational, but the exercise proves helpful in keeping me abreast of current issues, hot topics, and debated matters in the larger religious world. On a number of occasions I have heard preachers warn their listeners about groups in society that are harmful, destructive to faith, and even diabolical. One pastor made the following comments (I'm paraphrasing, of course): "Now, friends and brothers and sisters, stay on your toes. Keep your eyes open. Be especially wary of groups that proselytize, that travel from door to door seeking converts. Some of these people are led by powerful personalities who simply prey upon ignorance and do whatever they need to do to win followers. Never put your trust in cult leaders like Jim Jones or Joseph Smith." I about swallowed my tongue! I couldn't believe the speaker would assign Joseph Smith and the Latter-day Saints to a cultic category like unto the one that resulted in the suicide deaths of many people. I found the comments to be not only insulting but ignorant.

During the 1980s, I served for a time on a ministerial council in a small town in one of the Southern states. Over the years I learned to appreciate the gifts and talents of many of my colleagues on the council, leaders of Roman Catholic, Orthodox, mainstream Protestant, Evangelical, Jewish, and Islamic organizations in the area. There developed a congenial spirit and mutual respect among the group, and the monthly meetings actually became quite enjoyable. At one point the chair of the group announced a grave concern: members of Rev. Moon's Unification Church had moved into the area and were seeking representation on the council. I sat quietly and listened as my friends conjured up a list of requirements that would easily exclude them inasmuch as they were a cult. After much animated conversation and note taking, one of my associates noticed that I had been especially quiet during the preceding half hour. He asked why. I commented: "Well, I suppose I haven't had much to say because I feel a bit uncomfortable. If my memory serves me well, almost every item of exclusion you have put forward for the Unification Church could be applied to the Latter-day Saints."

Before we get too far into this discussion, the *New Shorter Oxford English Dictionary* (Clarendon, 1993) offers the following definitions of a cult (in this order): (1) "Worship; reverential homage rendered to a divine being"; (2) "A system of religious worship, especially as expressed in ceremonies, ritual, etc."; (3) "Devotion or homage paid to a person or thing, especially a fashionable enthusiasm"; (4) "a transient fad." It is not until we turn to the word *cultish* that we find the definition "Of the nature of, resembling, or belonging to a cult, especially one regarded as eccentric or unorthodox." Frankly, any religious group would be considered a cult under definitions 1, 2, or 3. Number 4 describes a movement that is short-lived. And I suppose that words like "eccentric" or "unorthodox" are not flattering terms.

Oddly enough, however, in recent decades, for someone to refer to one's faith tradition as a cult has become a considerable insult. Further, some people are not able to distinguish between what is cult is what is the *occult*. Thus it is not uncommon at all for someone to associate the "cult" of Mormonism with devil worship, voodoo, or bizarre spiritualism. One of the underlying premises of the anti-Mormon production *The Godmakers*, is that in spite of the clean looking, religiously devout, and service-minded model citizen your Mormon neighbor appears to be, there is in reality some kind of slick, slimy underbelly beneath it all; in other words, as some have said, "Well you just need to know the difference between public Mormonism and private Mormonism." I have been a Latter-day Saint all my life. I was raised as a Mormon in Louisiana and spent my first eighteen years there. I have since lived in

New York, New Jersey, Massachusetts, Connecticut, Idaho, Florida, Georgia, and Utah, and I have been intimately involved in the work of the Church through the years. Since 1973 I have been employed by the LDS Church as a marriage and family counselor, religion instructor for both high school and college students, a professor of religion at the Church's 33,000-student university, and dean of religious education at BYU. I have seen the Church from all sides—from right to left, and from top to bottom. I have worked closely with rank-and-file members and Church leaders at all levels of administration. In all that time I have never encountered but one brand of Mormonism—the public version. I'm not sure where the secret brand of Mormonism—the one advertised by our critics as scheming, mischievous, power-hungry, occultish, and violent—is to be found, but I haven't come across it. The reader would do well to be discerning and discriminating when it comes to some of the rather exotic assaults made upon the LDS Church by its critics.

So-called countercult movements have been on the rise for the last twenty or thirty years, all seeking to uphold the beloved tradition of their godfather, Walter Martin. In one of Martin's last books, *The New Cults* (Regal Books, 1980), he describes cults as follows: (a) they are started by strong and dynamic leaders; (b) they believe in additional scripture; (c) they have rigid standards for membership; (d) they proselyte new converts; (e) the leaders or officials of the cult are not professional clergymen; (f) they believe in ongoing and continual communication from God; and (g) they claim some truth not available to other individuals or groups.[1] Fascinating list, isn't it? Only a moment's reflection, however, will reveal the fact that the first-century Christian Church meets all of the requirements to be classified as a "new cult." And, indeed, from a Jewish or Roman perspective, that's just what the followers of "the Way," the followers of Jesus, were. Not only did they meet requirements (a) through (g), they were also considered eccentric and unorthodox.

I have appreciated the efforts of a growing number of religious leaders and scholars who have chosen to jettison the word cult in describing Mormonism, fully cognizant of the pain and offense it causes to Latter-day Saints and equally aware of how grievously misleading the word can be to those who know precious little about the Church. In his book, *I Love Mormons* (Baker, 2005), Professor David L. Rowe, an Evangelical Christian who has lived in Salt Lake City for many years, pointed out how some of his own thinking needed to evolve to better understand the heart of Mormonism. "We [previously] thought of them in terms of orthodoxy and not in terms of ethnicity, depreciated their aberrant beliefs, and did not appreciate their colorful lifeways. We reduced their movement to a cult and did not recognize it as a culture."[2]

The editors of a book entitled *Encountering New Religious Movements* (Kregel, 2004) observe in their introduction: "The end of the twentieth and beginning of the twenty-first centuries witnessed the continued growth and development of a variety of new religious movements. These groups are often called 'cults' in popular evangelical discourse, but throughout this book we will use the term 'new religious movements.' This choice of terminology is a carefully calculated one. There are a variety of differing definitions of 'cult' in evangelical literature, but more importantly, there are serious problems with the use of the term. It can be argued that to speak of 'the cults' is to engage in an overgeneralization that ignores the great complexity and diversity found in a variety of groups and movements. Perhaps more importantly, adherents within new religions consider the term pejorative. It is the desire of the editors and contributors not to add unnecessary stumbling blocks to the offense of the gospel, and this necessitates sensitivity in our choice of terminology. We also wish to move beyond the often confrontational and aggressive tone adopted by many evangelicals in formulating responses to new religious movements."[3]

In the years that I have been involved in working with persons of other faiths, I have learned a few things that have made a real difference in my life and have opened new vistas of understanding and communication. It is easy to dismiss with a wave of the hand another person who sees things differently, but extremely difficult (yet rewarding) to pay the price to understand what they *really* believe and feel. It is so easy to pigeonhole, categorize, marginalize, or even demonize someone you don't know very well. Unfortunately, we tend to be down on whatever we're not up on. On the other hand, it is much more difficult to assume the worst about someone you have come to befriend, trust, and love. In that spirit, let me also acknowledge that surely many Latter-day Saints, both purposefully and unwittingly, have borne false witness against our neighbors whenever we have caricatured or misrepresented their beliefs.

I believe today, more so than I ever have, that God is our Father; that He loves all of His children; that He will do all within His power to bring greater light and truth into our lives; and that he does indeed, as we sing in the hymn, "work in mysterious ways his wonders to perform." I am persuaded that God is working through His Spirit to lead and empower individuals and groups to recognize and cherish light and knowledge wherever it may be found—particularly light and knowledge concerning God and His plan for the salvation of the world. I am not talking about some kind of broad ecumenical movement in which treasured doctrines are compromised or sacred practices are jettisoned; too often this merely results in a kind of shared impotence.

Rather, I have reference to what my friend Richard Mouw calls *convicted civility*. "Being civil," Rich has written, "isn't just trying to be respectful toward the people we know. It is also to care about our common life." Further, "The quest for empathy can be helped along by a good dose of *curiosity*. We ought to want to become familiar with the experiences of people who are different from us simply out of a desire to understand the length and breadth of what it means to be human." "We cannot place artificial limits on how God may speak to us." We should "be open to the possibility that they will help us discern the truth more clearly. Being a civil Christian means being open to God's surprises." That is not likely to come through argument, debate, or browbeating one another with "facts."[4] As John Stackhouse points out: "God cares about people more than he cares about 'truth' in the abstract. Jesus didn't die on the cross to make a point. He died on the cross to save people whom he loves. We, too, must represent our Lord with love to God and our neighbor always foremost in our concerns."[5]

Many have accused the Latter-day Saints of seeking to put on a new face, of enlarging the name of Jesus Christ in our Church logo, of placing greater emphasis upon the mercy, grace, and atoning work of the Savior, all in an effort to convince onlookers that we really are Christian. Let me suggest an analogy. Suppose a very devout Pentecostal minister, the only one in his community, were to encounter stiff opposition from a man who simply disliked Pentecostals. Suppose the critic began a smear campaign that took the form of brochures, booklets, books, and video presentations that stated in no uncertain terms that Pentecostals are not only not Christian, but atheists! The Pentecostal minister might initially even smile at the ridiculous propaganda and dismiss it with a wave of the hand, concluding that no sane listener or viewer would give the anti-Pentecostal materials a moment's thought. But let's complicate the picture by suggesting further that after a decade of constant chants of "Pentecostals are not Christian!" or "Pentecostals are atheists!" a noticeable percentage of the public began to believe or at least attend to the propaganda. What then? What should the minister do? Would it be inappropriate or beneath his dignity to begin a similar campaign to set the record straight? Not at all.

The problem with saying that Latter-day Saints are not Christian, as I pointed out early in this work, is that such a statement is in many ways untrue and almost always misleading. While there are certainly differences between the LDS conception of Jesus Christ and the more traditionally Christian view, to say that we are not Christian is to lead some who know very little of us to the conclusion that we are un-Christlike, anti-Christian, opposed to the teachings of Jesus, or that we do not accept the message of the New Testament. It is to place us in the same category as Buddhists, Hindus, or Muslims. The Church of Jesus Christ of Latter-day Saints has begun to stress its heartfelt acceptance of Jesus as the Christ, so that people in society may not misunderstand its fundamental beliefs. We believe what is in the New Testament, and we believe what we feel God has revealed in the latter days concerning Christ. Such belief, such teachings, did not spring into existence within the last few years; they have been in the Book of Mormon, Doctrine and Covenants, Pearl of Great Price, and teachings of Church leaders from the beginning.

Let me illustrate the challenge the Church faces. Several years ago a colleague and I were asked if we would be willing to participate in an interview with representatives of a Christian organization. We were informed that they were preparing a video presentation on The Church of Jesus Christ of Latter-day Saints. My interview—which consisted basically of my response to a series of questions—lasted for about an hour and a half. We covered much ground, including the role of prophets, our views concerning the Bible, the person and nature of God the Father, and our teachings on Jesus Christ. For at least twenty or thirty minutes I described our understanding of the Atonement and of the necessity of the mercy and grace of Christ. When the video presentation was released several months later, I felt that it portrayed quite accurately, for the most part, our fundamental beliefs and, of course, the differences between LDS and other Christian beliefs. One part was, however, particularly troublesome to me: The narrator stated quite emphatically that the Latter-day Saints do not believe in salvation by the grace of Christ.

Months later we met once again with representatives of this group. They were eager to know our feelings concerning the video. We commented that it was nice that Latter-day Saints had been allowed to express themselves. At the same time, I voiced my disappointment in what was said about our lack of belief in grace. I said, essentially, "If you want to say that the Latter-day Saints have an *unusual* view of grace, or a *different* view of grace, or a *deficient* view of grace, we can live with that, for we obviously have differences between our two faiths. But to say that we have *no* view of grace is a serious misrepresentation that confuses and misleads people."

In my encounters with Christians of various sorts, I've discovered what I perceive to be a double standard. On the one hand, in an effort to avoid the appearance that anything at all is to be added to the wondrous gift of Atonement, many Christians declare emphatically that salvation comes *merely* by the confession of one's sin and the profession of Jesus Christ as Savior. For example, in the eighth chapter of Acts, Philip encounters an Ethiopian eunuch who is reading the 53rd chapter of Isaiah, perhaps the most powerful and detailed messianic prophecy in the Old Testament. Philip asks the eunuch whether he understands what he is reading, to which the eunuch sweetly and humbly responds: "How can I, except some man should guide me?" Philip does just that: He reads the passage and explains how it is fulfilled in the redeeming work of Jesus of Nazareth. At this point the two men encounter a body of water, and the eunuch asks what would prevent him from being baptized, to which Philip answers: "If thou believest with all thine heart, thou mayest." The eunuch comes back: "I believe that Jesus Christ is the Son of God." He is then baptized into the Christian faith, and Philip is led by the Spirit to other fields of labor.

On Paul's second missionary journey, he and Silas find themselves in a prison in Philippi. At midnight the two of them begin to sing and pray, and then God intervenes: He causes an earthquake, dramatically shakes the prison, opens the doors of the prison, and looses the bands of the prisoners. The Philippian jailer, sensing that this incident will probably result in his own execution by his superiors, prepares to take his own life. Paul stops him from doing so. The jailer then asks: "Sirs, what must I do to be saved? And they say, Believe on the Lord Jesus Christ, and thou shalt be saved, and thy house." Paul and Silas then taught the household the gospel of Jesus Christ and baptized them (see Acts 16:25–33). In short, salvation comes to those who admit their spiritual plight and accept Jesus Christ as Lord and Savior. Nothing more is or can be required for salvation. As Paul wrote to the Roman saints, "If thou shalt confess with thy mouth the Lord Jesus, and shalt believe in thy heart that God hath raised him from the dead, thou shalt be saved.... For whosoever shall call upon the name of the Lord shall be saved" (Romans 10:9, 13).

On the other hand, religious and academic colleagues who are traditional Christians have told me, in no uncertain terms, that, as a Latter-day Saint, I am not a Christian. Why? Because of doctrinal differences, additional scripture, or the fact that Mormonism cannot trace its historical roots through the Reformation into the New Testament church. In other words, I can be saved by professing and accepting Jesus Christ, but I am excluded from being a Christian for doctrinal and historical reasons. It strikes me as being a little odd. According to the Amsterdam Declaration (2000), "A Christian is a believer in God who is enabled by the Holy Spirit to submit to Jesus Christ as Lord and Savior in a personal relationship of disciple to master and to live the life of God's kingdom. The word Christian should not be equated with any particular cultural, ethnic, political, or ideological tradition or group. Those who know and love Jesus are also called Christ-followers, believers and disciples."[6]

I agree with the Amsterdam Declaration on what constitutes a Christian. Doctrine does matter. It matters a great deal. But no one of us knows all things or can comprehend or articulate the doctrines of salvation perfectly; consequently, the depth of one's conviction to Christ and his gospel should not and cannot be measured by the perceived "correctness" of their doctrinal pronouncements. Perhaps more than any other world religion, Christianity is all about a relationship— a relationship between a person and the Person of Jesus Christ. And that's what counts.

ENDNOTES

1. Martin, *The New Cults*, 17–21.

2. Rowe, *I Love Mormons*, 29.

3. Hexham, Rost, and Moorehead, eds., *Encountering New Religious Movements*, 17–18.

4. Mouw, *Uncommon Decency*, 25, 63, 67.

5. Stackhouse, *Humble Apologetics*, 142.

6. In Packer and Oden, eds., *One Faith*, 121–22.

TEN

By What Authority?

JOSEPH SMITH ONCE REMARKED that "a man can do nothing for himself unless God direct him in the right way; and the priesthood is for that purpose."[1] From an LDS perspective, the New Testament clearly teaches the need for divine authority. Jesus ordained the Twelve Apostles (John 15:16), gave to them the keys of the kingdom of God (Matthew 16:18–19; 18:18), and empowered his servants to perform miracles and take the gospel to all nations (Matthew 10:1, 5–8; 28:19–20). Later, after the Lord's death, the apostles commissioned others to serve in the ministry (Acts 6:1–6; 13:1–3; 14:23; 1 Timothy 4:14; 2 Timothy 1:6; Titus 1:5) and to insure that the saving ordinances (sacraments) were performed only by those properly ordained (Acts 19:1–6, 13–16).

This was a power that no man could assume, take upon himself, or even purchase; it came through the laying on of hands by those holding proper authority (Acts 8:18–20; Hebrews 5:4). Latter-day Saints believe that with the death of the apostles, within one hundred years of the crucifixion of Jesus, this authority, the power to act in the name of God, was lost from the earth. It was Hegesippus, the second-century Jewish-Christian writer, who noted that "when the sacred band of the apostles had in various ways reached the end of their life, and the generation of those privileged to listen with their own ears to the divine wisdom had passed on, then godless error began to take shape."[2]

Similarly, J. B. Phillips observed that the differences between present-day Christianity and the young Church of the first century are readily apparent. The early Christians "did not make 'acts of faith,' they believed; they did not 'say their prayers,' they really prayed. They did not hold conferences on psychosomatic medicine, they simply healed the sick.... We in the modern Church have unquestionably lost something. Whether it is due to the atrophy of the quality which the New Testament calls 'faith,' whether it is due to a stifling churchiness, whether it is due to our sinful complacency over the scandal of a divided Church, or whatever the cause may be, very little of the modern Church could bear comparison with the spiritual drive, the genuine fellowship, and the gay unconquerable courage of the Young Church."[3] The story is told that on one occasion the pope "pointed to his gorgeous Papal Palace and said [to St. Francis], 'Peter can no longer say "Silver and gold have I none"'; and the Spanish friar answered, 'No, and neither can he now say, "Rise and walk."'"[4]

While Catholic and Orthodox Christians claim apostolic succession (that the bishops of the ancient Church have conveyed their priesthood powers down to the pope and patriarch in our time), Latter-day Saints teach that God's divine authority was not to be found in the Old World by the middle of the second century A.D. Other than the formal break between western (Roman) and eastern (Orthodox) Christianity in A.D. 1054, the Roman Church had control of the Christian faith until the sixteenth century, when courageous men objected to, opposed, and broke away from Catholicism. Again from Brother Joseph: "It is in the order of heavenly things that God should always send a new dispensation into the world when men have apostatized from the truth and lost the priesthood; but when men come out and build upon other men's foundations, they do it on their own responsibility, without authority from God."[5]

Roger Williams, later in his life, renounced the views of the Baptists and "turned seeker, i.e., to wait for new apostles to restore Christianity." He felt the need "of a special commission, to restore the modes of positive worship, according to the original institution." Williams concluded that the Protestants were "not...able to derive the authority...from the apostles,...[and] conceived God would raise up some apostolic power."[6] In short, Williams held that there was "no regularly constituted church of Christ, on earth, nor any person authorized to administer any church ordinance, nor can there be until new apostles are sent by the great head of the Church, for whose coming I am seeking."[7]

John Wesley was a marvelous preacher and religious leader in the eighteenth century and became essentially the father of Methodism. His brother Charles, probably less well known, is responsible for many of the magnificent hymns sung in Christianity today. Though they were very close as brothers, on one occasion Charles criticized his brother John when the latter ordained a man to an office without authority to do so. Charles wrote:

> How easily are bishops made
> By man or woman's whim:
> Wesley his hands on Coke hath laid,
> But who laid hands on him?[8]

Let's be clear, however, when we speak of the LDS notion of an apostasy of the primitive Church. "In our assertion that the church had apostatized," Alexander Morrison has written, "we must *not* conclude that all virtue had left the world. We must *not* for even a moment think that with the apostasy a blanket of spiritual darkness, keeping out all light and truth, descended upon humankind, suffocating and choking off every good and worthy thought and deed, erasing Christ from every heart. That just didn't happen, and we do a grave injustice to all Christians, including ourselves, if we think otherwise."[9] John Taylor declared that there were persons during medieval times who "could commune with God, and who, by the power of faith, could draw aside the curtain of eternity and gaze upon the invisible world…, have the ministering of angels, and unfold the future destinies of the world. If those were dark ages I pray God to give me a little darkness, and deliver me from the light and intelligence that prevail in our day."[10]

In speaking of the primitive church, Boyd K. Packer observed that "the flame flickered and dimmed….

"But always, as it had from the beginning, the Spirit of God inspired worthy souls.

"We owe an immense debt to the protesters and the reformers who preserved the scriptures and translated them. They knew something had been lost. They kept the flame alive as best they could. Many of them were martyrs."[11] On another occasion he taught: "The line of priesthood authority was broken. But mankind was not left in total darkness or completely without revelation or inspiration. The idea that with the Crucifixion of Christ the heavens were closed and they opened in [Joseph Smith's] First Vision is not true. The Light of Christ would be everywhere present to attend the children of God; the Holy Ghost would visit seeking souls. The prayers of the righteous would not go unanswered."[12]

But let's go back to the question of authority. I have pondered frequently upon the Protestant assertion that Mormons aren't Christian because we are not a part of the historic Christian tradition, because we cannot trace our lineage back through the Reformation, through Catholic Christianity, to the first-century Church. The irony of this indictment for me is this: Neither can Protestants! How can one claim to be a part of the Christian line of authority when that line was broken in the days of the Reformers? How can one, like Martin Luther, an Augustinian monk, then assert and assume a "priesthood of all believers," thereby denouncing the need for a priestly hierarchy and thus apostolic succession back to Peter? Joseph Smith taught: "I will illustrate it [the situation in the Christian world in regard to divine authority] by an old apple tree. Here jumps off a branch and says, I am the true tree, and you are corrupt. If the whole tree is corrupt, are not its branches corrupt? If the Catholic religion is a false religion, how can any true religion come out of it?"[13]

"In becoming a Catholic," Richard Neuhaus observed, "one is braced for certain criticisms. Among the most common, usually coming from Protestant sources, is that the person who becomes a Catholic has a 'felt need for authority.' This is usually said in a somewhat condescending manner by people who say they are able to live with the ambiguities and tensions that some of us cannot handle. But *to say* that I have a felt need for authority is no criticism at all. Of course I have, as should we all. The allegedly autonomous self who acknowledges no authority but himself is abjectly captive to the authority of a tradition of Enlightenment rationality that finally collapses into incoherence. Whether in matters of science, history, religion, or anything else of consequence, we live amid a storm of different and conflicting ideas claiming to be the truth. Confronted by such truth claims, we necessarily ask, 'Sez who?' By what authority, by whose authority, should I credit such claims to truth? Answering the question requires a capacity to distinguish between the authoritative and the authoritarian."[14]

Orson F. Whitney, an LDS apostle, told the following story: "Many years ago a learned man, a member of the Roman Catholic Church, came to Utah and spoke from the stand of the Salt Lake Tabernacle. I became well-acquainted with him, and we conversed freely and frankly. A great scholar, with perhaps a dozen languages at his tongue's end, he seemed to know all about theology, law, literature, science and philosophy. One day he said to me: 'You Mormons are all ignoramuses. You don't even know the strength of your own position. It is so strong that there is only one other tenable in the whole Christian world, and that is the position of the Catholic Church. The issue is between Catholicism and Mormonism. If we are right, you are wrong; if you are right, we are wrong; and that's all there is to it. The Protestants haven't a leg to stand on. For, if we are wrong, they are wrong with us, since they were a part of us and went out from us; while if we are right they are apostates whom we cut off long ago. If we have the apostolic succession from St. Peter, as we claim, there is no need of Joseph Smith and Mormonism; but if we have not that succession, then such a man as Joseph Smith was necessary, and Mormonism's attitude is the only consistent one. It is either the perpetuation of the gospel from ancient times, or the restoration of the gospel in latter days.'"[15]

Further, one need only survey the Christian world today to note significant differences in doctrine among the various religious groups, such as: whether God has complete foreknowledge; whether man has freedom of will or is predestined to salvation or damnation; whether man is morally depraved and thus unable to choose God; whether good works play a role in the salvation process; whether baptism is completely necessary and how (mode) and to whom (believers only or children also) it is administered; and the place of spiritual gifts in the Church. Others have pointed out that alterations in doctrine took place during the Reformation as well, theological shifts away from the teachings of the primitive Church in the days of Jesus and the apostles. Such doctrines as predestination, man's inability to come unto Christ on his own, salvation by grace alone (with no need for good works), and *sola scriptura*, the notion of the sufficiency of written scripture—each of which is a vital element within current Christian thinking—do not reflect the teachings and doctrine of the first few centuries of the Christian Church. So while Latter-day Saints believe that the Protestant Reformation provided some measure of correction to the Christian Church, it was not sufficient. A complete restoration was needed.

While translating the Book of Mormon in May 1829, Joseph Smith and his scribe encountered repeatedly the concept of divine authority and the need for the same to operate and oversee the Church. Joseph and Oliver Cowdery went into a grove of trees and knelt in prayer on the banks of the Susquehanna River in Harmony, Pennsylvania. According to both of their accounts, a heavenly messenger who introduced himself as John the Baptist, the same who prepared for and baptized Jesus in the New Testament, appeared, laid his hands upon their heads, and conferred upon them what is known as the Aaronic or Lesser Priesthood. A few weeks later they were visited by Peter, James, and John, apostles of Jesus Christ in the first century, who conferred on them the Melchizedek or Higher Priesthood, including the power of the Holy Apostleship, the power they had received under the hands of the Savior himself some eighteen hundred years earlier. On 6 April 1830 the Church was organized in Fayette, New York.

Ordination to this priesthood authority has continued in rightful succession from Joseph Smith down to the present day. For example, my own "line of authority" in the Church is as follows:

- Robert L. Millet was ordained a high priest by Roy O. Warburton on 29 August 1976;

- he was ordained a high priest by Delbert L. Stapley on 1 May 1960;

- he was ordained an apostle by George Albert Smith on 5 October 1950;

- he was ordained an apostle by Joseph F. Smith on 8 October 1903;

- he was ordained an apostle by Brigham Young on 8 October 1867;

- he was ordained an apostle by the three witnesses of the Book of Mormon (Oliver Cowdery, David Whitmer, and Martin Harris) on 14 February 1835;

- they were called to choose the first quorum of the Twelve Apostles by Joseph Smith (D&C 18:23–27, 37);

- he and Oliver Cowdery were ordained to the holy apostleship by Peter, James, and John in 1829;

- they were ordained apostles by the Lord Jesus Christ (John 15:16).

Latter-day Saints feel strongly that the Church of Jesus Christ should and must be built upon the foundation of *living* apostles and prophets, with Jesus Christ himself as the chief cornerstone (Ephesians 2:19–20). As marvelous as it is to have the writings and witness of the first-century apostles in the New Testament, one does not derive apostolic authority from a book, even a sacred book. For that reason, The Church of Jesus Christ of Latter-day Saints is presided over by fifteen men who profess to hold the apostolic office.

The president of the Church is sustained and upheld as the prophet of God and the senior apostle by the confidence and prayers of the members of the Church throughout the world. In that weighty assignment he is assisted by two counselors. These three men constitute what is called the First Presidency. Under their direction are twelve men who have been ordained apostles; they constitute what is called the Quorum of the Twelve Apostles. The apostles are charged to be "special witnesses of the name of Christ in all the world." Further, they are tasked to "build up the church, and regulate all the affairs of the same in all nations" (D&C 107:23, 33).

When one is ordained an apostle, there is conferred upon him the keys of the kingdom of God, the same power Jesus gave to the Twelve in his day (Matthew 16:19; 18:18). But since keys represent the right of presidency, the right to preside, the directing power, these keys in their fullness lie dormant within that individual unless or until he lives to become the senior apostle of God on earth (seniority determined by date of ordination to the Twelve). Thus succession in the presidency, apostolic succession, takes place automatically. When the president of the Church dies, the First Presidency is dissolved and the fourteen living apostles preside over the Church until a formal reorganization of the First Presidency takes place. The senior apostle becomes the President of the Church, and he then chooses, generally from among the living apostles, two counselors. Thus there is no jockeying for position, no political maneuvering, for each man understands very clearly just who is his senior and who is his junior within the Quorum.

There are those who have raised questions concerning the men chosen to serve as apostles in the LDS Church and their suitability to stand as witnesses of the resurrected Redeemer. "Some years ago," Harold B. Lee (an apostle and the eleventh president of the Church) stated, "two missionaries came to me with what seemed to them to be a very difficult question. A young…minister had laughed at them when they had said that Apostles were necessary today in order for the true Church to be upon the earth. They said that the minister said, 'Do you realize that when the Apostles met to choose one to fill the vacancy caused by the death of Judas they said it had to be one who companied with them and had been a witness of all things pertaining to the witness and resurrection of the Lord? How can you say you have Apostles, if that be the measure of an Apostle?' And so these young men said, 'What shall we answer?'

"I said to them, 'Go back and ask your minister friend two questions. First, how did the Apostle Paul gain what was necessary to be called an Apostle? He didn't know the Lord, and had no personal acquaintance. He hadn't accompanied the Apostles. He hadn't been a witness of the ministry nor of the resurrection of the Lord. How did he gain his testimony sufficient to be an Apostle? And the second question you ask him is: How does he know that all who are today Apostles have not likewise received that witness? I bear witness to you that those who hold the apostolic calling may, and do, know of the reality of the mission of the Lord."[16]

The general officers of the Church preside over all local officers and members. Elder Jeffrey R. Holland, a modern LDS apostle, declared: "Thus the apostolic and prophetic foundation of the Church was to bless in all times, but *especially* in times of adversity or danger, times when we might feel like children, confused or disoriented, perhaps a little fearful, times in which the devious hand of men or the maliciousness of the devil would attempt to unsettle or mislead. Against such times as come in our modern day, the First Presidency and Quorum of the Twelve are commissioned by God and sustained by you as 'prophets, seers, and revelators,' with the President of the Church sustained as *the* prophet, seer, and revelator, the *senior* Apostle, and as such the only man authorized to exercise all of the revelatory and administrative keys for the Church. In New Testament times, in Book of Mormon times, and in modern times these officers form the foundation stones of the true Church, positioned around and gaining their strength from the chief cornerstone, 'the rock of our Redeemer, who is [Jesus] Christ, the Son of God,' He who is the great Apostle and High Priest of our profession' (Hebrews 3:1).... Such a foundation in Christ was and is always to be a protection in days 'when the devil shall send forth his mighty winds, yea, his shafts in the whirlwind, yea, when all his hail and his mighty storm shall beat upon you.' In such days as we are now in—and will more or less always be in—the storms of life 'shall have no power over you... because of the rock upon which ye are built, which is a sure foundation, a foundation whereon if men build they cannot fall'"(Helaman 5:12).[17]

ENDNOTES

1. Smith, *TPJS*, 364.

2. Eusebius, *History of the Church*, Penguin, 96.

3. Phillips, *The Young Church in Action*, 11, 20–21; cited in Morrison, *Turning from the Truth*, 51–52.

4. Cited in G. K. Chesterton, *St. Thomas Aquinas*, 34–35.

5. Smith, *TPJS,* 375.

6. Cited in Williams Cullen Bryant, ed., *Picturesque America or the Land We Live In* (New York: D. Appleton, 1872–74), 1:502; see also Jeffrey R. Holland, CR, October 2004, 6.

7. Cited in Richards, *A Marvelous Work and a Wonder,* 29; see also Backman, *American Religions and the Rise of Mormonism,* 180–81.

8. *Representative Verse of Charles Wesley,* sel. Frank Baker (The Epworth Press, 1962), 368; see also Jeffrey R. Holland, CR, April 2005, 48.

9. Morrison, *Turning from the Truth,* 52.

10. Taylor, *JD* 16:197.

11. Packer, CR, April 2000, 7.

12. Packer, "The Light of Christ," 11.

13. Smith, *TPJS,* 375.

14. Neuhaus, *Catholic Matters,* 70, emphasis added.

15. Whitney, cited in Richards, *A Marvelous Work and a Wonder,* 3–4.

16. *Teachings of Harold B. Lee,* 546–47.

17. Holland, CR, October 2004, 5.

ELEVEN

Is That in the Bible?

THERE IS NO QUESTION but that the Holy Bible holds a place of distinctive preeminence within the Judaeo-Christian world. It is sacred scripture, the holy book, the word of God. One might be inspired through reading Lloyd C. Douglas's *The Robe* or Hawthorne's *The Scarlet Letter.* One might be moved emotionally by a score of books that have religious themes or that point the reader toward the higher path. But the Bible is the book of books. It contains teachings that pertain to personal improvement, moral betterment, and even the salvation of the human soul, lessons that are both timely and timeless. A significant price has been paid by thousands upon thousands of noble men and women to preserve the scriptures, and it is my feeling that the Bible will continue to serve as a normative guide for people throughout the earth as long as time exists.

Even though I was raised as a Latter-day Saint, my first exposure to holy scripture was with Bible stories from the Old and New Testaments. While attending vacation Bible school with some Baptist friends, I learned to appreciate the importance of the messages of the Bible and came to feel the soothing influence that hearing its messages brings. But because I was LDS, I became aware of the fact that people of my faith were different in their acceptance of additional books of scripture. Even to this day many of my dearest friends and colleagues of other faiths who have come to know me best are downright astonished when they learn of my love for, memorization of, and regular citation of the Bible, especially the New Testament. In other words, my acceptance of the Book of Mormon, Doctrine and Covenants, and Pearl of Great Price does not in any way mar the image of the Bible in my own eyes, nor do I feel any less reverence or respect for biblical texts as a result of my acceptance of LDS scripture.

Over the years it has been quite interesting to try to explain Mormonism to persons unacquainted with my faith. I remember very well telling Joseph Smith's story of his first vision, and of the translation of the Book of Mormon, to a Roman Catholic friend of mine when I was about sixteen years old. I was surprised at his reaction: Not only was he incensed that I should believe in the need for anything beyond the Bible, but automatically assumed that I did not therefore love and revere that great book. I tried to use analogies to illustrate my devotion to both ancient and modern scripture; I suggested, for example, that one need not denigrate the Old Testament in order to fully appreciate the value of the New. I suppose what I am suggesting is that it is an incorrect notion that Mormons devalue the Bible; if in fact they do, they do so without divine authorization and in complete ignorance. There are few things I would rather do more than read and reflect upon the Gospel of John or Paul's epistle to the Romans, and those who know me best know that.

I can still remember when I was quite young trying to tell someone about Joseph Smith's prophetic call when I was abruptly interrupted with the question: "Where's that in the Bible?" And then came the even more fascinating question: "Where does the Bible even mention Joseph Smith?" I almost didn't know how to respond to that question, given that Joseph Smith wasn't even born until centuries after the establishment of the biblical canon. It reminded me of the person who was so insistent on staying with their own biblical translation and refusing a different rendering of the text that they spoke these words: "Look, if the King James Version was good enough for Jesus, it's good enough for me."

I enrolled in a doctoral course entitled Seminar on Biblical Studies in the late 1970s. There were eight of us in the course, as I recall, from various religious backgrounds—two Southern Baptists, a couple of Methodists, a Reform Jew, a Roman Catholic, a Nazarene, and a Latter-day Saint. It was an excellent class and helped introduce me to the vocabulary of the academic study of religion as well as to some of the problems and challenges of biblical scholarship. The professor, a former Methodist minister, was a superb instructor. He was organized, well prepared, and considerate of students. He responded well to questions and was always available for consultation. We studied various topics, including the nature of scripture, covenant, prophecy, interpretation, authorship, and the dating of scriptural records. One of the things that stands out in my mind is our discussion of the canon of scripture. We had covered in some detail the historical roots of the Old and New Testament canons and discussed the relationship between canonicity and authority of scripture; that is, we had debated whether a document belonged in the canon because it was considered authoritative, or whether it was considered authoritative because it was included in the canon.

For two periods the instructor had emphasized that the word *canon*—referring, of course, to the biblical books that are generally included in the Judaeo-Christian collection—implied the rule of faith, the standard against which we measure what is acceptable. Further, he stated that the canon, if the word meant anything at all, was *closed, fixed, set,* and *established*. I look back at my notes decades later and realize that he must have stressed those four words at least ten times. I noticed in our second session on this topic that the instructor seemed a bit uneasy. I remember thinking that something must be wrong. Without warning, he stopped what he was doing, banged his fist on the table, turned to me and said: "Mr. Millet, will you please explain to this group the Latter-day Saint concept of canon, especially given your acceptance of the Book of Mormon and other books of scripture?" I was startled, caught off guard, certainly surprised. I paused for several seconds, looked up at the board, saw the now very familiar four words written under the word canon, and said somewhat shyly: "Well, I suppose you could say that the Mormons believe the canon of scripture is *open, flexible,* and *expanding!*" We spent much of the rest of the period trying to make sense out of what I had just said.

Joseph Smith loved the Bible. It was pondering upon a biblical passage that began his quest to know the will of the Almighty. Most of his sermons, writings, and letters are laced with quotations or paraphras-

ing summaries of biblical passages and precepts, from both the Old
and New Testaments. Joseph once remarked that one can "see God's
handwriting in the sacred volume; and he who reads it oftenest will like
it best."[1] He believed the Bible represented God's word to humanity,
and he gloried in the truths and timeless lessons it contained.

From his earliest days, however, Joseph did not believe the Bible
was complete, nor did he feel that religious difficulties could necessarily
be handled quickly by turning to the Old or New Testaments for help.
After speaking of how James 1:5–6 had made such a deep impression
upon his soul, he wrote: "I reflected on it again and again, knowing
that if any person needed wisdom from God, I did; for the teachers of
religion of the different sects understood the same passages of scripture
so differently as to destroy all confidence in settling the question by an
appeal to the Bible" (Joseph Smith-History 1:12). On another occasion
he declared:

"From what we can draw from the Scriptures relative to the teaching
of heaven, we are induced to think that much instruction has been given
to man since the beginning which we do not possess now. This may not
agree with the opinions of some of our friends who are bold to say that
we have everything written in the Bible which God ever spoke to man
since the world began, and that if He had ever said anything more we
should certainly have received it.... We have what we have, and the Bible
contains what it does contain: but to say that God never said anything
more to man than is there recorded, would be saying at once that we
have at last received a revelation: for it must require one to advance thus
far, because it is nowhere said in that volume by the mouth of God that
He would *not,* after giving what is there contained, speak again; and if
any man has found out for a fact that the Bible contains all that God ever
revealed to man he has ascertained it by an immediate revelation."[2]

In an 1833 letter to his uncle, Silas Smith, Joseph wrote:

Seeing that the Lord has never given the world to understand by
anything heretofore revealed that he had ceased forever to speak to
his creatures when sought unto in a proper manner, why should it be
thought a thing incredible that he should be pleased to speak again
in these last days for their salvation? Perhaps you may be surprised at

this assertion that I should say "for the salvation of his creatures in these last days" since we have already in our possession a vast volume of his word [the Bible] which he has previously given. But you will admit that the word spoken to Noah was not sufficient for Abraham.... Isaac, the promised seed, was not required to rest his hope upon the promises made to his father Abraham, but was privileged with the assurance of [God's] approbation in the sight of heaven by the direct voice of the Lord to him....

"I have no doubt but that the holy prophets and apostles and saints in the ancient days were saved in the kingdom of God.... I may believe that Enoch walked with God. I may believe that Abraham communed with God and conversed with angels.... I may believe that Elijah was taken to heaven in a chariot of fire with fiery horses. I may believe that the saints saw the Lord and conversed with him face-to-face after his resurrection. I may believe that the Hebrew Church came to Mount Zion and unto the city of the living God, the heavenly Jerusalem, and to an innumerable company of angels. I may believe that they looked into eternity and saw the Judge of all, and Jesus the Mediator of the new covenant; but *will all this purchase an assurance for me,* or waft me to the regions of eternal day with my garments spotless, pure, and white? Or, must I not rather obtain for myself, by my own faith and diligence, in keeping the commandments of the Lord, an assurance of salvation for myself? And *have I not an equal privilege* with the ancient saints? And will not the Lord hear my prayers, and listen to my cries as soon [as] he ever did to theirs, if I come to him in the manner they did? Or is he a respecter of persons?"[3]

One of Mormonism's articles of faith states: "We believe the Bible to be the word of God as far as it is translated correctly. We also believe the Book of Mormon to be the word of God" (Articles of Faith 1:8). It appears that Joseph Smith meant to convey what is generally associated with the term *transmitted;* there was certainly more involved in how we got the Bible than translation matters, including copying, adding to, taking from, and interpretation as well as problems of translation from the ancient tongues. In 1843 he added: "I believe the Bible as it ought to be, as it came from the pen of the original writers."[4] He felt that many plain and precious truths had been taken from the Bible before the documents were compiled into what we now know as the Old and New Testaments. This was one of the reasons Joseph Smith felt called to initiate a *restoration* of truth and power, not simply a reformation of existing religious matters.

Neither Joseph Smith nor his followers have held to a view of biblical inerrancy. For one thing, the Latter-day Saints do not find the doctrine of scriptural inerrancy to be particularly helpful. As I understand the concept, it could be stated as follows: Scriptural inerrantists believe that the original autographs (the first Old or New Testament manuscripts) were without error or flaw. The problem, of course, is that we do not have the original manuscripts, and so inerrancy is not really a statement about the accuracy of today's Bible. Joseph believed, to be sure, that the essential message of the Bible was true and from God. We could say that he believed it was "God's word." I am not so certain that he or modern Church leaders would be convinced that every sentence recorded in the testaments necessarily contains "God's words," meaning a direct quotation or a transcription of divine direction. Joseph taught, and his successors have emphasized, that it is the spirit of revelation within the one called of God that is the energizing force and that in most instances God places the thought into the mind or heart of the revelator, who then assumes the responsibility to clothe the oracle in language. Certainly there are times when a prophet records the words of God directly, but very often the "still, small voice" (1 Kings 19:12) whispers to the prophet who then speaks for God. For that matter, I am fairly certain that most thinking Latter-day Saints would not feel that the Book of Mormon is without flaw or error either (see, for example, Title Page; Mormon 8:17).

In short, an LDS view might be stated as follows: When God chooses to speak through a person, that person does not become a holy ventriloquist, a mindless instrument, an earthly sound system through which God can voice himself. Rather, the person becomes enlightened and filled with intelligence or truth. Nothing could be clearer in the Old Testament, for example, than that many factors impacted the prophetic message—personality, experience, vocabulary, literary talent. The word of the Lord as spoken through Isaiah is quite different from the word of the Lord as spoken through Luke, and both are different from that spoken by Jeremiah or Mark. I fully understand and appreciate why many Christians choose to adopt such a position: If the Bible cannot be trusted in all things, they feel, it cannot be trusted at all. Latter-day Saints do not believe such an extreme position is necessary.

Further, it is worth noting that stone, leaves, bark, skins, wood, metals, baked clay, and papyrus were all used anciently to record inspired messages. The Mormon concern with the ancients is not the perfection with which such messages were recorded but with the inspiration of the message. More specifically, Latter-day Saints are interested in the fact that the heavens were opened to the ancients, that they had messages to record. In other words, knowing that God is the same yesterday, today, and forever (see Hebrews 13:8), the fact that he spoke to them at all, however well or poorly it may have been recorded, attests that he can speak to men and women in the here and now. After all, the Bible is only black ink on white paper until the Spirit of God manifests its true meaning to us; if we have obtained that, there is little need to quibble over the Bible's suitability as a history or science text.

So often I encounter religious persons who state emphatically that their position is based entirely upon "the authority of scripture." The fact is, God is the source of any reputable religious authority. In the words of N. T. Wright, "The risen Jesus, at the end of Matthew's gospel, does not say, 'All authority in heaven and on earth is given to the books you are all going to write,' but 'All authority in heaven and on earth is given to me.'" In other words, "scripture itself points—authoritatively, if it does indeed possess authority!—away from itself and to the fact that final and true authority belongs to God himself, now delegated to Jesus Christ."[5]

Lee M. McDonald, a Baptist pastor who has taught at Fuller Theological Seminary, posed some probing questions relative to the present closed Christian canon of scripture. "The first question," he writes, "and the most important one, is whether the church was right in perceiving the need for a closed canon of scriptures." McDonald also asks: "Did such a move toward a closed canon of scriptures ultimately (and unconsciously) limit the presence and power of the Holy Spirit in the church? More precisely, does the recognition of absoluteness of the biblical canon minimize the presence and activity of God in the church today?… On what biblical or historical grounds has the inspiration of God been limited to the written documents that the church now calls its Bible?" While McDonald poses other issues, let me refer to his final question: "If the Spirit inspired only the written documents of the first century, does that mean that the same Spirit does not speak today in the church about matters that are of significant concern …?"[6]

For Joseph Smith and his followers, the traditions of the past regarding scripture, revelation, and canon were altered dramatically by the appearance of God the Father and His Son Jesus Christ in Joseph's First Vision. They believed God had spoken again and a "new dispensation" of truth was under way. The ninth article of faith states: "We believe all that God has revealed, all that He does now reveal, and we believe that He will yet reveal many great and important things pertaining to the Kingdom of God" (Articles of Faith 1:9). The LDS canon of scripture, called the "standard works," consists of the Bible, Book of Mormon, Doctrine and Covenants, and Pearl of Great Price.

Over three years passed from the time of Joseph Smith's first visionary experience, and during that interim he had simply refrained from joining any of the existing churches in the area. One evening Joseph knelt in prayer to determine his standing before God, inasmuch as he had enjoyed no further communication with God since 1820. In his own words: "On the evening of the 21st of September, A.D. 1823, while I was praying unto God, and endeavoring to exercise faith in the precious promises of Scripture, on a sudden a light like that of day, only of a far purer and more glorious appearance and brightness, burst into the room, indeed, the first sight was as though the house was filled with consuming fire; the appearance produced a shock that affected the whole body; in a moment a personage stood before me surrounded with a glory yet greater than that with which I was already surrounded."[7] The angel announced himself as Moroni and explained that "God had a work for me to do and that my name should be had for good and evil among all nations, kindreds, and tongues, or that it should be both good and evil spoken of among all people. He said there was a book deposited, written upon gold plates, giving an account of the former inhabitants of this continent, and the source from whence they sprang.

He also said that the fullness of the everlasting Gospel was contained in it, as delivered by the Savior to the ancient inhabitants" (Joseph Smith-History 1:34). In describing the plates as well as the manner in which he translated them, Joseph Smith said in 1842:

"These records were engraven on plates which had the appearance of gold, each plate was six inches wide and eight inches long, and not quite so thick as common tin. They were filled with engravings, in Egyptian characters, and bound together in a volume as the leaves of a book, with three rings running through the whole. The volume was something near six inches in thickness, a part of which was sealed.... With the records was found a curious instrument, which the ancients called 'Urim and Thummim,' which consisted of two transparent stones set in the rim of a bow fastened to a breast plate. Through the medium of the Urim and Thummim I translated the record by the gift and power of God."[8]

For the Latter-day Saints, the Book of Mormon is an additional book of scripture, Another Testament of Jesus Christ. The majority of the Book of Mormon deals with a group of Hebrews (descendants of the tribe of Joseph, son of Jacob) who leave Jerusalem in the first year of the reign of King Zedekiah (ca. 600 B.C.), anticipating (being divinely directed concerning) the overthrow of Judah by the Babylonians. The people travel south and eventually set sail for a "promised land," a land "choice above all other lands," the land of America. The early story highlights the dissension between Nephi, a righteous and obedient leader of his people, and his rebellious and murmuring brothers, Laman and Lemuel. Prophet after prophet arises to call the people to repentance and declare the message of salvation. The Nephites are told repeatedly of the coming of Jesus, the Messiah, and the prophet leaders constantly strive to turn the hearts of the people to Christ. Eventually the internal squabbles result in a total break of the migrants into two separate bodies of people—the followers of Nephi (Nephites) and the followers of Laman (Lamanites). The remainder of the Book of Mormon is essentially a story of the constant rise and fall of the Nephite nation (not unlike the accounts of the children of Israel contained in 2 Kings), as the people either choose to obey God or yield to the enticings of riches and pride.

The book of 3 Nephi, chapters 11–28, contains an account of a visit and brief ministry of Jesus Christ to the Nephites in America, following his death, resurrection, and ascension in the Holy Land. While teaching and comforting these "other sheep" (see John 10:14–16; 3 Nephi 15:21), Jesus organizes a church and establishes standards for a Christian community. An era of peace and unity follows for almost two hundred years as the people see to the needs of one another through having "all things in common." The misuse of material blessings eventually leads to pride and class distinctions, resulting in a continuation of the former struggles between good and evil. The story of the Book of Mormon culminates in a final battle between the Nephites and the Lamanites in which the former (who had proven over time to be more wicked than their idolatrous enemies) are exterminated. The history and divine dealings of the people from the time of Nephi had been kept by the prophets or civic leaders, and the final task of completing and then editing the thousand-year collection of metal plates remained for the prophet-leader Mormon (for whom the book/collection is named) and his son, Moroni, in about A.D. 400. Joseph Smith stated that it was this same Moroni who returned as an angel with the plates in 1823. It is, by the way, because of the Latter-day Saints' acceptance of the Book of Mormon that they have come to be known as "Mormons."

Many persons in the nineteenth century claimed revelation from God, claimed visions and oracles. But the Book of Mormon made Joseph's claims somewhat unusual, inasmuch as it represented to many a tangible evidence of divine intervention in history. People "touched the book," as Richard Bushman has written, "and the realization came over them that God had spoken again. Apart from any specific content, the discovery of additional scripture in itself inspired faith in people who were looking for more certain evidence of God in their lives."[9] In fact, Jan Shipps observed that as important as the First Vision was to the early Saints, "it was this 'gold bible' that first attracted adherents to the movement. As crucial to the success of the whole Latter-day Saint enterprise as is Joseph Smith, it must never be forgotten that in the early years it was not the First Vision but the Book of Mormon that provided the credentials that made the prophet's leadership so effective."[10]

Inasmuch as Joseph Smith claimed divine authority to speak for

God, it was but natural that revelations and oracles given to him would be recorded. In fact, in a revelation given in November 1831, we find a demonstration of the broadened concept of scripture, one still held by the Latter-day Saints. This revelation stated that the elders of the Church "shall speak as they are moved upon by the Holy Ghost. And whatsoever they shall speak when moved upon by the Holy Ghost shall be scripture, shall be the will of the Lord, shall be the mind of the Lord, shall be the word of the Lord, shall be the voice of the Lord, and the power of God unto salvation" (Doctrine and Covenants 68:3–4; cited as D&C). In 1831 the leaders of the Church began to compile the revelations received by Joseph Smith to date, and by 1833 that collection was known as *A Book of Commandments for the Government of the Church of Christ*, a volume consisting of approximately sixty-four of the present sections of the Doctrine and Covenants. Mob violence in Missouri led to the destruction of the press and the loss of all but a few copies of the Book of Commandments. In August 1835, Joseph Smith published the first edition of the Doctrine and Covenants, an expanded form of the Book of Commandments, a collection that contained an additional forty-five revelations. Today the Doctrine and Covenants consists of 138 divisions called "sections" and two "official declarations."

A perusal of the Doctrine and Covenants demonstrates that most of the revelations recorded were received during the Ohio era of the Church's history, over twenty were received in Missouri, and fewer than ten were recorded in the Doctrine and Covenants in Illinois. In addition to the revelations through Joseph Smith, there is in the Doctrine and Covenants one revelation received by Brigham Young, one by Joseph F. Smith, sixth president of the Church (1901–18), and official declarations from Wilford Woodruff (fourth president, 1899–1901) and Spencer W. Kimball (twelfth president, 1973–85).

At the April 1976 general conference of the Church, two revelations were added to the canon. One had been received by Joseph Smith in January 1836 but had never been placed in the canon. Another was received by Joseph F. Smith in October 1918. Mormons believe that both of these oracles were inspired of God—that is, they represent the will, mind, voice, and word of the Lord, even from the time they were delivered and recorded. That is, since 1836 or 1918 they were *scripture*.

But in 1976 they were added to the standard works, the canon, by a vote of the Church, thus making them *canonized scripture*. As such they become binding upon the Saints, and the members of the Church are expected to read and study them and to govern their beliefs and practices according to them.

In 1850, Franklin D. Richards, a young member of the Quorum of Twelve Apostles, was called to serve as president of the British mission of the Church. He discovered a paucity of either LDS scripture or Church literature among the Saints in England, this in spite of the fact that a larger number of members resided in the British Isles at this time than in the United States. In 1851 he published a mission tract entitled *Pearl of Great Price*, a collection of translations and narrations from Joseph Smith, essentially a type of prophetic potpourri. Interest in and appreciation for the tract grew over the years, and by 1880 the entire Church voted to accept the Pearl of Great Price as the fourth standard work, the fourth book of scripture in the LDS canon. The Pearl of Great Price contains: (1) doctrinal details concerning Adam (and the Creation and Fall), Enoch, Noah, Moses, and Jesus' Olivet Discourse (Matthew 24) as made known to Joseph Smith; (2) more of God's dealings with Abraham; (3) an excerpt from Joseph Smith's 1838 history of the Church; and (4) thirteen statements of religious belief by Joseph Smith, called the Articles of Faith.

The scriptures are to be read and searched and studied; the reader of scripture is encouraged to open himself or herself to inspiration and to "liken the scriptures" unto their own life situation. In short, though the study of scripture may not be considered a sacramental act, Latter-day Saints believe that one essential key to the receipt of *individual* revelation—to know the mind and will of God in one's life—is the study of *institutional* revelation. "We read scripture," N. T. Wright has observed, "in order to be refreshed in our memory and understanding of the story within which we ourselves are actors, to be reminded where it has come from and where it is going to, and hence what our own part within it ought to be."[11] Elsewhere Wright declared: "Reading scripture, like praying and sharing in the sacraments, is one of the means by which the life of heaven and the life of earth interlock. (This is what older writers were referring to when they spoke of 'the means of grace.' It isn't that we can control God's grace, but that there are, so to speak, places to go where God has promised to meet with his people, even if sometimes when we turn up it feels as though God has forgotten the date. More usually it's the other way around.) We read scripture in order to hear God addressing us—*us*, here and now, today."[12]

A modern Mormon apostle counseled Church leaders as follows: "Faith is...born of scriptural study. Those who study, ponder, and pray about the scriptures, seeking to understand their deep and hidden meanings, receive from time to time great outpourings of light and knowledge from the Holy Spirit.... However talented men may be in administrative matters; however eloquent they may be in expressing their views; however learned they may be in worldly things—they will be denied the sweet whisperings of the Spirit that might have been theirs unless they pay the price of studying, pondering, and praying about the scriptures."[13] "When this fact is admitted," Joseph Smith said in 1834, "that the immediate will of heaven is contained in the Scriptures, are we not bound as rational creatures to live in accordance to all [their] precepts?"[14]

Gordon B. Hinckley spoke of the value of scripture study in coming to know the Lord. "If you wish to know of the Savior," he said, "read of the Savior. Read the New Testament, study it. Read the words of the Lord. Read the Epistles of Paul that speak of Him in wonder and glory and awe. Read the Book of Mormon. Pray about it. Get on your knees, ask the Lord for a testimony of the truth of this most important of all knowledge—the divinity and the reality of the Lord Jesus Christ."[15]

A final thought regarding the LDS expansion of the canon. As important as the Bible is:

1. How certain are we that it is the final manifestation of God's word?

2. Why should we suppose that the ignorance and confusion and doubt and cynicism of our day do not demand current and continuing divine direction, perhaps even additional scripture?

3. The Protestant notion of *sola scriptura* (the scripture alone),

highlighted in the Reformation, is a position that is indefensible from the Holy Bible itself. That is to say, well-intended people, people who desperately desire for the Bible to be cherished and loved and read and applied, are making claims for the Bible that the Bible never makes for itself. The Roman Catholic Church has suggested additional legs to the stool of scriptural understanding—the tradition of the church, as well as the majesterium, the interpretations and pronouncements of presiding Church officers. Besides, the Bible is not a self-interpreting document; if it were, the Christian world would certainly not be as divided as it is today.

Scott Hahn, a man raised as an Evangelical Protestant but who later converted to Catholicism, wrote that "when our nation's founders gave us the Constitution, they didn't leave it at that. Can you imagine what we'd have today if all they had given us was a document, as good as it is, along with a charge like, 'May the spirit of Washington guide each and every citizen'? We'd have anarchy—which is basically what…Protestants do have when it comes to Church unity. Instead, our founding fathers gave us something besides the Constitution; they gave us a government—made up of a President, Congress and a Supreme Court—all of which are needed to administer and interpret the Constitution. And if that's just enough to govern a country like ours, what would it take to govern a worldwide Church?"[16]

The Bible is a magnificent tool in the hands of God, but it is too often used as a club or a weapon in the hands of men and women. For a long time now, the Bible has been used to settle disputes of every imaginable kind, even those that the prophets never intended to settle. Creeds and biblical interpretations in the nineteenth century served as much to distinguish and divide as they did to inform and unite. "At some level, Joseph's revelations indicate a loss of trust in the Christian ministry," historian Richard Bushman has pointed out. "For all their learning and their eloquence, the clergy could not be trusted with the Bible. They did not understand what the book meant. It was a record of revelations, and the ministry had turned it into a handbook. The Bible had become a text to be interpreted rather than an experience to be lived. In the process, the power of the book was lost.... It was the power thereof that Joseph and the other visionaries of his time sought to recover. Not getting it from the ministry, they looked for it themselves.

"To me," Bushman continues, "that is Joseph Smith's significance for our time. He stood on the contested ground where the Enlightenment and Christianity confronted one another, and his life posed the question, Do you believe God speaks? Joseph was swept aside, of course, in the rush of ensuing intellectual battles and was disregarded by the champions of both great systems, but his mission was to hold out for the reality of divine revelation and establish one small outpost where that principle survived. Joseph's revelatory principle is not a single revelation serving for all time, as the Christians of his day believed regarding the incarnation of Christ, nor a mild sort of inspiration seeping into the minds of all good people, but specific, ongoing directions from God to his people. At a time when the origins of Christianity were under assault by the forces of Enlightenment rationality, Joseph Smith returned modern Christianity to its origins in revelation."[17]

ENDNOTES

1. Smith, *TPJS*, 56.

2. Ibid., 61, emphasis added.

3. Smith, in *Personal Writings of Joseph Smith*, 321–24, emphasis added.

4. Smith, *Words of Joseph Smith*, ed. Ehat and Cook, 256.

5. Wright, *Last Word*, xi, 24.

6. McDonald, *Formation of the Christian Biblical Canon*, 254–56.

7. *History of the Church* 4:536.

8. Ibid., 4:537.

9. Bushman, *Joseph Smith and the Beginnings of Mormonism*, 142.

10. Shipps, *Mormonism: The Story of a New Religious Tradition*, 33.

11. Wright, *Last Word*, 115.

12. Wright, *Simply Christian*, 188, emphasis in original.

13. McConkie, address to Regional Representatives, April 1982; cited in *Doctrines of the Restoration*, 238.

14. Smith, *TPJS*, 54.

15. Hinckley, from Regional Conference, St. George, Utah, 24 November 2002; in *Church News*, 3 December 2005, 2.

16. Scott and Kimberly Hahn, *Rome Sweet Home*, 73.

17. Bushman, *Believing History*, 274.

TWELVE

Solid Doctrine or Pop Theology?

THERE IS POWER IN doctrine, power in the word, power to heal the wounded soul, power to transform human behavior. "True doctrine, understood, changes attitudes and behavior," Boyd K. Packer explained. "The study of the doctrines of the gospel will improve behavior quicker than a study of behavior will improve behavior. That is why we stress so forcefully the study of the doctrines of the gospel."[1] Another modern Church leader, Neal A. Maxwell, pointed out that "doctrines believed and practiced do change and improve us, while insuring our vital access to the Spirit. Both outcomes are crucial."[2]

A Baptist minister was in my office one day. We were chatting about a number of things, including doctrine. He said to me, "Bob, you people believe in such strange things!"

"Like what?" I asked.

"Oh, for example," he said, "you believe in blood atonement. And that affects Utah's insistence on retaining death by a firing squad."

I responded: "No we don't."

"Yes you do," he came right back. "I know of several statements by Brigham Young and other early LDS Church leaders that teach such things."

"I'm aware of those statements," I said. I then found myself saying something that I had never voiced before: "Yes, they were taught, but they do not represent the doctrine of our Church. We believe in the blood atonement of Jesus Christ, and that alone."

My friend didn't skip a beat: "What do you mean they don't represent the doctrine of your Church? They were spoken by major Church leaders."

I explained that such statements were made, for the most part, during the time of what has come to be known as the Mormon Reformation and are examples of a kind of "revival rhetoric" in which the leaders of the Church were striving to "raise the bar" in terms of obedience and faithfulness. I assured him that the Church, by its own canonical standards, does not have the right or the power to take a person's life because of disobedience or even apostasy (D&C 134:10). I read to him a passage from the Book of Mormon in which the prophets had resorted to "exceeding harshness, ...continually reminding [the people] of death, and the duration of eternity, and the judgments and the power of God, ...and exceedingly great plainness of speech" in order to "keep them from going down speedily to destruction" (Enos 1:23).

This seemed to satisfy him to some extent, but then he said: "Bob, many of my fellow Christians have noted how hard it is to figure out what Mormons believe. They say it's like trying to nail green Jell-O to the wall! What do you people believe? How do you decide what is your doctrine and what is not?" I suggested that he consider the following three ideas:

1. The teachings of the Church today have a rather narrow focus, range, and direction; central and saving doctrine is what we teach and emphasize, not tangential and peripheral ideas.

2. Very often what is drawn from Church leaders of the past is, like the matter of blood atonement mentioned above, either misquoted, misrepresented, or taken out of context. Further, not everything that was ever spoken or written by a Church leader in the past is a part of what we teach today.

3. In determining whether something is a part of the doctrine of the Church, we might ask: Is it found within the four standard works—the Bible, Book of Mormon, Doctrine and

Covenants, and Pearl of Great Price? Within official declarations or proclamations? Is it taught or discussed in general conference (held in April and October in Salt Lake City each year) or other official gatherings by general Church leaders today? Is it found in the general handbooks or approved curriculum of the Church today? If it meets at least one of these criteria, we can feel secure and appropriate in teaching it. A significant percentage of anti-Mormonism focuses on statements by Church leaders of the past that deal with peripheral or noncentral issues. No one criticizes us for a belief in God; in the divinity of Jesus Christ or his atoning work; in the literal bodily resurrection of the Savior and the eventual resurrection of mankind; in baptism by immersion; in the gift of the Holy Ghost; the sacrament of the Lord's Supper, etc.

While we love the scriptures and thank God regularly for them, we believe that one can have sufficient confidence and even reverence for holy writ without believing that every word between Genesis 1:1 and Revelation 22:21 is the word-for-word dictation of the Almighty or that the Bible now reads as it has always read. Indeed, our own scriptures attest that plain and precious truths and many covenants of the Lord were taken away or kept back from the Bible before it was compiled (1 Nephi 13:20–29; Moses 1:40–41; Articles of Faith 1:8). We still cherish the sacred volume, however, recognize and teach the doctrines of salvation within it, and seek to pattern our lives according to its timeless teachings.

In like manner, we can sustain with all our hearts latter-day prophets and apostles without believing that they are perfect or that everything they say or do is exactly what God wants said and done. In short, we do not believe in apostolic or prophetic infallibility. Moses made mistakes, but we love and sustain him and accept his writings nonetheless. Peter made mistakes, but we still honor him and study his words. Paul made mistakes, but we admire his boldness and dedication and treasure his epistles. James pointed out that Elijah "was a man subject to like passions as we are" (James 5:17), and the prophet Joseph taught that "a prophet [is] a prophet only when he [is] acting as such."[3] On another occasion Joseph declared: "I told them I was but a man, and they must not expect me to be perfect; if they expected perfection from me, I should expect it from them; but if they would bear with my infirmities and the infirmities of the brethren, I would likewise bear with their infirmities."[4] "I can fellowship the president of the Church," said Lorenzo Snow, "if he does not know everything I know.... I saw the...imperfections in [Joseph Smith].... I thanked God that he would put upon a man who had those imperfections the power and authority he placed upon him...for I knew that I myself had weakness, and I thought there was a chance for me."[5] Every member of the Church, including those called to guide its destiny, has the right to be wrong at one time or another—to say something that simply isn't true. They also have the right to improve their views, to change their minds and correct mistakes as new light and new truth become available.

Being called as an apostle or even as president of the Church does not remove the man from mortality or make him perfect. David O. McKay, ninth president of the Church, explained that "when God makes the prophet He does not unmake the man."[6] "I was this morning introduced to a man from the east," Joseph Smith stated. "After hearing my name, he remarked that I was nothing but a man, indicating by this expression, that he had supposed that a person to whom the Lord would see fit to reveal his will, must be something more than a man. He seemed to have forgotten the saying that fell from the lips of James, that [Elijah] was a man subject to like passions as we are, yet he had such power with God, that he, in answer to his prayers, shut the heavens that they gave no rain for the space of three years and six months."[7]

"I have worked with seven presidents of this Church," Gordon B. Hinckley explained. "I have recognized that all have been human. But I have never been concerned over this. They may have had some weaknesses. But this has never troubled me. I know that the God of heaven has used mortal men throughout history to accomplish His divine purposes."[8] On another occasion President Hinckley taught that "as we continue our search for truth...we look for strength and goodness rather than weakness and foibles in those who did so great a work in their time. We recognize that our forebears were human. They doubtless made mistakes.... There was only one perfect man who ever walked the earth. The Lord has used imperfect people in the process of building his perfect society. If some of them occasionally stumbled, or if their characters may have been slightly flawed in one way or another, the wonder is the greater that they accomplished so much."[9]

Some time ago a colleague and I were in Southern California speaking to a group of about five hundred people, both Latter-day Saint and Protestant. During the question-and-answer phase of the program, someone asked the inevitable: "Are you really Christian? Do you, as many claim, worship a different Jesus?" I explained that we worship the Christ of the New Testament, that we believe wholeheartedly in his virgin birth, his divine Sonship, his miracles, his transforming teachings, his atoning sacrifice, and his bodily resurrection from the dead. I added that we also believe in the teachings of and about Christ found in the Book of Mormon and modern revelation. After the meeting an LDS woman came up to me and said: "You didn't tell the truth about what we believe!"

Startled, I asked: "What do you mean?"

She responded: "You said we believe in the virgin birth of Christ."

"Well, we do," I retorted.

She then said with a great deal of emotion: "I want to believe you, but I was told that God the Father had sexual relations with Mary and thereby Jesus was conceived."

I looked her in the eyes and said: "I'm aware of that idea, but that is not the doctrine of the Church; that is not what we teach in the Church today. Have you ever heard the leaders of the Church teach it in conference? Is it in the standard works, the curricular materials, or the handbooks of the Church? Is it a part of an official declaration or proclamation?" I watched as an enormous weight seemed to come off her shoulders, as tears came into her eyes, and she simply said: "Thank you, Brother Millet."

Once Pastor Greg Johnson and I met with an Evangelical Christian church just outside Salt Lake City. The minister there asked us to come and make a presentation (An Evangelical and a Latter-day Saint in Dialogue) that Greg and I have made several times before in different parts of the country. There were many, many hands in the air when we opened for questions. I called on a woman close to the front of the church. Her question was: "How do you deal with the Adam-God doctrine?"

I responded: "Thank you for that question. It gives me an opportunity to explain a principle early in our exchange that will lay the foundation for other things to be said." I took a few moments to address the questions, What is our doctrine? What do we teach today? I indicated if some teaching or idea was not in the standard works, not among official declarations or proclamations, was not taught currently by living apostles or prophets in general conference or other official gatherings, or was not in the general handbooks or official curriculum of the Church, it is probably not a part of the doctrine or teachings of the Church.

I was surprised when my pastor friend then said to the group: "Are you listening to Bob? Do you hear what he is saying? This is important! It's time for us to stop criticizing Latter-day Saints on matters they don't even teach today." At this point in the meeting, two things happened: First, the number of hands of questioners went down, and second, the tone of the meeting changed quite dramatically. The questions were not baiting or challenging ones, but rather efforts to clarify. For example, the last question asked was by a middle-aged man. He stood up and said: "I for one would like to thank you for what you have done here tonight. This thrills my soul. I think this is what Jesus would do. I have lived in Utah for many years, and I have many LDS friends. We get along okay; we don't fight and quarrel over religious matters. But we really don't talk with one another about the things that matter most to us, that is, our faith. I don't plan to become a Latter-day Saint, and I'm certain my Mormon friends don't plan to become Evangelical, but I would like to find more effective ways to talk heart to heart. Could you two make a few suggestions on how we can deepen and sweeten our relationships with our LDS neighbors?"

I have no hesitation telling an individual or a group "I don't know" when I am asked why men are ordained to the priesthood and women are not; why Blacks were denied the blessings of the priesthood for almost a century and a half; and several other matters that have neither been revealed nor clarified by those holding the proper keys. The difficulty comes when someone in the past has spoken on these matters, has put forward ideas that are out of harmony with what we know and teach today, and when those teachings are still available, either in print or among the everyday conversations of the members, and have never been corrected or clarified.

It's inevitable that some persons, either LDS or those of other faiths, who are told that not everything stated by an LDS prophet or apostle is a part of the doctrine of the Church and of what we teach today, will be troubled and ask follow-up questions: "Well then, what else did this Church leader teach that is not considered doctrine today? How can we confidently accept anything else he taught? What other directions taken or procedures pursued by the Church in an earlier time do we not follow in our day?" The fact is, one need not take such an approach. This is like throwing the baby out with the bathwater. We must never allow ourselves to overgeneralize and thus overreact. Nor must we be guilty of discounting all that is good and uplifting and divinely given because of an aberration. After all, because a Church leader or preacher once expressed an opinion or perhaps even put forward a doctrinal view that needed further clarification or even correction, does not invalidate all else that he did or said. I would certainly hate to be judged that way and have no desire to be guilty of doing the same to those I believe to be divinely called. God calls his servants, and God corrects them. He knows their strengths, and he knows their weaknesses.

Those of other faiths who leap to criticize the Church and question its truthfulness because of past teachings from Church leaders that are not accepted as doctrine today would do well to ask themselves if they are prepared to apply the same standards of judgment to their own tradition, their own prominent speakers, or their own past. This is like asking someone, "Would you like to better understand Roman Catholicism today? Then study carefully the atrocities of the Crusades or the horrors of the Inquisition." Or: "Would you like a deeper glimpse into the hearts of Lutherans today? Then make it your business to study the anti-Semitic writings of Martin Luther." Or: "Would you care to better understand where Southern Baptists are coming from? Then simply read the many sermons of Baptist preachers during the time of the Civil War who utilized biblical passages to justify the practice of slavery." Again, doctrine means teaching. If we do not teach something today, it is not part of our doctrine today. Was Jesus married? The scriptures do not provide an answer. So whether he was or was not is not part of the doctrine of the Church. I state to my classes regularly that it is as important for us to know what we do not know as it is for us to know what we know. Far too many things are taught or discussed or even argued about that fit into the realm of the unrevealed and thus the unresolved. Such matters, particularly if they do not fall within that range of revealed truth we teach today, do not edify or inspire. Often, very often, they lead to confusion and sow discord.

This does not in any way mean that we should not seek to study and grow and expand in our gospel understanding. Peter explained that there needs to be a reason for the hope within us (1 Peter 3:15). Our knowledge should be as settling to the mind as it is soothing to the heart. Apostle Hugh B. Brown once observed: "I am impressed with the testimony of a man who can stand and say he knows the gospel is true. But what I would like to ask is 'But, sir, do you know the gospel?' …Mere testimony can be gained with but perfunctory knowledge of the Church and its teachings…. But to retain a testimony, to be of service in building the Lord's kingdom, requires a serious study of the gospel and knowing what it is."[10] Again, the issue is one of focus, one of emphasis—where we choose to spend our time when we teach the gospel.

Elder Maxwell explained that "Deeds do matter as well as doctrines, but the doctrines can move us to do the deeds, and the Spirit can help us to understand the doctrines as well as prompt us to do the deeds." He also noted that "when weary legs falter and detours and roadside allurements entice, the fundamental doctrines will summon from deep within us fresh determination. Extraordinary truths can move us to extraordinary accomplishments."[11] The teaching and application of sound doctrine are great safeguards to us. Understanding true doctrine and being true to that doctrine can keep us from ignorance, from error, and from sin.

ENDNOTES

1. Packer, CR, October 1986, 20.

2. Maxwell, *One More Strain of Praise*, x.

3. Smith, *TPJS*, 278.

4. Ibid., 268.

5. Snow, cited in Neal A. Maxwell, CR, October 1984, 10.

6. McKay, CR, April 1907, 11–12; October 1912, 121; April 1962, 7.

7. Smith, *TPJS*, 89.

8. Hinckley, CR, April 1992, 77.

9. Hinckley, "The Continuous Pursuit of Truth," 5.

10. Brown, letter to Robert J. Matthews, cited in "Using the Scriptures," 124.

11. Maxwell, *That My Family Should Partake*, 87.

THIRTEEN

Body and Mind

AS WE INDICATED IN chapter 4, the LDS concept of the Fall is somewhat different from the more traditional Christian view. While LDS scriptures certainly speak at length of the toll taken by the Fall—men and women's utter inability to forgive their own sins or change their own nature, and thus of the absolute necessity for an atonement whose reach is as deep and broad as the Fall—yet, Mormons do not subscribe to a traditional view of human depravity. We claim that the early Christian Church believed in the goodness and potential of human beings (i.e., that men and women are created in the image and likeness of God) while at the same time acknowledging our need for redemption, renewal, and reconciliation with the Father (since that image has been somewhat marred by the Fall).

Elaine Pagels observed that "Augustine, one of the greatest teachers of western Christianity, derived many of [his views of human depravity] from the story of Adam and Eve: that sexual desire is sinful; that infants are infected from the moment of conception with the disease of original sin; and that Adam's sin corrupted the whole of nature itself. Even those who think of Genesis only as literature, and those who are not Christian, live in a culture indelibly shaped by such interpretations as these." Pagels continues: "Augustine's theory of original sin…offered an analysis of human nature that became, for better and worse, the heritage of all subsequent generations of western Christians and the major influence on their psychological and political thinking. Even today, many people, Catholics and Protestants alike, regard the story of Adam and Eve as virtually synonymous with original sin."[1]

Because Latter-day Saints believe in a "fortunate fall" and thus deny that children are "born in sin," they do not baptize infants nor do they view the body through negative lenses. Joseph Smith took a stand that would have been a bit unusual in the nineteenth century. He taught that the physical body was not something to be spurned, transcended, or ashamed of. Rather, the body was an integral part of the human soul (the soul equals the body plus the spirit, D&C 88:15) and that a fullness of joy comes only through the inseparable union of body and spirit in the resurrection (D&C 93:33). "We came to this earth that we might have a body and present it pure before God in the celestial kingdom [the highest heaven]. The great principle of happiness consists in having a body. The devil has no body, and herein is his punishment. He is pleased when he can obtain a tabernacle of man and when cast out by the Savior he asked to go into the herd of swine, showing that he would prefer a swine's body to having none."[2]

This belief is not, of course, inconsistent with the LDS belief that our Father in heaven possesses a physical or corporeal body. Latter-day Saints have been taught that there are experiences and feelings to be had in this second estate, had through the instrumentality of the physical body, that could come to us in no other way. In a revelation given to Joseph Smith in August 1831 we find the following: "Yea, all things which come of the earth, in the season thereof, are made for the benefit and use of man, both to please the eye and to gladden the heart; yea, for food and for raiment, and for taste and for smell, to strengthen the body and to enliven the soul. And it pleaseth God that he hath given all these things unto man; for unto this end were they made to be used." (D&C 59:18–20). And so men and women are expected to enjoy, within established bounds, the beauties and pleasures of the physical body.

At the same time, the children of God are expected to learn to become disciples of the Lord Jesus Christ, to discipline their appetites and passions, to gain control over the flesh and over fleshly yearnings. True joy in life comes through bridling one's passions and bringing one's will into conformity with a Higher Will. While Latter-day Saints do not subscribe to any form of asceticism, they do practice the principle and law of the fast, for example, as a means of gaining victory over the self and thereby acquiring deeper spirituality.

In spite of changing trends in society, the Latter-day Saints are taught to observe the Ten Commandments, including the laws of morality and decency that have proven the bulwark of successful civilizations of the past. Mormons take the law of chastity seriously: All sexual relations of any kind are to be enjoyed only within the bonds of matrimony. The Church teaches complete abstinence from sexual relations before marriage and even cautions against indecent or uncontrolled forms of sexual behavior after marriage. In addition, Latter-day Saints believe that the union of one man and one woman within marriage is for the bearing and rearing of children and for the strengthening and nurturing of marital relationships. Marital fidelity is expected of members in good standing, while those who violate the laws of morality are subject to appropriate Church discipline. "Know ye not that ye are the temple of God, and that the spirit of God dwelleth in you? If any man defile the temple of God, him shall God destroy; for the temple of God is holy, which temple ye are" (1 Corinthians 3:16–17).

Susan W. Tanner, general president of the young women program of the Church, stated that Satan "tries to do everything he can to get us to abuse or misuse this precious gift [the physical body]. He has filled the world with lies and deceptions about the body. He tempts many to defile this great gift of the body through unchastity, immodesty, self-indulgence, and addictions. He seduces some to despise their bodies; others he tempts to worship their bodies. In either case, he enticed the world to regard the body merely as an object. In the face of so many satanic falsehoods about the body, I testify that the body is a gift to be treated with gratitude and respect....

"The pleasures of the body can become an obsession for some; so too can the attention we give to our outward appearance. Sometimes there is a selfish excess of exercising, dieting, makeovers, and spending money on the latest fashions.

"I am troubled by the practice of extreme makeovers. Happiness comes from accepting the bodies we have been given as divine gifts and enhancing our natural attributes, not from remaking our bodies after the image of the world. The Lord wants us to be made over—but in His image, not in the image of the world, by receiving His image in our countenances."[3]

In 1833, Joseph Smith introduced to the Church what has come to be known as the Word of Wisdom, a Mormon health code the Saints believe has both physical and spiritual benefits. Members in good standing abstain from alcohol, tobacco, harmful drugs, coffee, and tea. In recent years, studies by cancer experts have shown a significantly lower cancer rate for the Utah population than the United States in general. James E. Enstrom, UCLA epidemiologist, conducted a study on ten thousand nonsmokers and nondrinkers. "It illustrates a group of individuals [that] have healthy practice in regard to diet because of the large Mormon population. There is an absence among most of the population [and] alcohol is not consumed. These are factors that are often related to cancer risk."[4]

Because the body and the spirit are both so critical to the full development of the individual, members believe that spirituality is adversely affected by the consumption of harmful substances. In the revelation on the Word of Wisdom is found this promise: "And all saints who remember to keep and do these sayings, walking in obedience to the commandments, shall receive health in their navel and marrow to their bones; and shall find wisdom and great treasures of knowledge, even hidden treasures; and shall run and not be weary, and shall walk and not faint. And I, the Lord, give unto them a promise, that the destroying angel shall pass by them, as the children of Israel, and not slay them." (D&C 89:18–21.) The body and the spirit are closely linked.

Early LDS apostle Parley P. Pratt wrote that the Spirit "quickens all the intellectual faculties, increases, enlarges, expands, and purifies all the natural passions and affections, and adapts them, by the gift of wisdom, to their lawful use. It inspires, develops, cultivates, and matures all the fine-toned sympathies, joys, tastes, kindred feelings, and affections of our nature. It inspires virtue, kindness, goodness, tenderness, gentleness, and charity. It develops beauty of person, form, and features. It tends to health, vigor, animation, and social feeling. It invigorates all the faculties of the physical and intellectual man. It strengthens and gives tone to the nerves. In short, it is, as it were, marrow to the bone, joy to the heart, light to the eyes, music to the ears, and life to the whole being."[5]

Further, LDS theology teaches that "the glory of God is intelligence, or, in other words, light and truth" (D&C 93:36). The mind is a precious thing, a blessing and a stewardship that we are expected to cultivate, utilize, and expand. Learning and education are eternal pursuits, and thus they are a vital part of the religion of Mormonism. First and foremost, Latter-day Saints are expected to immerse themselves in the scriptures and to become more than distant acquaintances with holy writ. Church leaders have for many years now encouraged the Saints to be involved in regular personal and family scripture study during the week and to make this a significant part of their group study and worship on the Sabbath. Young people ages fourteen to eighteen are encouraged to involve themselves in weekday religious education in a program known as seminary. A large percentage of LDS youth arise well before school starts in order to attend seminary each weekday morning. Similarly, college and university students may attend weekday religious instruction at what are called institutes of religion, spiritual educational facilities adjacent to most institutions of higher learning around the world.

It is worthwhile to notice the order and breadth of instruction given to the early Latter-day Saints in regard to their educational endeavors: "And I give unto you a commandment that you shall teach one another the doctrine of the kingdom. Teach ye diligently and my grace shall attend you, that you may be instructed more perfectly in theory, in principle, in doctrine, in the law of the gospel, in all things that pertain unto the kingdom of God, that are expedient for you to understand." And then to indicate the extent of learning that is associated closely with building the kingdom of God, note what follows: "Of things both in heaven and in the earth, and under the earth; things which have been, things which are, things which must shortly come to pass; things which are at home, things which are abroad; the wars and the perplexities of the nations, and the judgments which are on the land; and a knowledge also of countries and of kingdoms" (D&C 88:77–79).

For some time now, studies have indicated that higher education tends to have a strong negative influence on religiosity. Various explanations have been offered, but perhaps the most popular is the secularizing effect of post–high school study on one's commitment to the faith. British physicist Paul Davies observed: "If the church is largely ignored today it is not because science has finally won its age-old battle with religion, but because it has so radically reoriented our society that the biblical perspective of the world now seems largely irrelevant."[6] A related explanation posits that "higher education tends to both expand one's horizons and increase exposure to countercultural values. Such exposure works to erode the traditional plausibility structures which maintain the poorly understood religious convictions so typical of American religion. In other words, poorly grounded religious beliefs have simply been unable to stand in the face of challenges generated by modern science and higher education."[7]

Since their beginnings, the Latter-day Saints have placed tremendous stress on the value of education; it is a religious principle that men and women should strive to gain all of the education and training possible to better themselves and their circumstances in life. Thus for both males and females, the percentage of Latter-day Saints who have completed post–high school education or training is significantly higher than in the nation as a whole. Research demonstrates that 53.5% of LDS males have some type of post–high school education, compared to 36.5% for the U.S. population. For females, 44.3% have received some post–high school education, 27.7% for the U.S. population. In addition, the Mormons defy the long-held thesis concerning higher education and religiosity. Weekly attendance at church for males works as follows: Those with only a grade-school education attended 34% of the time, while Mormon males with post–high school education attended 80% of the meetings. The same results followed in such other areas of religiosity as financial contributions, frequency of personal prayer, and the regularity of personal scripture study. In short, the secularizing influence of higher education does not seem to hold for the Mormons.[8]

Assisting members in meeting their needs, both temporal and spiritual, entails more in this complex age than seeing to a proper diet; social, emotional, occupational, and literacy needs are just as important, and so the Church maintains formal programs as an aid to individuals and families to become independent and self-reliant. Finally, it might be observed that through the fast offering program the LDS Church (a monthly fast accompanied by a generous offering to be used for the less fortunate) has in the past been able to send tons of supplies—food, clothing, bedding, etc.—to needy people in such areas as Germany following World War II, and more recently to Africa, India, Iraq, Indonesia, and the Gulf States in the U.S. In recent years the Church has established what is called the Perpetual Education Fund. It is an opportunity for members and interested persons to contribute to a fund that assists young people to receive the needed education and training in their native land to secure gainful employment. Funds for education/training are loaned to the participants, and then repaid in order to keep the corpus healthy and intact and make similar opportunities available to others. Tens of thousands of young people are now involved in this program.

Unlike so many in the religious world, the Latter-day Saints anticipate celestial life on a material world. Elder Orson Pratt eloquently made the point as follows: "A Saint who is one in deed and truth, does not look for an immaterial heaven, but he expects a heaven with lands, houses, cities, vegetation, rivers, and animals; with thrones, temples, palaces, kings, princes, priests, and angels; with food, raiment, musical instruments, etc., all of which are material. Indeed, the Saints' eternal home is a redeemed, glorified, celestial material creation, inhabited by glorified material beings, male and female, organized into families, embracing all the relationships of husbands and wives, parents and children, where sorrow, crying, pain, and death will be known no more." On this earth, Elder Pratt continued, the Saints of God "expect to live, with body, parts, and holy passions; on it they expect to move and have their being." In short, "Materiality is indelibly stamped upon the very heaven of heavens, upon all the eternal creations; it is the very essence of all existence."[9]

ENDNOTES

1. Pagels, *Adam, Eve, and the Serpent*, xix, xxvi; see also 97, 130.
2. Smith, *TPJS*, 181.

3. Tanner, CR, October 2005, 12–13.

4. Cited in *Latter-day Saint Social Life*, ed. James T. Duke, 441–71.

5. Pratt, *Key to the Science of Theology*, 61.

6. Davies, *God and the New Physics*, 2.

7. Albrecht, "The Consequential Dimension to Mormon Religiosity," 100.

8. Albrecht and Heaton, "Secularization, Higher Education, and Religiosity," 49–54.

9. *Masterful Discourses of Orson Pratt*, 62–63.

FOURTEEN

Pure Religion

IKE MEMBERS OF ALL churches, the
Latter-day Saints try their best to live their
religion but fall short. They teach and reach
toward the ideal, but the ideal is still, with most, an unblemished reality. Nevertheless, we keep trying and plead with God to transform our
weakness into strength.

Latter-day Saints do not believe their actions in society and any
good that may come from Christian labors can be separated from their
doctrine. To begin with, Mormons believe that a people cannot really
be built upon Christ's gospel if they do not believe in the divinity of
Jesus Christ. Those who labor tirelessly to lighten burdens or alleviate
human suffering, but at the same time deny the fact that Jesus Christ
is God, cannot have the lasting impact on society that they could have
through drawing upon those spiritual forces that center in the Lord.
Those in our day who focus endlessly upon the moral teachings of Jesus
but who downplay the divine Sonship miss the mark.

For many the doctrine of Christ has been replaced by the ethics
of Jesus. The problem with a social gospel, for the Latter-day Saints,
is that it is inherently deficient as far as engaging the real problems
of human beings. It almost always focuses on symptoms rather than
causes. Ethics is not the essence of the gospel. Ethics is not necessarily righteousness. The very word *ethics* has come to connote socially
acceptable standards based on current consensus as opposed to absolute truths based on God's eternal laws. Ethics is too often to virtue and
righteousness what theological jargon is to religion—a pale and wimpy

substitute. Indeed, ethics without that virtue that comes through the cleansing powers of the Redeemer is like religion without God, at least the true and living God.

"It is one thing," Bruce R. McConkie has written, "to teach ethical principles, quite another to proclaim the great doctrinal verities, which are the foundation of true Christianity and out of which eternal salvation comes. True it is that salvation is limited to those in whose souls the ethical principles abound, but true it is also that Christian ethics, in the full and saving sense, automatically become a part of the lives of those who first believe Christian doctrines." In summary, "It is only when gospel ethics are tied to gospel doctrines that they rest on a sure and enduring foundation and gain full operation in the lives of the saints."[1]

The Latter-day Saints are occasionally criticized for expending so much of the resources of the Church on missionary work or the construction of temples. Some indicate that the institutional Church should be more involved in leading or officially supporting this or that crusade, in laboring for this or that social cause. Bruce Hafen pointed out that "the ultimate purpose of the gospel of Jesus Christ is to cause the sons and daughters of God to become as Christ is. Those who see religious purpose only in terms of ethical service in the relationship between man and fellowmen may miss that divinely ordained possibility. It is quite possible to render charitable—even 'Christian'—service without developing deeply ingrained and permanent Christlike character. Paul understood this when he warned against giving all one's goods to feed the poor without charity.... While religious philosophies whose highest aim is social relevance may do much good, they will not ultimately lead people to achieve the highest religious *purpose,* which is to become as God and Christ are."[2]

Latter-day Saints believe that when people have been true to their trusts and live worthy of the gifts and influence of the Holy Spirit, then the works of the Father—the works of righteousness, the actions and behaviors of the faithful, including deeds of Christian service—flow forth from regenerate hearts. Those works are not alone the works of mortals, but rather the doings of persons who have become new creatures in Christ. Their works are therefore the works of the Lord, for they have been motivated by the power of his Spirit. To the Philippian Saints the apostle Paul beckoned: "Work out your own salvation with fear and trembling. For *it is God which worketh in you* both to will and to do of his good pleasure" (Philippians 2:12–13; emphasis added). In short, Latter-day Saints believe that only when ethical behaviors are founded on doctrine will the change in individuals and society be lasting.

In the 1930s and during the time of the Great Depression, many members of the LDS Church found themselves in the same plight as their neighbors. The leader of one of the ecclesiastical units in Salt Lake City found, for example, that of the 7,300 people under his care, 4,800 were receiving some form of government welfare assistance. The leader, Harold B. Lee (who became the eleventh president of the Church in 1972), with his counselors, set about to establish a program of assistance for the members that would preserve their dignity and allow them to work for what they received. His welfare program was successful, was eventually implemented churchwide, and he was asked to oversee what came to be known as the Church Welfare Services Program. The primary purpose of the program, as announced by Church leaders in 1936, was "to set up...a system under which the curse of idleness would be done away with, the evils of a dole abolished, and independence, industry, thrift, and self-respect be once more established amongst our people. The aim of the Church is to help the people to help themselves. Work is to be re-enthroned as the ruling principle of the lives of our Church membership."[3]

Members of the Church are asked to pay 10 percent of their income as a tithing. These funds are used to build chapels, temples, and finance missionary service. In addition, members are asked to fast from food and drink (two meals) once per month and then donate the equivalent cost to a fast offering, to be used for the care of the poor. Those who are in need are expected to exhaust every personal, family, and extended family resource before turning to the Church; having surveyed all options, members should feel no hesitation in seeking temporary assistance from the Church, as administered by the local bishop (pastor). This use of fast offering is a vital part of the Church Welfare Program. Further, the Church maintains employment centers as well as social services agencies that provide foster care, unwed mother care, adoptions, and individual and family counseling.

I have met many noble sons and daughters of God, many people who may not be able to explain the intricacies of the Atonement, but who nonetheless have the image of Christ in their countenances. I have become acquainted with men and women who constitute that vast body of souls we know as the rank and file of the Church, who by divine standards embody gospel greatness. Many of these choice individuals have lived lives of quiet goodness. Their righteousness is unpretentious, their service spontaneous, unpremeditated, and silent. They love as the Lord loves. They are not immune from life's challenges. They agonize over children who stray. They wrestle with personal weaknesses. But they love as the Lord loves. Their lives bring to mind the story told by Luke of a woman—a sinner by some self-righteous standards—who washed Jesus' feet with her tears, anointed them with ointment, and then wiped his feet with her hair. Responding to the thoughts of those who prejudged her and were incensed that the Master would allow such a one to minister to him, Jesus said: "Her sins, which are many, are forgiven; for she loved much: but to whom little is forgiven, the same loveth little. And he said unto her, Thy sins are forgiven.... Thy faith hath saved thee; go in peace" (Luke 7:37–50).

It just may be that the Keeper of the gate, the Holy One of Israel, will not be as interested in what we know at the great day of judgment or how busy we have been than he is in what we have become. Our mortal medals and our temporal acquisitions may prove to be far less significant in the eternal scheme of things than the enduring personal relationships we have developed and nurtured. Holy writ attests to the fact that the depth of our conversion is and should be reflected in the way we view and treat one another. The apostle John wrote: "Beloved, let us love one another: for love is of God; and every one that loveth is born of God, and knoweth God" (1 John 4:7). A modern Mormon apostle, Marvin J. Ashton, pointed out that "the way we treat each other is the foundation of the gospel of Jesus Christ." Further, "When we truly become converted to Jesus Christ, committed to Him, an interesting thing happens: our attention turns to the welfare of our fellowmen, and the way we treat others becomes increasingly filled with patience, kindness, a gentle acceptance, and a desire to play a positive role in their lives. This is the beginning of true conversion."[4]

To love and be loved is a glorious thing, especially in a world where in recent years men's and women's hearts have grown cold. I have come to know that the love of God—what the scriptures denominate as charity, the pure love of Christ (Moroni 7:47)—is not of this world. It is not man-made, and it cannot be manufactured. It is not something that can be programmed. It is of God. It is bestowed by him. I have had a few experiences with this divine principle that attest to its power and influence for good.

Some years ago my wife Shauna received word from a few of her high school friends that her class would be holding a reunion. She was excited to go and be a part of it. She asked me if I would be willing to go with her, and so I dutifully smiled and said it sounded like a lot of fun. (To be honest, I couldn't think of anything that might be more deadly than spending five or six hours with a group of people I didn't know from Adam and Eve!) The plans went forward and the long-anticipated day came. The evening was all I had sensed it would be. My wife is a very loving person and has been so forever, and so she has loads of friends. She shook hands and hugged and greeted people with excitement for hours. Once in a while she would say to me: "Bob, could you wait here for just a second? I'll be right back. I want to go over and say something to Brenda or Bill or Becky." And so I would stand there, not so patiently, wringing my hands, wondering why time seemed to stand still.

During one of those occasions, at about nine o'clock, I began to feel some bitterness toward my wife for leaving me alone. And then something happened. Something unexpected. I began to be taught and chastened through the medium of memory. I began to sense things I had never sensed before, such as how very much my wife had given of herself to stand by me for so long, to bear and basically rear the children, and to move forward through terribly challenging years without complaint. I reflected with much pain about how often I had been the center of attention, how often I had been the one to win the accolades, while she quietly and in the background went about the task of supporting and sustaining. I pondered in much anguish of soul on the times I had been insensitive or just plain uncaring. I don't think I am a mean and vicious person by nature, but I suddenly remembered all the times through the years I had chosen not to call home and indicate I would be late for dinner, all the times in the name of physical exhaustion I had failed to assume my part of the parental obligation, and, most painful of all, the occasions I knew she needed to be alone, to rest, to have time to herself, but when I had elected to do something other than be thoughtful. I didn't have much to say during the rest of the night, though I tried to act interested in what was going on.

Worrying that perhaps I was not having a glorious time, just before midnight Shauna suggested that we go home. I nodded. As we drove away, few words were spoken. At a certain point on the way home she turned to me and said sweetly, "I'm so grateful for my life." I was moved to tears but refrained from saying anything. Shauna has the capacity to sit down and go to sleep in one motion, and so we were only home for a few moments before she dropped off to sleep. It was after a restless night of facing up to who and what I had been, after a sleepless period of hours with time spent on my knees begging for forgiveness and promising to be better, that I awoke to a new view of things.

Sparing the details, let me say simply that without warning I was endowed with a depth of love and caring and affection that was beyond anything earthly. For a period of days I was consumed with charity, the pure love of Christ. I loved my wife, my children, and, above all, the Lord and his work with all my soul. For three days I saw things as they really are. There is no way for me to describe the immersion into the heavenly element and the tenderness of feelings that accompanied what I can only label as a rebirth. I sang sacred hymns with a gusto and an emotion that I had never known. The opening hymn in Sunday's worship service was "Because I Have Been Given Much." I went to pieces. The sacrament hymn was "I Stand All Amazed at the Love Jesus Offers Me." I was unable to sing. The closing hymn was "How Great Thou Art." I could barely read the words of the hymn through my tears.

I read the scriptures with enlightened eyes. I prayed with real intent and with a sense of purpose that had seldom accompanied my petitions before. At the end of a glorious Sabbath day, as Shauna and I stood on our front porch on that breezy August evening, I turned to her and from the depths of my heart said: "For reasons that I do not fully understand, I have been given what I believe to be a foretaste of eternal life. If this is just a glimpse what it is like to dwell in the highest heaven with God, with my family, and among the Saints, then I will give everything, even my own life, to feel this forever."

Though I have not felt the same intensity of love since that time, except in flashes, the sobering and sacred memory and its effects linger. Nothing is quite the same to me now. I know, to some degree at least, what it means to be consumed with the love of God. I came to grasp something about the pure love of Christ, not alone as the motivation for acts of Christian service, but, more important, the means by which men and women are purified from sin and thereby become the sons and daughters of God (1 John 3:2–3). The scriptures teach that we do not come to love as the Lord loves merely because we work hard at it. It is true that we must serve others, that we must concern ourselves with others' needs more than with our own. But that service and that outreach cannot have lasting effect, nor can it result in quiet peace and rest in the giver, unless and until it is motivated from on high.

We must ask for God's love. We must plead for it. We must pray with all the energy of heart, that we might have it bestowed upon us (Moroni 7:48). As we do so, there will come moments of surpassing import, sublime moments that matter, moments in which we know that what we are feeling for God and his children is akin to what God feels for us. This dimension of love settles the hearts of individuals. It provides moral courage to those who must face difficult challenges. It unites husbands, wives, and children and grants them a foretaste of heaven. And, once again, it comes from that Lord who is the Source of all that is godlike. It is thus to Jesus Christ that we look in this endeavor, as in all others, to obtain charity, "the highest pinnacle the human soul can reach and the deepest expression of the human heart."[5] And, as the apostle Paul testified, there is a sacred sealing, a binding tie associated with that love. "I am persuaded," he wrote to the Romans, "that neither death, nor life, nor angels, nor principalities, nor powers, nor things present, nor things to come, nor height, nor depth, nor any other creature, shall be able to separate us from the love of God, which is in Christ Jesus our Lord" (Romans 8:38–39).

A friend and colleague of mine, now retired, told of his experience in the military in traveling to the beautiful land of Korea. He indicated that he fell in love with the people there and with their magnificent country in no time at all. As a PFC he was subject to the military's pecking order and thus found himself on many work details, including more than his share of KP duty. He noticed that a number of his American friends seemed to treat the Korean people condescendingly, as though the Americans should be served and honored by the Koreans. This was distasteful to my friend, and so he made it his business to be especially kind and deferential to the Koreans. It was little things that he chose to do: getting at the end of the line, stepping off the sidewalk onto the grass to allow the Koreans to walk past him, etc. This was their country, he reasoned, and we were their guests; he felt the American soldiers needed to act like guests. After being in the country for a few months, he took his place at the end of the line when it was mealtime and waited patiently until he could receive his chow. Sensing that it would be some time before he would ever make it to the front of the line, he and a buddy went and sat at a table until the line could thin out. Moments later he was startled by a Korean man who stood before him with a full tray of food. The man bowed and sweetly said: "I serve you. You number one Christian." My friend George was deeply moved by the sweet gesture and vowed from that time on to live up to that impossible ideal, to be a "number one Christian."

While there are definitely fundamental doctrines necessary to the definition of "mere Christianity," it is doubtful that the Judge of all the earth will give to each one of us a theological exam at the bar of judgment. In terms of theology, there are some things that would be *nice to know*. There are things that we probably *should know*. And then there are those things—the central saving doctrines—that we *must know*. But far more important than what we know is who we are and what we have become. I believe Rick Warren is correct when he suggests that the first question God will ask us at the time we stand before him to be judged may well be, "What have you done with my Son?" I would suppose that not too far down the list of divine inquiries will be a question that pertains to the manner in which we have come to emulate and imitate our Master, the extent to which we have come to love and cherish and serve God's children. It was James who taught that "pure religion and undefiled before God and the Father is this, To visit the fatherless and widows in their affliction, and to keep [ourselves] unspotted from the world" (James 1:27). Again, God is in the business of people, and if our eye is single to his glory (Matthew 6:22; D&C 88:67), so are we.

ENDNOTES

1. McConkie, *A New Witness for the Articles of Faith*, 699.
2. Hafen, *The Broken Heart*, 196–97.
3. Heber J. Grant, CR, October 1936, 3.
4. Ashton, CR, April 1992, 25–26.
5. Howard W. Hunter, *Conference Report*, April 1992, 85.

FIFTEEN

Some Things Just Don't Change

T
HE APOSTLE PAUL PROPHESIED of our day, and many of the elements of that prophecy are pathetically present in today's newspaper. "This know also," he wrote, "that in the last days perilous times shall come. For men shall be lovers of their own selves, covetous, boasters, proud, blasphemers, disobedient to parents, unthankful, unholy, without natural affection, trucebreakers, false accusers, incontinent, fierce, despisers of those that are good, traitors, heady, highminded, lovers of pleasures more than lovers of God; having a form of godliness; but denying the power thereof: from such turn away." Perhaps as an indication of the source of the problem in our day, Paul concluded that such souls would be "ever learning, and never able to come to the knowledge of the truth" (2 Timothy 3:1–7).

We live in the day of an information explosion, a time when raw knowledge is being processed and disseminated far faster than we can incorporate or inculcate. But we also live in a time of moral erosion, indicating clearly that our decency has not kept pace with our discoveries. As a world, and more particularly as a nation, we have drifted from our moral moorings, strayed from the faith of our fathers and mothers. That the decline in society is due to a moral decay is perhaps obvious to most of us. I desire, however, to take a step beyond that premise. I suggest that the lack of scriptural or theological literacy and the subsequent lack of doctrinal depth are at the heart of our problem.

149

Very often what we believe and know affect what we do. I suggest that when men and women comprehend the great plan of happiness—the plan of salvation, the gospel—many begin to see themselves within that plan as a vital part of God's program. They then begin to govern their actions accordingly.

I would like now to discuss some key factors that have contributed to our doctrinal desensitization and thereby our moral decline. We could choose any number of things that have hacked away at the roots of our religious heritage, but I will focus on three: (1) the trivialization of religion; (2) the loss of a moral sense; and (3) a denial of personal responsibility. In subsequent sections we will consider some solutions to our problem.

1. *The Trivialization of Religion*

Whereas a hundred years ago religion was central to the outlook of most Americans, we have in the last four decades become prey to a growing secularism, a worldview that seeks to make sense of life without reference to God or the divine. If there is no real purpose to life, no God, no system of salvation, no hope of a life beyond the grave, and no divine parameters by which to distinguish right from wrong—in short, if anything goes—then eventually everything goes.

In the early 1960s a strange and to some frightful sound was heard throughout the academic world of religious studies—the cry that "God is dead." Protestant, Roman Catholic, and even Jewish theologians spoke often of godless theologies, Christless Christs, and Christian atheism, phrases that at first blush seem meaningless and absurd. The essence of their rhetorical requiem was that God had died in the hearts of men and women, that "God [had] passed out of our existence and become a dead entity for us because we crowded him out of our consciousness in creating and worshiping idols of our own ethnic likenesses."[1] How strikingly similar are the words found in the first section of the Doctrine and Covenants concerning the state of things at the time of Joseph Smith: "They seek not the Lord to establish his righteousness, but every man walketh in his own way, and after the image of his own god, whose image is in the likeness of the world, and whose substance is that of an idol, which waxeth old and shall perish in Babylon, even

Babylon the great, which shall fall" (D&C 1:16).

The Death of God movement, though not necessarily characteristic of the rank and file of the religious world (or even typical of the views or feelings of the average priest, minister, or rabbi), nevertheless symbolized a growing dis-ease in society, a loss of confidence in religious life, and a gradual distancing from religious values and time-honored traditions. Though the pendulum would yet swing to the religious right during the 1970s with the rise of the Charismatic Movement and Christian Fundamentalism, yet the age of existential anguish, of moral malaise, of cynicism and skepticism and doubt would take its terrible toll.

In recent times, where religion has not been rejected outright, it has been either ignored or in many cases trivialized. As Stephen L. Carter has pointed out, "One sees a trend in our political and legal cultures toward treating religious beliefs as arbitrary and unimportant, a trend supported by a rhetoric that implies that there is something wrong with religious devotion. More and more, our culture seems to take the position that believing deeply in the tenets of one's faith represents a kind of mystical irrationality, something that thoughtful, public-spirited American citizens would do better to avoid.... The consistent message of modern American society is that whenever the demands of one's religion conflict with what one has to do to get ahead, one is expected to ignore the religious demands and act...well...*rationally*."

"One good way," Carter points out, "to end a conversation—or start an argument—is to tell a group of well-educated professionals that you hold a political position (preferably a controversial one, such as being against abortion or pornography) because it is required by your understanding of God's will. In the unlikely event that anyone hangs around to talk with you about it, the chances are that you will be challenged on the ground that you are intent on imposing your religious beliefs on other people. And in contemporary political and legal culture, nothing is worse."[2]

2. *The Loss of a Moral Sense*

Certain problems arise whenever people either deny or ignore absolute truths. One Protestant writer has stated: "I believe that one of the prime reasons this generation is setting new records for dishonesty, disrespect, sexual promiscuity, violence, suicide, and other pathologies, is because they have lost their moral underpinnings; their foundational belief in morality and truth has been eroded.... At one time, our society, by and large, explained the universe, humanity, and the purpose of life from the Judaeo-Christian tradition: a belief that truth existed, and everyone could know and understand it. A clear understanding of what was right and wrong gave society a moral standard by which to measure crime and punishment, business ethics, community values, character, and social conduct....

"That has changed dramatically, however. Our children are being raised in a society that has largely rejected the notions of truth and morality, a society that has somewhere lost the ability to decide what is true and what is right. Truth has become a matter of taste; morality has been replaced by individual preference."[3]

"If modern man has taken seriously the main intellectual currents of the last century or so," James Wilson has written, "he would have found himself confronted by the need to make moral choices when the very possibility of making such choices had been denied. God is dead or silent, reason suspect or defective, nature meaningless or hostile. As a result, man is adrift on an uncharted sea, left to find his moral bearings with no compass and no pole star, and so able to do little more than utter personal preferences, bow to historical necessity, or accept social conventions." Further, "If the moral sense is the result of nothing more significant than a cultural or historical throw of the dice, then it will occur to some people ...that they are free to do whatever they can get away with by practicing indulgent self-absorption or embracing an angry ideology."[4]

In the 1960s a second movement began to take shape—hand in hand with the Death of God Movement—one that has had its flowering in our own time. It was known as situational ethics or ethical relativism. Inspired by the writings of Bishop John A. T. Robinson and Professor Joseph Fletcher, this movement proposed that any moral system is too shallow to provide answers to all situations and that every man and women must decide what is right. It was a time when all were told to open themselves to the "new morality." Many of you will remember how common it was to hear young people spout off with

"It's all relative" or the even more common dictum, "There are no absolutes" (a pretty absolute statement, to be sure!). Though we hear fewer chants and may notice fewer crusades for ethical relativism today, the die is cast and what was once parlor conversation or even college colloquy is now applied theology.

We seem to be caught in a vicious cycle. Knowing and sensing the things of God tend to prevent (or at least slow down) profligate wickedness. We cannot, however, come to know the things of God while we are sinning, for the Spirit of Truth will have difficulty penetrating the barriers we have erected through disobedience. Thus the need to declare repentance, to set forth the great plan of happiness, to teach of things eternal, to bring our lives and our lifestyles into harmony with the mind and will of the Almighty. We simply cannot be guilty of moving the standards, shifting the anchors, or diluting the doctrine (especially the hard doctrine) in order to enhance our public image. Indeed, if those called to be the salt of the earth—those who have come out of the world by covenant—lose their savor, either by mixture or by contamination, wherewith shall the world be salted or the people be saved? (Matthew 5:13; D&C 101:39–40).

3. A Denial of Personal Responsibility

The growth of the behavioral sciences in the last century has been phenomenal. Humankind seems at least as eager to understand the behavior and motivation of men and women as they are to understand light waves and black holes and the mysteries of DNA. The application of scientific principles to the study of human behavior—in an effort to formalize and objectify that study—has resulted in the superimposition of a cause-effect model on man and woman. Though it may be healthy and in some cases helpful to search for root causes, the cause-effect, stimulus-response model for understanding man will forevermore yield deficient and perhaps even perverse results, so long as we ignore the role of personal moral agency in that process. I say that, not only in regard to behaviorism, but also any other system, humanistic or Freudian, that attempts to define the cause of human behavior solely in terms of inner mechanisms, self-actualization, id or ego functions, or even genetic predisposition.

Our fascination with causes ancillary to human agency has led us to paint ourselves into a corner in today's world. "Whereas in the late nineteenth century," James Wilson has written, "crime rates seem to have decreased during periods of economic growth, in the last few decades they have often increased during such periods. Over the course of the last hundred years the world has experienced a shift from an era in which crime chiefly responded to material circumstances to one in which it responds to cultural ones. That shift has many causes, but one is the collapse in the legitimacy of what once was respectfully called middle-class morality but today is sneeringly referred to as 'middle-class values.'

"The moral relativism of the modern age," Wilson continues, "has probably contributed to the increase in crime rates, especially the increases that occur during prosperous times. It has done so by replacing the belief in personal responsibility with the notion of social causation and by supplying to those marginal persons at risk for crime a justification for doing what they might have done anyway."[5] Add to this movement the gradual attack our society has made on guilt—the inner monitor by which we sense within ourselves that we have violated the laws of God or the norms of society—and we find ourselves in a precarious position. "That kind of thinking," John MacArthur has observed, "has all but driven words like *sin, repentance, contrition, atonement,* and *redemption* out of public discourse. If no one is supposed to feel guilty, how could anyone be a sinner? Modern culture has the answer: people are *victims.* Victims are not responsible for what they do; they are casualties of what happens to them. So every human failing must be described in terms of how the perpetrator has been victimized."[6] To be sure, there are real victims in society—abused children or spouses, persons who suffer at the hands of racism or sexism—and they deserve our empathy, our support, and our zealous defense against such tragedies. My specific concern is with men and women who do wrong, who knowingly violate the laws of decency and morality, and then seek refuge behind the growing wall of victimization.

We begin with the certain assurance that we cannot solve spiritual maladies through temporal solutions. Our problem in the world today is a detachment from morality, and morality cannot, in the long run, be severed from religion. Religion is a most interesting word. It means literally "to tie back to." It is related to the word ligament, that which ties the bone to the muscle. Religion is thus that which ties us back to God and to sacred things. To define morality in terms of utility (what works) or in terms of consensus (what most people believe) is to fall short of what was, is, and is to be.

Some things are. They just are. Neither congressional decisions nor popular opinion changes absolute truth. All the people in the world may decide that abortion is humane, homosexuality is merely an alternative lifestyle, and assisted suicide is compassionate, but that does not change the fact that these matters are wrong and contrary to the great plan of the Eternal God. They cannot bring happiness. They cannot result in peace. Every religious body on the globe may conclude that God is uninvolved in the daily doings of men and women, and that men and women will prosper according to their genius and not through the divine assistance of a Savior. But such sentiments do not matter a snap of the finger in the eternal scheme of things; what God is, does, and accomplishes among his children through the mediation of his Beloved Son is in the realm of absolute truths. These things we know from scripture, from prophets, and by the still, small voice of conscience.

"We know instinctively," one Christian writer has observed, "that some things are right and some things are wrong. Let [a young woman] discover, for example, that her soccer shoes were stolen from her school locker and she'll feel wronged. She would not argue that the thief is entitled to his opinion of right and wrong; she would appeal to an objective sense of justice because she would claim that she had suffered an injustice. In so doing, of course, she would appeal to a moral law that she believes everyone—not just herself—ought to follow."[7] That is to say, while many who yearn to speak of ethical relativism or situational ethics do so from their philosophical perch above the real world, those same persons expect others to treat them according to a model of truth and morality that reflects a more objective and absolute way of knowing what is right or wrong. If it is true that "there are no atheists in foxholes," then it is also true that "there are no relativists who expect to be treated relatively."[8]

So many people, as C. S. Lewis observed, seek to "invent some sort of happiness for themselves outside God, apart from God. And out of that hopeless attempt has come nearly all that we call human history—money, poverty, ambition, war, prostitution, classes, slavery—the long terrible story of man trying to find something other than God which will make him happy.

"The reason why it can never succeed is this.... God designed the human machine to run on *Himself.* He Himself is the fuel our spirits were designed to burn, or the food our spirits were designed to feed on. There is no other. That is why it is just no good asking God to make us happy in our own way without bothering about religion. *God cannot give us a happiness and peace apart from Himself,* because it is not there. There is no such thing."[9] Similarly, Neal A. Maxwell pointed out that "mankind has not had much success in keeping the second commandment by loving our neighbors as ourselves, without also keeping the first great commandment, loving God with all of our heart, might, mind, and strength. Try as mankind may to achieve the brotherhood of man without the Fatherhood of God, it is cosmetic and *does not last!*"[10]

Let me propose what might be a rather typical discussion between a parent and child:

> Father: "Billy, is it wrong to steal?"
> Son: "Yeah, Dad, it's wrong to steal."
> Father: "Why is it wrong?"
> Son: "Because you taught us that it's wrong."
> Father: "That's right, Son, we did. But why did we teach you that?"
> Son: "Because the Church teaches us that it's not right to steal."
> Father: "Right again. But why does the Church teach that?"
> (Then there is a long pause.)
> Son: "I don't know, Dad. Is it because Heavenly Father doesn't want us to steal?"
> Father: "You're absolutely right, Billy. Heavenly Father does not want us to steal. Why doesn't he want us to steal?"
> (This time there is a longer and even more uncomfortable pause.)
> Son: "I don't really know, Dad."

This fictional encounter highlights a problem we face in teaching one another (and especially our children) the principles of morality and decency. Notice that the PRECEPT of "Thou shalt not steal" is pretty clear in this young man's mind. He has been taught the commandments and is able to articulate what he understands. A little less clear is that which underlies the precept, namely the PRINCIPLE, in this case the principle of honesty. Our young man knows what has been forbidden (to steal), and he senses that the major reasons it is forbidden is because his parents, his Church, and his God have condemned it. Now those are all fine sources for the precept and the principle, but are they the ultimate or absolute source? No, for beneath the principle is the PERSON of God. A vital part of the great plan of happiness is the nature and kind of Being we worship. Fundamental to the purpose of life and the hope for glory hereafter is the knowledge concerning God—his character, his attributes, his perfections, his relationship to us, and the knowledge that we should strive with all our might and seek for spiritual transformation and divine enabling power to become holy and pure as our Heavenly Father is.

To complete our conversation,

> Father: "Billy, we are commanded not to steal [the Precept] because the Lord wants his people to be honest [the Principle]. He wants us to be honest because he is a God of truth [the Person]. We are sent to earth to strive as best we can to become as he is. Only as we become a people of truth can we ever hope to be like our Heavenly Father."

It is one thing to teach that honesty is the best policy (utility) or to teach that it is best to be honest because most people in society expect us to deal respectfully and responsibly with one another (consensus). Both utility and consensus have done much in the past to maintain some semblance of order in our world. But with changing times and the erosion of time-honored values, many look about hopelessly for a more solid and enduring foundation. That foundation is doctrinal; it is the foundation of faith and theology. Our children deserve answers to the hard question of why. And the only lasting and satisfying answer to why we do what we do or why we do not do other things is to be found in the understanding of God and humanity, in the clear statement of our eternal possibilities here and hereafter.

In a pastoral role, I have had occasion to listen as young people discuss their major moral transgressions. I have been asked about why the violation of the law of chastity, for example, is so serious. I have been interested as they have spoken of disappointing their parents, postponing a temple marriage or full-time missions, bearing children out of wedlock, and contracting deadly diseases—all of which, from the perspective of utility or consensus are darned good reasons to stay morally clean. But there is more to it, much more, and it is that added light and added knowledge that come from divinely given doctrine to which we turn for the greatest preventive medicine against serious sin.

I learned something very valuable many years ago when my wife and I timidly approached the much dreaded but needed conversation about the facts of life with our oldest child, our daughter Angie. We sweated and stewed for weeks. We read. We prepared charts and graphs and pictures of the human reproductive system. We had also prayed earnestly for inspiration. We dived into the presentation and discovered to our surprise that it was going in a direction that neither my wife nor I had anticipated. For about an hour we spoke of God's plan of salvation—of who we are, where we came from, why we are here, and where we are going when we die. We spoke of physical bodies and experiences and Satan and opposition and relationships and children and families. At the end of that most unusual hour, I asked: "Now, sweetheart, do you understand why it is so very important to stay morally clean?" She nodded.

President Boyd K. Packer explained to LDS Church educators: "Young people wonder 'why?'—Why are we commanded *to do* some things, and why are we commanded *not* to do other things? A knowledge of the plan of happiness, even in outline form, can give young minds a 'why.'

"A parent once angrily scolded a child for a serious mistake, saying, 'Why on earth did you do such a thing?'

"The child answered, 'If I'd had a Why, I wouldn't have done it.'

"Providing your students [or, we might add, our children] with a collection of unrelated truths will hurt as much as it helps. Provide a basic feeling for the whole plan, even with just a few details, and it will help them ever so much more. Let them know what it's all about, then they will have the 'why.'

"Most of the difficult questions we face in the Church right now... cannot be answered without some knowledge of the plan as a background....

"You will not be with your students or your own children at the time of their temptations. At those dangerous moments they must depend on their own resources. If they can locate themselves within the framework of the gospel plan, they will be immensely strengthened.

"The plan is worthy of repetition over and over again. Then the purpose of life, the reality of the Redeemer, and the reason for the commandments will stay with them."[11]

Having said this, I hasten to add that even with a knowledge of God's plan before them, men and women, boys and girls often choose to walk in the ways of the world and thus settle for less than what they could be. But I have a conviction that the proper teaching of the Father's plan will do much to hold on to those who are children of the covenant.

Let me conclude where I began—with the sobering prophecy of the apostle Paul. You recall that he warned of such sins in the last days as pride, blasphemy, disrespect for parents, ingratitude, dishonesty, immorality, and perversion. Finally, he spoke of persons who are "ever learning, and never able to come to the knowledge of the truth" (2 Timothy 3:1–7). The visible disarray in our world is but symptomatic of the invisible decay, an evidence that our moral foundation is under attack. It seems clear to me that "the knowledge of the truth" of which Paul wrote constitutes the sure foundation upon which true believers must build their houses of faith. It is worth noting that the apostle Paul did not leave us without comfort or recourse. Later in that same chapter he wrote to Timothy: "But evil men and seducers shall wax worse and worse, deceiving, and being deceived. But continue thou in the things which thou hast learned and hast been assured of, knowing of whom thou hast learned them; and that from a child thou hast known the holy scriptures, which are able to make thee wise unto salvation through faith which is in Christ Jesus. All scripture is given by inspiration of God, and is profitable for doctrine, for reproof, for correction, for instruction in righteousness: that the man of God may be perfect, thoroughly furnished unto all good works" (2 Timothy 3:13–17, emphasis added).

The scriptures. The word of God. The doctrines of salvation—these are the means by which we come to know the Precepts, the Principles, and the Person of God. They set forth what we must and must not do, as well as who we are and what we may become. There is a power, a supernal power associated with the teaching of God's plan for happiness. There is peace, consummate peace that comes into our lives when we erect our divine domiciles on the foundation of doctrine and faith. Therein is our safety. Therein is our hope.

ENDNOTES

1. Gabriel Vahanian, in Ice and Carey, eds., *The Death of God Debate*, 16.

2. Carter, *The Culture of Disbelief*, 6–7, 13, 23.

3. Josh McDowell, *Right from Wrong*, 12–13.

4. Wilson, *The Moral Sense*, 5, 9.

5. Ibid., 10.

6. MacArthur, *The Vanishing Conscience*, 21.

7. McDowell, *Right from Wrong*, 78.

8. Ibid., 78.

9. Lewis, *Mere Christianity*, 54, emphasis added.

10. Maxwell, "This Is a Special Institution," 9.

11. Packer, "The Great Plan of Happiness," 3.

SIXTEEN

On Knowing

A MONTHLY FAST FROM FOOD and drink for two meals (coupled with paying a generous fast offering for the care of the needy) is linked to attendance at the "fast and testimony meeting." In this particular gathering, after singing, praying, and partaking of the Sacrament of the Lord's Supper, members are encouraged to stand spontaneously and "bear testimony" of the truthfulness of such things as the reality of God, the divinity of Jesus Christ, the restoration of the ancient gospel through the instrumentality of Joseph Smith, and the guiding hand of the Almighty in the work of the Church today. This meeting proves to be a strengthening and bonding experience for members, as they bear witness of the goodness of God and affirm their faith publicly.

Not long ago I sat in my home ward (congregation) and listened with much interest as four children moved to the front of the chapel and in turn bore their testimonies. The first one could not have been more than seven years old, and yet she spoke with a confidence that one might expect from a seasoned adult member of the Church. She said, essentially, "I want to bear my testimony that I know that Jesus is our Savior, that the Church is true, that Joseph Smith was a prophet of God, and that President Gordon B. Hinckley is our living prophet today." She then shared some personal feelings and sat down. I pondered on her words, on the depth of sincerity evident in her voice, and I wondered: Does she know? Does she *really* know? How much could she know? Later during the day I reflected on the experience again and again, and had affirmed to my mind and heart that little children can come to know the things of God, by the power of the Spirit of God (1 Corinthians 2:11–14) and can speak words of truth and wisdom just as their adult counterparts can (Alma 32:23). A testimony is not something you either have or don't have, but rather an impression of the Spirit as to the truthfulness of eternal things, an inner awareness that ranges along a spiritual continuum from a simple peaceful feeling to a perfect knowledge.

It has wisely been observed that the strength of the LDS Church lies not alone in the powerful witnesses of the fifteen men we sustain as prophets, seers, and revelators, but rather the deep reassurance and resolve that rest in the souls of individual Saints from Alabama to Zanzibar. A testimony may begin through trusting in and relying upon the witness of another, of one who knows for sure; to believe on the faith of another is indeed a spiritual gift, a gift that can lead to eternal life (D&C 46:13–14). Latter-day Saints are often reminded of a statement by Heber C. Kimball, who served for many years as a counselor to Brigham Young. Brother Kimball warned of a test to come, a test that would separate out those who professed membership in the Church but did not possess a personal testimony sufficient to see them through hard times. "The time will come when no man or woman will be able to endure on borrowed light," he said. "Each will have to be guided by the light within himself. If you do not have it, how can you stand?"[1]

How does one know? How is my belief in present-day healing, for example, affected by what did or did not take place in the first century? Can I believe that the power to heal is real in our own day if in fact such powers were not operative in the first century or in the days of Joseph Smith's Nauvoo, if the stories of the healing of the blind, the halt, the maim, and even the dead being raised are prevarications? Faith is based on evidence, and the stronger the evidence the stronger the faith. To what extent can I trust in a power of redemption if in fact Jesus was not the Savior of humankind? How should I view death if in fact Jesus did not rise from the tomb three days after his crucifixion? To what degree do my religious beliefs need to be both true and reasonable? One Protestant theologian affirmed: "There is an excellent objective ground to which to tie the religion that Jesus sets forth. Final validation of this can only come experientially"—we would say, by revelation. "But it is desperately important not to put ourselves in such a position that the event-nature of the resurrection depends wholly upon 'the faith.' It's the *other way* around. The faith has its starting point in the event, the objective event, and only by the appropriation of this objective event do we discover the final validity of it....

"The Christian faith is built upon Gospel that is 'good news,' and there is no news, good or bad, of something that didn't happen. I personally am much disturbed by certain contemporary movements in theology which seem to imply that we can have the faith regardless of whether anything happened or not. I believe absolutely that the whole Christian *faith* is premised upon the fact that at a certain point of time under Pontius Pilate a certain man died and was buried and three days later rose from the dead. If in some way you could demonstrate to me that Jesus never lived, died, or rose again, then I would have to say I have no right to my faith."[2] Indeed, to what degree can we exercise saving faith in something that did not happen? The Book of Mormon prophets declare that "faith is not to have a perfect knowledge of things; therefore if ye have faith ye hope for things which are not seen, *which are true*" (Alma 32:21, emphasis added).

Can Jesus be a Galilean guru and not the Son of God? Can he play the role of Samaritan Socrates and not be divine? In short, what of the idea so prevalent among the humanists that Jesus was a great moral teacher, a mere man, albeit a brilliant and inspired man, but not the Promised Messiah? In short, is there a difference between the "historical Jesus" and the "Christ of faith"? Do the extant sources allow such a distinction? Did Jesus? There's a simple syllogism that applies to Jesus. It goes something like this: He was a great moral teacher. He claimed to be the Son of God. He was not the Son of God. Therefore, he could not be a great moral teacher.

A few years ago a Baptist minister friend and I were driving through Boston in an effort to get to the LDS Institute of Religion at Cambridge. My colleague commented on a matter that we had discussed several times, namely the idea that Latter-day Saints are more prone to rely upon feelings than tangible evidence for truth of religious claims. Being just a bit frustrated, I asked: "Do you believe in the literal bodily resurrection of Jesus Christ?"

"Of course I believe in the resurrection, Bob; I'm an ordained minister."

I followed up: "Why do you believe in the resurrection? How do you know it really happened?"

He answered: "Because the New Testament teaches of the resurrection of Jesus." I shot right back: "But how do you know the New Testament accounts are reliable? How do you know the Bible can be trusted? Maybe someone just made all of this up. Maybe the Bible is a giant hoax."

"No," he said. "There is strong evidence to support the truthfulness of the Bible."

"Like what?" I asked.

"Well, there are archaeological, historical, and cultural evidences that what is being described actually happened."

I then queried, "And so that's how you know the resurrection is real?"

"Yeah, I suppose so," he said.

At this point my mind began to race. I found myself saying something I hadn't planned to say. "You know, I feel a great sense of sadness right now."

My evangelical friend was surprised and asked "Sadness? Why are you sad?"

"I was just thinking of a good friend of mine, an older woman in Montgomery, Alabama."

My partner asked: "What about her?"

I then said, "Well, I was thinking of how sad it is that this wonderful and devoted Christian, a person who has given her life to Jesus and studied and memorized her Bible like few people I know, a woman whose life manifests her complete commitment to the Savior, is not really entitled to have a witness of the truthfulness of the Bible."

"Why is that?" he followed up.

"Well, she knows precious little about archaeology or languages or culture or history or manuscripts, and so I suppose she can't know within her heart that the Bible really is the word of God."

"Of course she can," he said. "She can have her faith, her personal witness that the Bible is true."

I turned to him, smiled, and stated: "Do you mean that she can have the power of the Holy Spirit testify to her soul that her Bible is trustworthy and can be relied upon as God's word?"

"Yes, that's what I mean." My smile broadened as I added: "Then we've come full circle."

"What do you mean by that?" he asked.

I said: "You're telling me that this good woman, one who has none of the supposed requisite background or knowledge of external evidence, can have a witness of the Spirit, including deep personal feelings about the Bible and that those feelings are genuine and heaven-sent."

At that point my friend looked into my eyes and he smiled. "I see where you're going with this." We then engaged in one of the most productive conversations of our time together as friends. We agreed between us that it is so easy to yield to the temptation to categorize and pigeonhole and stereotype persons whose faith is different than our own. It is so easy to overstate, to misrepresent, to create "straw men" in an effort to establish our own point.

We agreed that Evangelical Christians and Latter-day Saint Christians both base their faith upon evidence—both seen and unseen. While, as we observed earlier, saving faith is always built upon that which is true, upon an actual historical moment in time, upon something that really existed in the past, true believers will never allow their faith to be held hostage by what science has or has not found at a given time. I know, for example, that Jesus fed the five thousand, healed the sick, raised the dead, calmed the storm, and rose from the dead—not just because I have physical evidence for each of those miraculous events (because I do not), nor even because I can read of these things in the New Testament, which I accept with all my heart. But I know these things actually happened because the Spirit of the Living God bears witness to my spirit that the Lord of Life did all the scriptures say he did, and more.

Noted New Testament scholar Tom Wright has pointed out that "over the last generation in Western culture, truth has been like the rope in a tug-of-war contest. On the one hand, some want to reduce all truth to 'facts,' things which can be proved in the way you can prove that oil is lighter than water, or even that two and two make four. On the other hand, some believe that all truth is relative, and that all claims to truth are merely coded claims to power." Wright then went on to explain regarding "knowing" the truthfulness of deeper things, things of God: "What we mean by 'know' is...in need of further investigation. To 'know' the deeper kinds of truth we have been hinting at is much more like 'knowing' a person—something which takes a long time, a lot of trust, and a good deal of trial and error—and less like 'knowing' about the right bus to take into town."[3]

"I believe because of the epiphanies, small and large," Randall Balmer has noted, "that have intersected my path—small, discrete moments of grace when I have sensed a kind of superintending presence outside of myself. I believe because these moments...are too precious to discard, and I choose not to trivialize them by reducing them to rational explanation. I believe because, for me, the alternative to belief is far too daunting. I believe because, at the turn of the twenty-first century, belief itself is an act of defiance in a society still enthralled by the blandishments of Enlightenment rationalism....

"The evangelical response to...intellectual challenges has been, in my judgment, utterly misguided. To these arguments about religious belief, informed by Enlightenment rationalism, evangelicals mounted counterarguments, also informed by Enlightenment rationalism. Evangelicals sent their best and most trustworthy students off to Cambridge and Harvard and Tübingen, and those who managed to return to the subculture with their doctorates in hand and largely unaffected by the experience were hailed as role models for having emerged from the lions' den unscathed. These 'doctors' were then paraded like show dogs in front of impressionable young evangelicals and told to teach courses in apologetics.

"Somehow, I don't think Jeffrey [who asks how he can know there is a God] wants me to rehearse the ontological, the teleological, and the cosmological arguments for the existence of God.... So instead of dusting off the teleological argument, I think I'll remind Jeffrey about Karl Barth, arguably the most important theologian of the twentieth century. Toward the end of his life, after he had written volume after volume on the transcendence of God and the centrality of Jesus, Barth was asked to sum up his work. The good doctor paused for a minute and no doubt looked out the window and played with the stubble on his chin before responding with the words of a Sunday school ditty: 'Jesus loves me, this I know, for the Bible tells me so.'"[4]

One professor of theology sounded a warning in our cynical age: "Perhaps enlightened, tolerant persons are willing to listen to ancient or even contemporary 'mystics' as if they were poets or dreamers; but the general effect of two or more centuries of sensory-based (empirical) rationality has made most of us skeptical of any religious or even quasi-religious thought that assumes the reality of presences or influences or relationships that cannot be explained by reference to data that is subject to 'scientific' (that is, empirical and controlled) investigation.

"Even if 'the modern mind' admits that there is much that we do not understand, and in that sense admits of 'mystery,' such a mind is likely to consider the unknown simply as that which *still remains to be known*, rather than as being permanently beyond the usual means of measurement. While possessors of such a mentality are usually tolerant of those who claim to have knowledge of God or to be in communion with the risen, living Christ through the mediation of the Holy Spirit and so forth, they harbor a strong suspicion of all such claims. Such claims are so completely inconsistent with the fact-oriented world of our daily experience as a people that when they are not regarded with open skepticism they are usually politely relegated to the realm of 'religion'—a realm which may or may not be respected, depending on differing social circumstances."[5]

Many years ago on a Sunday morning I opened the door and reached down to pick up the morning newspaper when I saw beside the paper a plastic bag containing a paperback book. I brought both inside and laid the newspaper aside as I browsed the paperback. The cover was a lovely picture of a mountain stream, but the title of the book revealed to me what in fact the book was all about—it was an anti-Mormon treatise. Many of the arguments in the book against The Church of Jesus Christ of Latter-day Saints were old and worn-out ones, dead horses that have been beaten since the 1830s. Latter-day Saints had responded to the issues posed scores of times, but they continued to crop up. One section of the book did prove, however, to be of some interest to me. Let me paraphrase what was essentially said. The author pointed out that eventually two Mormon missionaries would come to the reader's door. If they do come, he pleaded, don't let them in. If, however, you do let them in, then don't listen to them. If they are allowed to tell you about their message, about Joseph Smith and angels and golden plates, they will ask you to kneel and pray about the truthfulness of these things. Whatever you do, don't pray! The writer then made this unusual observation: In ascertaining the truthfulness of a religious claim, because of our fallen and unworthy condition, there are three things a person can never trust: (1) your thoughts; (2) your feelings; (3) your prayers.

I was all eyes and all ears at this point, wondering how we could ever know anything. I didn't have to wait long, for the writer then noted that the only thing that could be trusted was the Holy Bible itself. I shook my head and felt a deep sense of sadness for the author, for I wondered how indeed a person could even know of the truthfulness of the Bible if he or she could not think, feel, or pray. I had a collage of feelings at that moment. As indicated, I felt sad for the writer, for it was obvious that he could not see the blatant inconsistency and irrationality of his own words. I tried to put myself into the place of a reader who was not a Latter-day Saint and wondered how I might feel upon reading such things. To be honest, I would feel insulted, knowing that I could not be trusted enough in my pursuit of truth to rely upon my mind, my heart, or even the most tried and true method of obtaining divine direction—prayer itself.

My friend and colleague Craig Blomberg once observed: "You know, it's ironic: The Bible considers it praiseworthy to have a faith that does not require evidence. Remember how Jesus replied to doubting Thomas: 'You believe because you see; blessed are those who have not seen and yet believe.' And I know evidence can never compel or coerce faith. We cannot supplant the role of the Holy Spirit, which is often a concern of Christians when they hear discussions of this kind.

"But I'll tell you this; there are plenty of stories of scholars in the New Testament field who have not been Christians, yet through their study of these very issues have come to faith in Christ. And there have been countless more scholars, already believers, whose faith has been made stronger, more solid, more grounded, because of the evidence— and that's the category I fall into."[6]

True believers will always be challenged by those who refuse to see. In a very real sense, believing is seeing. Latter-day Saints have been instructed that no member of the Church need feel embarrassed when they cannot produce the golden plates or the complete Egyptian papyrus from which the Book of Abraham came. No member of the Church should ever feel hesitant to bear testimony of those verities that remain in the realm of faith, that are seen only with the eyes of faith. Neal A. Maxwell has written: "It is the author's opinion that all the scriptures, including the Book of Mormon, will remain in the realm of faith. Science will not be able to prove or disprove holy writ. However, enough plausible evidence will come forth to prevent scoffers from having a field day, but not enough to remove the requirement of faith. Believers must be patient during such unfolding."[7]

President Gordon B. Hinckley put things in proper perspective when he taught: "I can hold [the Book of Mormon] in my hand. It is real. It has weight and substance that can be physically measured. I can open its pages and read, and it has language both beautiful and uplifting. The ancient record from which it was translated came out of the earth as a voice speaking from the dust….

"The evidence for its truth, for its validity in a world that is prone to demand evidence, lies not in archaeology or anthropology, though these may be helpful to some. It lies not in word research or historical analysis, though these may be confirmatory. The evidence for its truth and validity lies within the covers of the book itself. The test of its truth lies in reading it. It is a book of God. Reasonable individuals may sincerely question its origin, but those who read it prayerfully may come to know by a power beyond their natural senses that it is true, that it contains the word of God, that it outlines saving truths of the everlasting gospel, that it came forth by the gift and power of God."[8]

Hugh Nibley, one of the greatest LDS apologists of the twentieth century, stated: "The words of the prophets cannot be held to the tentative and defective tests that men have devised for them. Science, philosophy, and common sense all have a right to their day in court. But the last word does not lie with them. Every time men in their wisdom have come forth with the last word, other words have promptly followed. The last word is a testimony of the gospel that comes only by direct revelation.

Our Father in heaven speaks it, and if it were in perfect agreement with the science of today, it would surely be out of line with the science of tomorrow. Let us not, therefore, seek to hold God to the learned opinions of the moment when he speaks the language of eternity."[9]

"True religion," Bruce R. McConkie attested, "deals with spiritual things. We do not come to a knowledge of God and his laws [solely] through intellectuality, or by research, or by reason.

"In their sphere, education and intellectuality are devoutly to be desired. But when contrasted with spiritual endowments, they are of but slight and passing worth. From an eternal perspective what each of us needs is a Ph.D. in faith and righteousness. The things that will profit us everlastingly are not the power to reason, but the ability to receive revelation; not the truths learned by study, but the knowledge gained by faith; not what we know about the things of the world, but our knowledge of God and his laws."[10]

ENDNOTES

1. Cited in Whitney, *Life of Heber C. Kimball*, 449–50.

2. John Warwick Montgomery, *History and Christianity*, 107, 108, emphasis added.

3. Wright, *Simply Christian*, 50, 51.

4. See Balmer, *Growing Pains*, 34, 42–43, 44–45, 61–62.

5. Douglas John Hall, *Why Christian?* 71–72, emphasis in original.

6. Blomberg, in Lee Strobel, *The Case for Christ*, 52–53.

7. Maxwell, *Plain and Precious Things*, 4.

8. Hinckley, *Faith, The Essence of True Religion*, 10–11.

9. Nibley, *The World and the Prophets*, 134.

10. McConkie, CR, April 1971, 99.

SEVENTEEN

Conversion to the Faith

A NUMBER OF YEARS ago an article appeared in *Christianity Today* entitled "Why Your Neighbor Joined the Mormon Church." Five reasons were given:

1. The Mormons show genuine love and concern by taking care of their people.

2. The Mormons strive to build the family unit.

3. The Mormons provide for their young people.

4. The Mormon Church is a layman's church.

5. The Mormons believe that divine revelation is the basis for their practices.

After a brief discussion of each of the above, the author of the article concludes: "In a day when many are hesitant to claim that God has said anything definitive, the Mormons stand out in contrast, and many people are ready to listen to what the Mormons think the voice of God says. It is tragic that their message is false, but it is nonetheless a lesson to us that people are many times ready to hear a voice of authority."[1]

In what some have called the post-Christian era, a time when men and women throughout the earth are leaving the faith of their parents and when churches are closing down in an ever-increasing number, the

Church of Jesus Christ of Latter-day Saints continues to grow in an unprecedented manner. What is it about our faith, this system of salvation we know as Mormonism, that has such appeal to people throughout the earth? For one thing, many in our day are weary of the shifting sands of secularity and the ever-mobile standards of society. They long for a return to time-honored values and absolute truths. Because wickedness is widening, honest truth seekers yearn for something to hold on to, something of substance, something that will stand when all else is falling. At the same time, they long to be a part of a religious organization that requires something of them. In fact, recent sociological studies attest that the churches that tend to be growing in our day are those that demand the most of its membership. Mormons do not apologize for our position in regard to chastity and virtue, nor do we hesitate to teach the Word of Wisdom or the need to pay our tithes and offerings. We know that one remains steadfast and immovable in the faith to the degree that he or she invests themselves in the faith. There is another significant appeal of the LDS Church, namely our doctrine, which we have discussed throughout this work. Such teachings as the place of the Book of Mormon as Another Testament of Jesus Christ, the premortal existence of spirits, life after death, degrees of glory hereafter, the eternal family, and the role of living apostles and prophets in the Church today—these are among the matters that attract persons throughout the world to Mormonism.

Just how does someone convert to Mormonism? How does a person become a member of The Church of Jesus Christ of Latter-day Saints? Well, one way is to be born into the Church. A baby that is blessed in a Church meeting (similar to "christening") becomes a member of record. At the age of eight years, the age of accountability (see D&C 68:25–27), the child is baptized, confirmed as a member of the Church, and given the gift of the Holy Ghost. If a person has no faith of their own or is investigating other churches, they may be taught about the doctrines, principles, and practices of the Church by the full-time missionaries in that area. The process of investigation, however, entails more than an intellectual enlargement, more than a theological conversation. Investigators are taught about God, Christ, the Holy Spirit, the need for a restoration and the call of Joseph Smith as a modern prophet, the Book of Mormon and modern scripture (Doctrine and Covenants and Pearl of Great Price), and the standards of Church membership.

The missionaries have the assignment to do more than inform; they are to testify and invite investigators to study, ponder, and pray upon the things they are taught. The burden of proof does not rest with the Latter-day Saints, nor is it dependent upon the charisma or power of persuasion of the missionaries. God knows all things, and so men and women are encouraged—even challenged—to ask in prayer, to seek for divine understanding, to knock at heaven's door for confirmation of what they have been taught. Only one who has received a witness, a testimony of the Spirit, and who commits to abide by the standards (e.g., church attendance, payment of tithing, moral behavior, abstaining from alcohol, tobacco, coffee, and tea) is prepared to be baptized. In addition, the missionaries begin early on to introduce the investigator to members of the local ward (congregation) and to the leaders of the ward, and the missionaries are responsible to assist in their socialization into Mormon culture. Like John the Baptist, the missionaries gradually decrease in their involvement with those they have taught, while the association with local Church members increases (see John 3:30).

As I indicated in the last chapter, critics of the LDS faith are eager to suggest that the Latter-day Saints play upon people's feelings, titillate the emotions in order to bring them into the Church. Well, of course emotion is linked to feeling, which is linked to conversion. How would a person come unto Christ without their feelings being affected? How could one enjoy a remission of sins by merely learning a few facts from the Bible? To be sure, no one is truly "born again" or becomes a "new creature in Christ" without their heart being changed and their mind being transformed (Romans 12:1–2). And so while I suppose there are some Latter-day Saints who are too hung up on emotion or too syrupy and sentimental than appropriate, the gaining of a testimony—that serves as a prompter to be baptized—involves all the human faculties, not just the tear ducts. For some people, conversion "is a deeply emotional experience; for others, it's a calm, clear-eyed resolution of matters long pondered. Our personalities are gloriously different, and God treats us all gloriously differently."[2]

Parley P. Pratt had been associated with Alexander Campbell and Sidney Rigdon before his acceptance of Mormonism. He was a serious student of the Bible who sought desperately for "the ancient order of things"—the teachings and practices of the primitive Christian Church. Brother Pratt writes in his autobiography:

> Arriving at Rochester, I informed my wife that, notwithstanding our passage being paid through the whole distance, yet I must leave the boat and her to pursue her passage to our friends; while I would stop awhile in this region. Why, I did not know; but so it was plainly manifest by the Spirit to me. I said to her, "We part for a season; go and visit our friends in our native place; I will come soon, but how soon I know not; for I have a work to do in this region of country, and what it is, or how long it will take to perform it, I know not; but I will come when it is performed."
>
> My wife would have objected to this; but she had seen the hand of God so plainly manifest in His dealings with me many times, that she dare not oppose the things manifest to me by His spirit. She, therefore, consented; and I accompanied her as far as Newark, a small town upwards of 100 miles from Buffalo, and then took leave of her, and of the boat. It was early in the morning, just at the dawn of day, I walked ten miles into the country, and stopped to breakfast with a Mr. Wells. I proposed to preach in the evening. Mr. Wells readily accompanied me through the neighborhood to visit the people, and circulate the appointment.
>
> We visited an old Baptist deacon by the name of Hamlin. After hearing of our appointment for evening, he began to tell of a *book*, a STRANGE BOOK, a VERY STRANGE BOOK! in his possession, which had been just published. This book, he said, purported to have been originally written on plates either of gold or brass, by a branch of the tribes of Israel; and to have been discovered and translated by a young man near Palmyra, in the State of New York, by the aid of visions, or the ministry of angels. I inquired of him how or where the book was to be obtained. He promised me the perusal of it, at his house the next day, if I would call. I felt a strange interest in the book. I preached that evening to a small audience,

who appeared to be interested in the truths which I endeavored to unfold to them in a clear and lucid manner from the Scriptures. Next morning I called at his house, where, for the first time, my eyes beheld the BOOK OF MORMON—that book of books— that record which reveals the antiquities of the *"New World"* back to the remotest ages, and which unfolds the destiny of its people and the world for all time to come;—that Book which contains the fulness of the gospel of a crucified and risen Redeemer;—that Book which reveals a lost remnant of Joseph, and which was the principal means, in the hands of God, of directing the entire course of my future life.

I opened it with eagerness, and read its title page. I then read the testimony of several witnesses in relation to the manner of its being found and translated. After this I commenced its contents by course. I read all day; eating was a burden, I had no desire for food; sleep was a burden when the night came, for I preferred reading to sleep. As I read, the Spirit of the Lord was upon me, and I knew and comprehended that the book was true, as plainly and manifestly as a man comprehends and knows that he exists. My joy was now full, as it were, and I rejoiced sufficiently to more than pay me for all the sorrows, sacrifices and toils of my life. I soon determined to see the young man who had been the instrument of its discovery and translation.[3]

Notice how Brigham Young described his own conversion: "If all the talent, tact, wisdom, and refinement of the world had been sent to me with the Book of Mormon, and had declared, in the most exalted of earthly eloquence, the truth of it, undertaking to prove it by learning and worldly wisdom, they would have been to me like the smoke which arises only to vanish away. But when I saw a man without eloquence, or talents for public speaking, who could only say, 'I know, by the power of the Holy Ghost, that the Book of Mormon is true, that Joseph Smith is a Prophet of the Lord,' the Holy Ghost proceeding from that individual illuminated by understanding, and light, glory, and immortality were before me. I was encircled by them, filled with them, and I knew for myself that the testimony of the man was true...

My own judgment, natural endowments, and education bowed to this simple, but mighty testimony."[4]

Similar stories could be told by millions of Latter-day Saints throughout the world. For example, my friend Carolyn Rasmus, a woman who was for many years a university professor, administrative assistant to the university president, and administrative assistant to the presidency of the general young women organization of the Church, reflects on her conversion as follows:

> The process of my conversion began at a very early age. Like Nephi [in the Book of Mormon], I was "born of goodly parents" (1 Nephi 1:1). I attended weekly Church services with my parents who, for as long as I can remember, either taught Sunday School or served in leadership positions in our community Lutheran Church. One of the most used books in our home was *Hurlbut's Story of the Bible for Young and Old.* I remember being read to from this book and recall studying the many pictures and illustrations. I loved the titles of the stories, "The First Baby in the World, and His Brother," "Jacob's Wonderful Dream," "The Promise of the Woman of Shunem," and many, many more.

> Following the example set by my parents, I found myself involved in teaching Sunday School and singing in the church choir during my college years and later as I taught in New York and Iowa. Most of my close friends, wherever I lived, were also Christians—people who were "doers of the word, and not hearers only" (James 1:22).

> While involved in a professional organization, I became acquainted with Dr. Leona Holbrook, a professor at Brigham Young University and then president of the American Association for Health, Physical Education, and Recreation. Each time I heard her speak I was impressed not only with what she said, but the manner with which she spoke. But more significantly, I was touched as I watched her interact with people. She seemed always to have time for others, to be genuinely interested in them, and to treat *everyone* with great dignity and respect. As I watched her it seemed that she literally "lifted" people and that they left her presence feeling better about themselves.

When I decided to pursue a doctoral degree I knew I wanted to study with Dr. Holbrook. I determined that the same books would be available at any university I attended, but that there were things I could learn from Leona Holbrook that couldn't be learned anywhere else or from anyone else. When I first told her of my interest in enrolling at Brigham Young University, she suggested I visit the campus before making a final decision. She knew of my smoking habit and that I dearly loved wine. Dr. Holbrook simply said, "BYU is a very unique place. Visit before you make your decision." More than a year before I became a student, I visited BYU. After a two-day visit I wrote, "My stop at BYU only served to convince me that I made the right decision. Having been there made me realize I'd even be able to give up my wine for what I'd receive in return."

The following August, at the conclusion of summer school, I was given a leatherbound triple combination [Book of Mormon, Doctrine and Covenants, and Pearl of Great Price] by a class of students who inscribed this message: "Dear Miss Rasmus, you have shared with us things that are important and close to you. In return, we would like to give you something that means a great deal to us. And we want you to know that we give it to you with a lot of love and respect. Sincerely, your fans, BYU Summer School, Second Session, 1970." It was to become the gift that made a difference. Though I could not begin to comprehend what it was they had really shared with me, I was touched that a group of students cared enough to present me with such a special gift. I tried reading the book, but it made little sense to me. Finally, instead of reading from the beginning, I read portions I'd heard others talk about or that I'd been told I should read. I remember reading Alma 32 and Moroni 10, but did not feel particularly impressed.

During the break between summer school and the beginning of fall semester, I drove to visit my family in Ohio, stopping to spend time with friends at Iowa State University. They were filled with questions about what Mormons were really like and what they did for fun. I felt I handled their inquiries with accuracy and good humor, but I was unprepared for a question asked me by one friend later that evening. "I've heard a lot about Joseph Smith," she began.

"Was he really a prophet? Did he receive gold plates from an angel? Where did the Book of Mormon come from? Is it true?"

The questions sounded simple enough, but I didn't know the answers. In fact, I had never really given much thought to these things. It was a long drive from Iowa back to Utah. I had a lot of time to think and question and wonder. Are these things true? How can I really know? Again, I tried reading the Book of Mormon, but I understood little. The names and circumstances were unfamiliar to me. I'd heard people say this book was "for our time," but it didn't seem like that to me. It certainly didn't "speak to me."

About a month after the beginning of the fall semester, several of my friends invited me to accompany them on an all-day hike one beautiful Saturday in October. I was eager to leave my studies and head for the mountains. But, as it neared 10:00 A.M. they began looking for a comfortable place to sit down. I didn't have any idea it was General Conference weekend; in fact, I didn't even know what General Conference was. I certainly didn't know my friends were equipped with a transistor radio. I was, without question, a captive audience, and although I said nothing to any of the hiking group, when I returned home that evening I wrote on my daily calendar, "Everything sounds so right."

Shortly after that experience I decided to fast for the first time in my life. It was a day when I was also studying for a statistics test. I was unsettled and unable to concentrate on studying for the test. Finally, I knelt down to pray. I have no recollection of the prayer I offered, but these thoughts came into my mind and I felt impressed to record them on a scrap of paper: "October 12, 1970, 8:45 A.M. Go now, my child, for there is much work to be done. I send my Spirit to be with you to enable you to work and think clearly, to accomplish all that lies before you this day. Go now and know that I am with you in all things, and later return to me, coming to me with real intent of prayer. Know that I am the Lord, that all things are possible to them who call upon my name. Take comfort in these words. Fill your heart with joy and gladness, not sorrow and despair. Lo, I am with you always, even unto the end of the world. Know me as Comforter and Savior."

That evening I wanted to be alone. I went to my student office on campus, locked the door, turned out the lights, and prayed. I wanted answers to the questions I'd been asking. I didn't expect an angel to appear, but I wanted some kind of manifestation that would prove, once and for all, that these things were true or false. Nothing happened! The experience earlier in the day had no particular meaning because I did not yet understand ...that the voice of the Lord can come into our mind. I also knew nothing about the principle of learning "by *study* and also by *faith*" (D&C 88:118).

I left my office determined to forget about Joseph Smith, the Book of Mormon, and everything associated with The Church of Jesus Christ of Latter-day Saints. But I couldn't. These things seemed to be constantly on my mind. Several months later I had the impression that I should begin to pay tithing. For more than three months, each time I received a paycheck I took 10 percent of my meager student-teacher wage and put the cash in a white envelope carefully hidden in a dresser drawer. I never had a desire to touch the money or to use it for something else. Although I wasn't sure how to give it to him, I believed it belonged to the Lord. I did other things that seemed and felt right. I would attend the Lutheran Church in the morning and then go with friends to sacrament meeting [the LDS worship service] and Sunday School. I stopped drinking coffee, which had always seemed harmless to me and which I had never understood was part of the honor code I had promised to keep when I enrolled at BYU. I spent many hours helping a friend memorize the missionary discussions before she left for her mission.

Only two weeks before I would join the Church, I sat in a sacrament meeting and the following words came pounding into my head: "Know that Joseph Smith was a prophet and that through him my Church has been restored in these latter days. Know that the Book of Mormon is the word of God. Know that my Church has been reestablished upon the earth in these latter days. Know that I intend for you to be baptized. Know, believe, do." These thoughts went through my head day and night for a week. The next Sunday during the sacrament service as I passed the bread to my neighbor, another thought came into my mind: "How much longer can you pass by the bread of life?" Six days later, on March 6, 1971, I was baptized and became a member of The Church of Jesus Christ of Latter-day Saints.

One of my faculty colleagues at BYU, Alonzo Gaskill, described his conversion as follows:

Prior to my conversion to The Church of Jesus Christ of Latter-day Saints, I was a practicing member of the Eastern Orthodox faith. As a freshman in college I had yet to ever read the Bible cover to cover. To my knowledge we didn't have a copy of it in our home. However, one Sunday our parish priest encouraged the congregation to read the scriptures. So, I purchased a KJV/NIV parallel Bible and began, first reading the New Testament, and then the Old. Much to my surprise, I began to find things in the Bible that appeared to contradict what I understood the official doctrine of the Orthodox Church to be. As opportunity allowed, I inquired of my priest regarding these seeming contradictions. His response was consistent but disappointing. To each doctrinal concern I raised, he responded with words akin to "Alonzo, we don't ask questions. We simply go on faith." Although his solutions to my spiritual inquiries were always disheartening, nevertheless, I had no intention of leaving the Orthodox faith over my little discoveries; perhaps his ability to sense that mind-set spawned his less-than-helpful comments.

Throughout my high school years my best friend was a Latter-day Saint, although he never aggressively attempted to proselytize me. While in my presence he would often tell others about his faith, but I don't recall ever feeling as though he had a strong interest in my conversion, nor was it apparent that he saw me as a potential proselyte. Owing to interactions with a handful of other high school friends (from various Christian denominations), I became rather anti-Mormon at about sixteen or seventeen years of age. My

LDS friend was patient with my references to Mormonism as a "cult," etc. And perhaps my apparent animosity was, in part, the cause of his hesitancy to engage in theological discussions with me. Although I did not believe the things I understood him to believe, nevertheless, I was always impressed with how he lived his life. He was as Christian in his behavior as anyone I knew.

In my freshman year of college I attended a university some distance from home. Not surprising was the fact that there was no Orthodox Church anywhere near the university. With one exception, my nine roommates were all Roman Catholic. Thus, I initially attended mass with them, but (with no criticism intended toward that great faith) I found that it left me wanting spiritually, and did not answer the myriad of doctrinal questions that began to flood my mind as I continued my first complete reading of the Bible.

My one non-Catholic roommate was an Evangelical Christian. He invited me to attend his Campus Crusade for Christ meetings, which I willingly did. I had a rather strange experience at one of these meetings that has left an indelible mark upon me. One evening a group of us were chatting. At one point I made a joke mocking Mormonism. Those in attendance roared with approving laughter. And yet the second I uttered those critical and mocking words a darkness enveloped me—it was almost tangible, to the degree that it could not go unnoticed. I tried to laugh with the others, but I was unable to ignore the strange experience of feeling as though someone or 'something' disapproved of my words and behavior.

I met a couple of missionaries and determined that it might be fun to chat with them regarding what I had read in the anti-Mormon literature I had acquired. I did so and went through a couple of sets of Elders. As the discussions progressed, the missionaries did their best to answer the questions I posed to them. Those they did not know, they promised to bring answers to during our next visit. And they were consistently good to their word.

At some point in my discussions with the LDS missionaries I turned the proverbial corner. For the first time it hit me: Regardless of why I was curious about this faith, the fact that they were claiming to be the "true" Church of Jesus Christ restored in these latter-days demanded that I take seriously their invitation to find out if what they were saying was true. In other words, my casual approach would no longer do. I didn't believe that Mormonism was "true"—and I frankly didn't think that it was very likely that it could be. I now felt an obligation, however, to see this through simply to confirm that it was appropriate to reject Mormonism. I somehow began to feel an accountability for what I was learning. Thus, although I had not done so up to that point, I determined that I would seek direction from God regarding the falsity or truthfulness of the things I was learning.

All of this was further complicated by the reality that my parents were not happy about my religious inquiries. They became uncomfortable when I first began reading the Bible and talking about questions I was having. But when they learned that I was attending the Catholic Church, Campus Crusade for Christ meetings, and entertaining LDS missionaries, they were livid. As I found myself becoming more and more dismissive of the anti-Mormon literature I was reading (primarily because of its inaccuracies and frequent misrepresentations), and as I became more and more convinced of the truthfulness of the doctrines I was learning from the Latter-day Saints, I began to feel a profound need to know for certain—from a divine source—whether or not what I was sincerely beginning to believe was right and true. I remember as clearly as though it were yesterday kneeling at the side of my bed and pleading with God to tell me what the truth was. As though it were necessary, I remember reminding the Lord that my parents would literally disown me should I convert, and thus the answer needed to be a clear one if I were to be expected to act upon it. At that instant, as clear as could be, I heard the following words pass through my mind: "Alonzo, you shall receive no witness until after the trial of your faith. You know it is true. Until you're willing to act upon that knowledge I can give you no more." I did not immediately recognize the origin of this phrase, but it was a passage from the Book of Mormon (Ether 12:6). Although I was hesitant, I felt I needed to move forward and be baptized, even though this could cause irreparable damage to my relationship with my parents. I kept thinking of Christ's teaching: "He that loveth father or mother more than me is not worthy of me" (Matthew 10:37). Although I was baptized on 25 November 1984, my conversion story does not end there.

From the point at which I realized that I needed to know for certain whether or not Mormonism was true, I began pleading with God for some very tangible witness—something I could trust and know to be more than simply my "feelings." I wouldn't say that I was seeking a "sign," as I was conscious that such would be offensive to God. But I did want a clear and strong empirical answer to my prayers so that I would know that I was not being deceived by the sophistries of men or my personal emotions. Approximately three weeks after my baptism a witness of that nature came. I was sitting at my desk studying materials for a theology course I was taking when that which I had sought came with a force and power unexpected. Although it would not be appropriate here to share the details of that experience, suffice it to say that it was a conversion in a very powerful sense. I felt God had rewarded my willingness to take a step into the unknown by giving me the very discernible experience I had desired prior to my baptism.

As the years have passed since my initial conversion, I have completed graduate work in religious studies at Catholic and Protestant universities. Upon enrolling, I fully expected to have my beliefs called into question and to discover things that would challenge my faith. Yet, I can honestly say that the exact opposite has been the case. Instead of finding things that provoked doubts, time and again my faith has been confirmed through my academic pursuits. In the Doctrine and Covenants—a book of revelations given by God to Joseph Smith (and his successors)—the following statement appears: "'seek learning, even by study and also by faith" (D&C 88:118; see also D&C 109:7, 14). My testimony of The Church of Jesus Christ of Latter-day Saints has really come through following this commission. I have faith in the restored gospel and its teachings, and that faith has come through scripture study, prayer, and personal revelation to my heart and mind. But I also have a belief in Mormonism based on an analytical, academic investigation of it. I'm as convinced intellectually of its claims to be the restored gospel as I am spiritually converted to that reality. Indeed, I can honestly say that I know it to be true "by study, and also by faith." For me, that ancient "law of witnesses" (i.e., "In the mouth of two or three witnesses shall every word be established," 2 Corinthians 13:1) has become a reality—I know it to be true by study, but also by faith.

We could multiply these kinds of stories many times over and gain distinctive insights from converts to Mormonism who came from other branches of Christianity, or who were Jewish, Muslim, or from any number of other world religions. But the above collection is sufficient for the reader to discern areas of commonality, specific points that interested individuals read, studied, tested, and had confirmed. Missionaries are just as likely to encounter and teach a CPA as they are a plumber, just as likely to baptize a construction worker as they are a college president. Conversion to Mormonism takes place all over the globe and is not confined to educational level, economic standing, or religious upbringing. People all across the spectrum of humanity are drawn to Latter-day Saint beliefs and way of life.

ENDNOTES

1. Shoemaker, "Why Your Neighbor Joined the Mormon Church," 11–13.
2. N. T. Wright, *Simply Christian*, 206.
3. *Autobiography of Parley P. Pratt*, 36–37.
4. Young, *JD* 1:90.

EIGHTEEN

Exclusive and Inclusive

I N THE SUMMER OF 1997 a colleague and
I sat with two Protestant ministers for a few
hours in what proved to be a delightful and
extremely enlightening conversation. Absent was any sense of defen-
siveness or any effort to argue and debate; we were earnestly trying
to understand one another better. Toward the end of the discussion,
one of the ministers turned to me and said: "Bob, it bothers you a
great deal, doesn't it, when people suggest that Latter-day Saints are
not Christian?"

I responded: "It doesn't just *bother* me. It *hurts* me, for I know how
deeply as a Latter-day Saint I love the Lord and how completely I trust
in him."

My Protestant friend then made a rather simple observation,
one that should have been obvious to me long before that particular
moment. He said: "How do you think it makes us feel when we know
of your belief in what you call the great apostasy, of the fact that Christ
presumably said to the young Joseph Smith that the churches on earth
at that time 'were all wrong,' that 'all their creeds [are] an abomination
in my sight,' that 'those professors were all corrupt' (Joseph Smith—
History 1:19), and that in your Doctrine and Covenants your church is
identified as 'the only true and living church upon the face of the whole
earth' (D&C 1:30)?" I can still remember the feelings that washed over
me at that moment: For a brief time I found myself, mentally speaking,
walking in their moccasins, seeing things through their eyes.

Roman Catholics often refer to the Catholic faith as the "only true church." What do Latter-day Saints mean when they use such language? What does this language mean relative to other faiths? First, let's chat briefly about what it *doesn't* mean.

It does not mean that men and women of other Christian faiths are not sincere believers in truth and genuine followers of the Christ. Latter-day Saints have no difficulty whatsoever accepting one's personal affirmation that they are Christian, that they acknowledge Jesus Christ as the divine Son of God, their Savior, the Lord and Master of their life.

I want to devote sufficient thought to this particular principle. "God, the Father of us all," Ezra Taft Benson said, "uses the men of the earth, especially good men, to accomplish his purposes. It has been true in the past, it is true today, it will be true in the future." Elder Benson then quoted the following from a conference address delivered by Apostle Orson F. Whitney in 1928: "*God is using more than one people for the accomplishment of His great and marvelous work* [see Isaiah 29:13–14]. *The Latter-day Saints cannot do it all.* It is too vast, too arduous for any one people."[1]

In June 1829, two early Church leaders, Oliver Cowdery and David Whitmer, were instructed to "contend against no church, save it be the church of the devil" (D&C 18:20). B. H. Roberts offered this insightful commentary upon this passage: "I understand the injunction to Oliver Cowdery to 'contend against no church, save it be the church of the devil' to mean that he shall contend against evil, against untruth, against all combinations of wicked men. They constitute the church of the devil, the kingdom of evil, a federation of unrighteousness; and the servants of God have a right to contend against that which is evil, let it appear where it will…. But, let it be understood, we are *not* brought necessarily into antagonism with the various sects of Christianity as such …. [O]ur relationship to the religious world is *not* one that calls for the denunciation of sectarian churches as composing the church of the devil." Now note the following: "All that makes for truth, for righteousness, *is of God;* it constitutes the kingdom of righteousness—the empire of Jehovah; and, in a certain sense at least, *constitutes the Church of Christ.* All that makes for untruth, for unrighteousness constitutes the kingdom of evil—the church of the devil. With the kingdom of righteousness we have no warfare. On the contrary, both the spirit of

the Lord's commandments to his servants and the dictates of right reason would suggest that we seek to enlarge this kingdom of righteousness
both by *recognizing* such truths as it possesses and *seeking* the friendship
and cooperation of the righteous men and women who constitute its
membership."[2] It is a gross exaggeration and misrepresentation to suggest that Latter-day Saints believe all of Christian practice and doctrine
since the time of the original apostles has been apostate. Noble and
God-fearing men and women who lived through the period that too
many have termed the "dark ages" sought to do good and maintain the
tenets of Christianity to the best of their ability.

It does not mean we believe that most of the doctrines in Catholic
or Protestant Christianity are false or that the leaders of the various
branches of Christianity have improper motives. Joseph Smith stated:
"The inquiry is frequently made of me, 'Wherein do you differ from
others in your religious views?' In reality and essence we do not differ
so far in our religious views, but that we could all drink into one principle of love. One of the grand fundamental principles of 'Mormonism' is to receive truth, let it come from whence it may."[3] "Have the
Presbyterians any truth?" he asked on another occasion. "Yes. Have the
Baptists, Methodists, etc., any truth? Yes.... We should gather all the
good and true principles in the world and treasure them up, or we shall
not come out true 'Mormons.'"[4]

It does not mean that the Bible has been so corrupted that it cannot be relied upon to teach us sound doctrine and provide an example
of how to live. We believe that the hand of God has been over the
preservation of the biblical materials such that what we have now is
what the Almighty would have us possess. Indeed, although Latter-day
Saints do not believe that the Bible now contains all that it once contained, the Bible is a remarkable book of scripture, one that inspires,
motivates, reproves, corrects, and instructs (2 Timothy 3:16). It is the
word of God.

While Latter-day Saints do not believe that one can derive divine
authority to perform the saving ordinances from the scriptures, we do
say that the Bible contains the fullness of the gospel in the sense that
(1) it teaches of groups of people in the past who enjoyed the full
blessings of the everlasting gospel; and (2) it teaches (especially the

New Testament) the good news or glad tidings of redemption in Christ through the Atonement.

It does not mean that Latter-day Saints desire to "do their own thing" or face social challenges on their own. To be sure, we strive earnestly to work together with men and women of other faiths to stand up and speak out against the rising tide of immorality and ethical relativism that are spreading in our world. With most Christian groups, we are persuaded that the changes to be made in our society can come about only "from the inside out"— through the transforming powers of Jesus Christ. Indeed, I am convinced that if we allow doctrinal differences, stereotyping, and demonizing of those who are different to prevent us from joining hands in halting the erosion of time-honored moral and family values, Lucifer will win a major victory.

What, then, does the statement in the Doctrine and Covenants mean when it states that The Church of Jesus Christ of Latter-day Saints is "the only true and living church upon the face of the whole earth" (D&C 1:30)?

"The word *only*," Neal A. Maxwell has written, "asserts a uniqueness and singularity" about the Church "as the exclusive ecclesiastical, authority-bearing agent for our Father in heaven in this dispensation."[5]

"When the Lord used the designation 'true,'" Elder Maxwell pointed out, "he implied that the doctrines of the Church and its authority are not just partially true, but true as measured by divine standards. The Church is not, therefore, conceptually compromised by having been made up from doctrinal debris left over from another age, nor is it comprised of mere fragments of the true faith. It is based upon the *fullness* of the gospel of him whose *name* it bears, thus passing the two tests for proving his church that were given by Jesus during his visit to the Nephites (3 Nephi 27:8).

"When the word *living* is used," Elder Maxwell observed, "it carries a divinely deliberate connotation. The Church is neither dead nor dying. Nor is it even wounded. The Church, like the living God who established it, is alive, aware, and functioning. It is not a museum that houses a fossilized faith; rather, it is a kinetic kingdom characterized by living faith in living disciples."[6]

It means that doctrinal finality rests with apostles and prophets, not theologians or scholars. There are simply too many ambiguous sections of scripture to "let the Bible speak for itself." This was, in fact, young Joseph Smith's dilemma: "The teachers of religion of the different sects understood the same passages of scripture so differently as to destroy all confidence in settling [his religious questions] by an appeal to the Bible" (Joseph Smith-History 1:12).

In many cases, neither linguistic training nor historical background will automatically produce the (divinely) intended meaning or clarification of a myriad of doctrinal or ecclesiastical matters on which hundreds of churches differ. Some of these matters are not exactly insignificant. Who decides which interpretation is that which Matthew or Paul or Jesus himself intended? Further, who decides who decides? "Some things in scripture are not perfectly clear," John MacArthur has written. "Sometimes we cannot reconstruct the historical context to understand a given passage. One notable example is the mention of 'baptism for the dead' in 1 Corinthians 15:29. There are at least forty different views about what that verse means. We cannot be dogmatic about such things."[7] What is the standard by which we judge and interpret? Who has the right to offer inspired commentary on words delivered by holy men of God who spoke or wrote anciently as they were moved upon by the Holy Spirit (2 Peter 1:21)? While each reader of holy writ should seek to be in tune with the Spirit enough to understand what is intended by the scripture, Latter-day Saints believe the final word on prophetic interpretation rests with prophets. As C. S. Lewis wisely remarked, "Unless the measuring rod is independent of the things measured, we can do no measuring."[8]

According to one of the accounts of Joseph Smith's First Vision, Joseph learned that "all their creeds were an abomination in his sight; that those professors were all corrupt; that 'they draw near to me with their lips, but their hearts are far from me, they teach for doctrines the commandments of men, having a form of godliness, but they deny the power thereof'" (Joseph Smith-History 1:19). This statement is, of course, considered to be harsh and hurtful to members of other Christian churches. Let's see if we can clarify things somewhat. For example, what were the "creeds" spoken of? Originally the Latin word *credo* meant simply "I believe." In Joseph Smith's day, the word creed referred to "a brief summary of the articles of Christian faith" or "that which is believed."[9] A modern dictionary defines a creed as "a system of religious belief" or "a set of opinions or principles on any subject" or "belief or confidence in; an article of faith."[10] As here defined, there is nothing wrong with a creed per se.

Alexander Campbell, a contemporary of Joseph Smith and the father of the Disciples of Christ and Church of Christ movements, was one who was particularly troubled by creeds. "Following the American Revolution," Milton Backman noted, "a number of theologians vehemently condemned all the popular creeds of Christendom. Urging all disciples of Christ to return to the purity of New Testament Christianity, these preachers taught that the Bible should be regarded as the only standard of faith, that every congregation should be autonomous, and that all men are endowed with the capacity to accept or reject God's gift of salvation. Although these resolute leaders were divided concerning the doctrine of the Godhead, they rejected the use of the term 'Trinity,' claiming that such a word was unscriptural."[11]

Joseph Smith was not necessarily opposed to religious creeds in general. In the preface to the first edition of the Doctrine and Covenants (1835) is found this fascinating remark: "There may be an aversion in the minds of some against receiving any thing purporting to be articles of religious faith, in consequence of there being so many now extant; but if men believe a system, and profess that it was given by inspiration, certainly, the more intelligibly they can present it, the better. It does not make a principle untrue to print it, neither does it make it true not to print it."

Latter-day Saints believe that the creeds spoken of in the First Vision were the post–New Testament creeds that sought to codify beliefs concerning God, Christ, the Holy Spirit, and their relationships, concepts that had evolved during the time following the deaths of the original apostles. To the extent that creeds teach or perpetuate falsehood, particularly concerning the nature of the Godhead, then of course our Father in heaven would be displeased with them. To the extent that creeds divide people, categorize people, exclude people, and even lead others to persecute them, one can appreciate why they would be viewed as undesirable. To the extent that they become a badge of belonging, the identifying mark by which a "true Christian" is known, the only way by which one can understand what the scriptures really mean about God and Christ—then to that extent the Christian circle is drawn smaller and smaller and that grace of God that makes salvation available to all humankind (Titus 2:11) is frustrated. "I cannot believe in any of the creeds of the different denominations," Joseph Smith observed, "because they all have some things in them I cannot subscribe to, though all of them have some truth. I want to come up into the presence of God, and learn all things; but the creeds set up stakes, and say, 'Hitherto shalt thou come, *and no further';* which I cannot subscribe to."[12] It seems to me that God and the Prophet Joseph were just as concerned with creedalism as they were with incorrect doctrine within the creeds.

The "professors" mentioned in the First Vision seem to be the antagonistic ministers in Joseph Smith's immediate surroundings. After describing the response of a Methodist minister to his First Vision that "it was all of the devil, that there were no such things as visions or revelations these days; that all such things had ceased with the apostles, and that there would never be any more of them," Joseph reported: "I soon found, however, that my telling the story had excited a great deal of prejudice against me among *professors of religion,* and was the cause of great persecution, which continued to increase… and this was common among all the sects" (Joseph Smith-History 1:21–22, emphasis added). In an account of the First Vision found in the Wentworth Letter (1842), Joseph indicates that "they [the Father and Son] told me that all religious denominations were believing in *incorrect doctrines,* and that none of them was acknowledged of God as His Church and kingdom: and I was expressly commanded to 'go not after them,' at the same time receiving a promise that the fullness of the Gospel should at some future time be made known unto me."[13]

Elder William Grant Bangerter once asked students and faculty at BYU: "Do we believe that all ministers of other churches are corrupt? Of course not. Joseph Smith certainly did not intend that. By reading the passage carefully, we find that the Lord Jesus Christ was referring to those ministers who were quarreling and arguing about which church was true—that is, the particular group with which Joseph Smith was involved....

"It is clearly apparent that there have been and now are many choice, honorable, and devoted men and women going in the direction of their eternal salvation who give righteous and conscientious leadership to their congregations in other churches. Joseph Smith evidently had many warm and friendly contacts with ministers of other religions. Quite a few of them joined the Church: Sidney Rigdon, John Taylor, Parley P. Pratt, and others in America and England. Some of them who carried the Christian attitude of tolerance did not join the Church. There are many others like them today."[14]

The question that arises from many of other faiths is this: Why should I join your church? What do you have to offer beyond my acceptance of Jesus Christ and the teachings of the Bible? Brigham Young declared that "We, the Latter-day Saints, take the liberty of believing *more* than our Christian brethren: we not only believe...the Bible, but...the whole of the plan of salvation that Jesus has given to us. Do we differ from others who believe in the Lord Jesus Christ? No, only in *believing more*."[15] How so? What is, in fact, the "more" of Mormonism?

1. *Restored Divine Authority*

As suggested earlier, one of the foundational teachings of Mormonism is that divine authority, known as the holy priesthood, was lost sometime following the deaths of the original apostles. This authority, including its keys—the directing power, the right of presidency—was necessary anciently to perform saving ordinances or sacraments, to oversee the performance of such sacraments, to properly interpret and propagate sound doctrine, and in general to officiate in the business of the Church. The restoration of divine authority through Joseph Smith in 1829 was therefore necessary in order that the restored church might be built upon the foundation of apostles and prophets, "Jesus Christ himself being the chief cornerstone" (Ephesians 2:19–20).

2. *Doctrinal Perspective*

Latter-day Saints believe that many of the truths restored through Joseph Smith provide a grander and more elevated perspective on life.

For example, to believe that men and women existed before this mortal sphere has immense implications for life here—our joys, our friendships and associations, our likes and dislikes, and our challenges and suffering. Also, consider what difference it makes to believe in "Christ's eternal gospel," the verity that the fullness of the gospel of Jesus Christ has been on earth since the beginning of time.

3. *Doctrinal Consolation*

What difference does it make to know that God has a plan and a timetable by which all of his children will have the opportunity to either accept or reject the message of salvation in Christ? What difference does it make to know that the sweetest associations of this life—marriage and family—can continue uninterrupted beyond the veil of death? What difference does it make to know that those who were unable to be married in this life to one with like passion for the faith, will have that opportunity hereafter?

4. *Doctrinal Clarification and Expansion*

Just as traditional Christians have no hesitation in viewing the events and teachings of the Old Testament through the lenses of the New Testament, so Latter-day Saints do not hesitate to read the Bible through the lenses of the Book of Mormon, modern scripture, and the words of living apostles and prophets. Supplementation is not the same as contradiction.

5. *Doctrinal Confirmation*

One of the major purposes of the Book of Mormon and modern scripture is to convince people "that the records of the prophets and of the twelve apostles of the Lamb are true" (1 Nephi 13:39). In the Book of Mormon we find the following: "Therefore repent, and be baptized in the name of Jesus, and lay hold upon the gospel of Christ, which shall be set before you, not only in this record but also in the record which shall come unto the Gentiles from the Jews [the Bible].... For behold, this [the Book of Mormon] is written for the intent that ye may believe that [the Bible]" (Mormon 7:8–9). In the Doctrine and Covenants we read that the Book of Mormon has been delivered in the last days for the purpose of "proving to the world that the holy scriptures are true, and that God does inspire men and call them to his holy work in this age and generation, as well as in generations of old; thereby showing that he is the same God yesterday, today, and forever" (D&C 20:11–12). In a day when people worldwide have come to doubt the historicity of biblical events, teachings, and values—especially the redemptive role of Jesus the Christ—Latter-day Saint scripture stands as a second witness to their truthfullness and reality.

I have often been challenged in public settings by people who are offended by the LDS notion of being the "only true church" or of our claim to possess the "fullness of the gospel of Jesus Christ." They feel it is unkind, exclusionary, and un-Christian. In response, doesn't Church A believe that it has a better insight into this or that doctrine found in the Bible than churches B, C, and D? Doesn't this denomination feel strongly that its beliefs and practices more closely mirror those of the church established by Jesus in the first century? Weren't Hus or Luther or Calvin or Zwingli or Wesley convinced that their efforts to reform the mother church—to cease the abuses of Roman Catholicism and to return to the scriptures—were inspired and heaven-directed, that their reforms and teachings brought them closer to what the Master had intended from the beginning?

Latter-day Saints cannot jettison what they believe to be the language of the Lord to Joseph Smith in 1820 in order to allay hurt feelings or court favor. We hold to the truth that God has spoken anew in our day and restored his everlasting gospel through living prophets. This is our distinctive position, our contribution to a world that desperately needs a belief in God, an understanding of his grand plan of salvation, the promise and hope that come from a Redeemer, and confirming evidence for the historical veracity of the Holy Bible. We can seek, as I have sought to do in this chapter, to better understand what was meant and intended, but we cannot relinquish the reason we have for being. President Gordon B. Hinckley remarked: "The Lord said that this is the only true and living Church upon the face of the earth with which He is well-pleased. I didn't say that. Those are His words. The Prophet Joseph was told that the other sects were wrong. Those are not my words. Those are the Lord's words. But they are *hard words* for those of other faiths. We don't need to exploit them. We just need to be kind and good and gracious people to others, showing by our example the great truth of that which we believe."[18]

"While one portion of the human race is judging and condemning the other without mercy," Brother Joseph Smith noted solemnly, "the Great Parent of the universe looks upon the whole of the human family with a fatherly care and paternal regard; He views them as His offspring, and without any of those contracted feelings that influence the children of men, causes 'His sun to rise on the evil and the good, and sendeth rain on the just and on the unjust.' He holds the reins of judgment in His hands; He is a wise Lawgiver, and will judge all men, not according to the narrow, contracted notions of men, but 'according to the deeds done in the body whether they be good or evil.... We need not doubt the wisdom and intelligence of the Great Jehovah."[19]

ENDNOTES

1. Whitney, CR, April 1928, 59; cited in Ezra Taft Benson, CR, April 1972, 49.
2. Roberts, CR, April 1906, 14–15, emphasis added.
3. Smith, *TPJS,* 313.
4. Ibid., 316.
5. Maxwell, *Things as They Really Are,* 45.
6. Ibid., 46.
7. MacArthur, *Why One Way?* 61.
8. Lewis, "The Poison of Subjectivism," in *Christian Reflections,* 100.
9. Noah Webster, *American Dictionary of the English Language,* s.v. "creed."
10. *The New Shorter Oxford English Dictionary,* s.v. "creed."
11. Backman, *Christian Churches in America,* 159.
12. Smith, *TPJS,* 327, emphasis added.
13. *History of the Church* 4:536, emphasis added.

14. Bangerter, "It's a Two-Way Street," 161.

15. Young, *JD* 13:56, emphasis added.

16. Smith, *TPJS*, 313.

17. Ibid., 314.

18. Hinckley, remarks delivered at the North Ogden, Utah Regional Conference, 3 May 1998; cited in *Church News*, 3 June 2000.

19. Smith, *TPJS*, 218.

NINETEEN

Unto All Nations

JESUS CHARGED HIS DISCIPLES to take his gospel message to all the known world, saying, "The kingdom of heaven is at hand" (Matthew 10:7), meaning that the Lord's kingdom had now come among them. They were to sound the call for people to repent of their sins and come unto Jesus, who was in fact the promised Messiah. At first they were cautioned to preach only to the Jews, "the lost sheep of the house of Israel" (Matthew 10:5–6; 15:24). As he ascended into heaven, however, the Lord expanded that charge: "Go ye therefore, and teach all nations, baptizing them in the name of the Father, and of the Son, and of the Holy Ghost: teaching them to observe all things whatsoever I have commanded you: and lo, I am with you always, even unto the end of the world" (Matthew 28:19– 20). Indeed, they were to "Go ye into all the world, and preach the gospel to every creature" (Mark 16:15).

For the most part, the disciples still confined their preaching and voice of warning to the Jews until Peter, the chief apostle, received a vision instructing him to broaden his perspective, recognize that God was no respecter of persons, and go to the Gentiles (Acts 10). Saul of Tarsus, at first a persecutor of the Christians, was struck down by Christ while on the road to Damascus. He was then and there commissioned to change his course and direction, accept Jesus of Nazareth as the Savior and Redeemer of humankind, and become the principal voice and later the apostle to the Gentiles. Saul, who came to be known as Paul, then devoted the remainder of his life traveling, teaching, preaching, and writing regulatory correspondence to the churches he established. He was finally able to preach the message of salvation to the people of Rome, where he was beheaded by order of Emperor Nero. But persecution did not put an end to the spread of Christianity. Christian missionaries now travel to all parts of the globe, preaching, making disciples, confirming the faith of others, translating and distributing the Bible, and in some cases giving their very lives for the cause they espouse.

On 6 April 1830, Joseph Smith met in company with a large group at Fayette, New York, to formally organize what was called on that day the Church of Christ. Later the name was changed to the Church of the Latter Day Saints, and in 1838 to The Church of Jesus Christ of Latter-day Saints. Joseph Smith was then and thereafter acknowledged and sustained by his followers as a prophet, seer, revelator, apostle, and first elder of the Church. Missionaries were sent out from the earliest days, and congregations of Saints (followers of Christ and baptized members of the Church) were established in New York and Pennsylvania. The command to spread the news of Christ's "restored gospel" came: "Go ye into all the world, preach the gospel to every creature, acting in the authority which I have given you, baptizing in the name of the Father, and of the Son, and of the Holy Ghost" (D&C 68:8).

By 1831 there were two church centers, one in Kirtland, Ohio, and one in Independence, Missouri. Severe persecution in Independence in 1833 and troubles in Ohio in the late 1830s forced the people into other parts of Missouri, and eventually the Mormons left the state and settled on the banks of the Mississippi River at Commerce, Illinois. There, from 1839–46, they enjoyed a brief season of peace and prosperity and built a city that came to be known as Nauvoo, the "city beautiful." During the time the Saints were there, Nauvoo grew to become the second largest city in Illinois.

Missionaries were sent abroad, and tens of thousands, especially from Great Britain, converted to Mormonism. Many of these left their homelands as a part of a modern gathering and came to America, the home of their newfound faith. But persecution and contention seemed to be ever a part of the lives of Joseph Smith and the Mormons. Fearing his increasing social and political strength and the capacity of the growing Church to wield more and more influence in the state—and being distressed by a number of the beliefs and practices of the Latter-day Saints, including plural marriage—the enemies of the Mormons (some from among dissident and disaffected members) eventually murdered Joseph Smith and his brother Hyrum in Carthage, Illinois, on 27 June 1844.

Many across the nation felt that Mormonism would, with the death of its charismatic leader, succumb to this final, stunning blow. But the Saints declared that their faith was not founded in one mortal man; by now the personal conviction of the truthfulness of that which Joseph had established was deep, while the vision was broad. There was left to Brigham Young the responsibility to regroup the Saints and prepare them for departure from Illinois and then an arduous and now-famous trek across the plains to the Great Basin in what is now Salt Lake City, Utah. The formal date of entry into the Salt Lake Valley was 24 July 1847.

Brigham served as the Church's second president for thirty years and during that time, although the Mormons enjoyed some degree of autonomy in their remote gathering place, there were ongoing struggles with the U.S. government over plural marriage and what was perceived to be the growing theocratic power of Brigham Young himself. Those struggles continued through the nineteenth-century until plural marriage was formally discontinued in 1890 and Utah became the forty-fifth state in the union in 1896. Growth and expansion throughout the world have characterized the twentieth century Church, and the movement set in motion by Joseph Smith continues to wield an influence in the twenty-first century.

As missionary work has intensified, the number of converts has steadily grown, to approximately 230,000 per year at the time of this writing. Whereas as recently as the 1950s Mormonism was viewed as largely a Western American Church, congregations of Mormons are now found in Africa, Asia, the Philippines, Europe, the islands of the Pacific, and in large numbers in Central and South America. Rodney Stark, a noted sociologist of religion, following a serious investigation of patterns of Mormon growth, observed in 1984 that "The Church of Jesus Christ of Latter-day Saints, the Mormons, will soon achieve a worldwide following comparable to that of Islam, Buddhism, Christianity, Hinduism, and the other dominant world faiths.... Indeed, today they stand on the threshold of becoming the first major faith to appear on earth since the Prophet Mohammed rode out of the desert." Stark then suggested that a 30 percent growth rate per decade will result in over 60 million Mormons by the year 2080. A 50 percent per decade growth rate, which is actually lower than the rate each decade since World War II, will result in 265 million Mormons by 2080. Some fifteen years later, Stark revisited his earlier and somewhat controversial projections and found that actual LDS growth had surpassed his highest optimistic projections by approximately a million members. That is, "So far membership is substantially higher than my most optimistic projection, the one that would result in 267 million Mormons worldwide in 2080."[1]

Whereas the way most people know of LDS missionary work is through the full-time missionaries—young men and women who are assigned throughout the world, leave their homes, and serve in a ministerial position for eighteen to twenty-four months—in point of fact the entire Church is encouraged to reach out, climb out of their comfort zone, be willing and prepared to answer others' questions, be an example, be a missionary. President David O. McKay, president of the Church from 1951–70, charged the Saints: "Every member a missionary." Therefore members are counseled to help identify people among their friends who might be approached by the full-time missionaries; the missionaries do the formal teaching.

In a general conference address delivered in April 1998 entitled "Are You Saved?" one of the LDS apostles, Dallin H. Oaks, stated: "A question that is repeatedly asked of the Latter-day Saints is this: 'Why do you send missionaries to preach to other Christians?' Sometimes this is asked with curiosity and sometimes with resentment.

"My most memorable experience with that question occurred some years ago in what we then called the Eastern Bloc. After many years of Communist hostility to religion, these countries were suddenly and miraculously given a measure of religious freedom. When that door opened, many Christian faiths sent missionaries. As part of our preparation to do so, the First Presidency sent members of the Quorum of the Twelve Apostles to meet with government and church leaders in these countries. Our assignment was to introduce ourselves and to explain what our missionaries would be doing.

"Elder Russell M. Nelson and I called on the leader of the Orthodox Church in one of these countries. Here was a man who had helped keep the light of Christianity burning through the dark decades of Communist repression. I noted in my journal that he was a warm and gracious man who impressed me as a servant of the Lord. I mention this so that you will not think there was any spirit of arrogance or contention in our conversation of nearly an hour. Our visit was pleasant and cordial, filled with the goodwill that should always characterize conversations between men and women who love the Lord and seek to serve Him, each according to his or her own understanding.

"Our host told us about the activities of his church during the period of Communist repression. He described the various difficulties his church and its work were experiencing as they emerged from that period and sought to regain their former position in the life of the country and the hearts of the people. We introduced ourselves and our fundamental beliefs. We explained that we would soon be sending missionaries into his country and told him how they would perform their labors.

"He asked, 'Will your missionaries preach only to unbelievers, or will they also try to preach to believers?' We replied that our message was for everyone, believers as well as unbelievers. We gave two reasons for this answer—one a matter of principle and the other a matter of practicality. We told him that we preached to believers as well as unbelievers because our message, the restored gospel, makes an important addition to the knowledge, happiness, and peace of all mankind. As a matter of practicality, we preach to believers as well as unbelievers because we cannot tell the difference. I remember asking this distinguished leader, 'When you stand before a congregation and look into the faces of the people, can you tell the difference between those who are real believers and those who are not?' He smiled wryly, and I sensed an admission that he had understood the point.

Elder Oaks continued: "Through missionaries and members, the message of the restored gospel is going to all the world. To non-Christians, we witness of Christ and share the truths and ordinances of His restored gospel. To Christians we do the same. Even if a Christian has been 'saved'…, we teach that there remains more to be learned and more to be experienced. As President Hinckley recently said, '[We are] not argumentative. We do not debate. We, in effect, simply say to others: Bring all the good that you have and let us see if we can add to it.'"[2]

So what are the reasons for such growth among the Latter-day Saints? What attracts people generally to The Church of Jesus Christ of Latter-day Saints? First of all, many persons in the world, weary of moral decline and what they perceive to be an erosion of time-honored values, are drawn to a church and a people who seem to be, as one journalist put it, "a repository of old-fashioned values, an American success story."[3] The Mormons hold to absolute truths concerning God, man, and right and wrong. Second, the Latter-day Saint doctrines concerning God's plan for his children, as well as the answers to such dilemmas as where we came from, why we are here, and where we are going—these things appeal to large numbers of men and women who are searching for meaning in life and for answers to the perplexities of our existence. The focus on the family is seen to be refreshing and badly overdue in a world that seems to be drifting rapidly from its moorings.

Though it may seem odd at first glance, there is another reason why the Church seems to be growing so rapidly—because of the requirements and the demands it makes upon its members. "Let us here observe," the early Mormons were taught, "that a religion that does not require the sacrifice of all things never has power sufficient to produce the faith necessary unto life and salvation."[4] In other words, a religion that does not ask anything of its congregants can promise very little to them. Easy religion and convenient theology are not satisfying to the soul. People yearn for something to which they can commit themselves completely, something worthy of their devotion and their investment of time, talents, and means.

My experience as a young missionary is replicated over and over by people who have taken the time to listen to the presentation of the missionaries. The missionaries teach them about God and his plan of salvation, about Christ's central role in that plan, about the importance of prophets through the ages, and of the call of a modern prophet, Joseph Smith. The burden of proof, the effort to find out, rests with honest truth seekers.

While missionary work is obviously a worthwhile enterprise in terms of expanding the ranks of Latter-day Saints, full-time missionary service has many other less obvious benefits. First, these young people devote themselves intensely to the service of others day in and day out; such a labor builds a feeling of love and appreciation, not only for the people in the country in which they serve directly, but also in terms of God's children everywhere. Second, the broadening experience that occurs as young single adults experience new cultures, new languages, new traditions, new religious ideas is far more extensive and valuable than any college education. Third, the intense work ethic, coupled with exposure to rejection, criticism, and disappointment, build an army that has learned to work hard and face challenges and emotional trauma in years to come. Fourth, the daily immersion in scripture study and prayer go a long ways toward preparing a cadre of future Church leaders who know their God, have a witness of their Savior, and are committed tenaciously to their faith tradition. Missionary work is clearly an invaluable investment in the Church's future. Those who are content with what they have are perfectly free to express the same to Mormon missionaries. Those who are curious, unsatisfied with their present faith or way of life, or those who may be seeking for answers to some of life's puzzling questions, may find an encounter with the Latter-day Saints worth their time and attention.

ENDNOTES

1. Stark, "The Rise of a New World Faith," 18–23; *Latter-day Saint Social Life*, ed. James T. Duke, chapters 1–2.

2. Oaks, CR, April 1998, 78–79; see also Oaks and Wickman, "The Missionary Work of The Church of Jesus Christ of Latter-day Saints," 247–75.

3. Peter Steinfels, "Despite Growth, Mormons Find New Hurdles," sec. 1, 1.

4. Smith, *Lectures on Faith* 6:7.

TWENTY

The City of God

W HILE ACCEPTANCE OF JESUS
Christ and his message of salvation is an
individual undertaking, heaven on earth
and heaven hereafter are to be brought to pass through the establishment of unity among people of goodwill. True it is that ultimate peace
and righteousness on earth cannot come until the King of kings returns
in glory and majesty and power, but true it is also that the people of
God should seek to rid their souls of pride and envy and thereby establish meaningful spiritual union in society. "It seems that we humans
were designed," N. T. Wright has written, "to find our purpose and
meaning not simply in ourselves and our own inner lives, but in one
another and in the shared meanings and purposes of a family, a street,
a workplace, a community, a town, a nation."[1]

As I have witnessed the growth of The Church of Jesus Christ
of Latter-day Saints since the year of my own birth (1947, when the
Church reached its first million members) to the present, I am blown
away by how bold the early LDS leaders were, how confident they were,
how optimistic they were about the future growth of this little kingdom of theirs. Try to imagine how a small group of Latter-day Saints
must have felt as they gathered together at the home of Peter Whitmer
Sr. for the formal organization of the Church on 6 April 1830. Try to
imagine what went through the minds of the early missionaries as they
were told by revelation that "the voice of the Lord is unto all men, and
there is none to escape; and there is no eye that shall not see, neither
ear that shall not hear, neither heart that shall not be penetrated....

And the voice of warning shall be unto all people, by the mouths of my disciples, whom I have chosen in these last days" (D&C 1:2, 4). Try to imagine the wonder and amazement that must have overcome the little flock as they were instructed that "the sound must go forth from this place unto all the world, and unto the uttermost parts of the earth—the gospel must be preached unto every creature, with signs following them that believe" (D&C 58:64). Truly, the arm of the Lord would be revealed "in convincing the nations…of the gospel of their salvation. For it shall come to pass in that day, that every man shall hear the fullness of the gospel in his own tongue, and in his own language, through those who are ordained unto this power" (D&C 90:10–11).

Wilford Woodruff described an early meeting of the Saints in Kirtland: "On Sunday night the Prophet called on all who held the Priesthood to gather into the little log school house they had there. It was a small house, perhaps 14 feet square. But it held the whole of the Priesthood of the Church of Jesus Christ of Latter-day Saints who were then in the town of Kirtland,…. When we got together the Prophet called upon the Elders of Israel with him to bear testimony of this work. …When they got through, the Prophet said, 'Brethren I have been very much edified and instructed in your testimonies here tonight, but I want to say to you before the Lord, that you know no more concerning the destinies of this Church and kingdom than a babe upon its mother's lap. You don't comprehend it.' I was rather surprised. He said 'it is only a little handful of Priesthood you see here tonight, but this Church will fill North and South America, it will fill the world.'"[2]

Joseph Smith stated only weeks before his death: "I calculate to be one of the instruments of setting up the kingdom of [God envisioned by] Daniel by the word of the Lord, and I intend to lay a foundation that will revolutionize the whole world." And how was this to be realized? "It will not be by sword or gun that this kingdom will roll on," the Prophet said. "The power of truth is such that all nations will be under the necessity of obeying the gospel."[3] Joseph Smith's vision of the Kingdom of God was cosmic. It consisted of more than preaching and study and Sabbath services; it entailed the entire renovation of the order of things on earth, the transformation of man and the elevation of society. And at the heart of that sublime scene was the doctrine of Zion, a doctrine and a worldview that would shape the early Church and point the Saints of the twentieth and twenty-first centuries toward the eschatological ideal. In this chapter, we will speak more broadly of the idea and the ideal—of Zion as a people or community of believers, Zion as a specific place, and Zion as a state of being, the pure in heart.

Joseph Smith seems to have first encountered the concept of Zion (in a sense other than the holy mount or holy city in Jerusalem) in his translation of the Book of Mormon. The Book of Mormon prophets spoke of Zion as a holy commonwealth, a *society* of the Saints, *a way of life* that was to be established or brought forth under God's direction; those who fought against it were to incur God's displeasure. The municipals "labor for the welfare of Zion" rather than for money. In addition, in the words of the resurrected Jesus found in the Book of Mormon, Zion was identified as a specific *place* in the land of America, a land of promise and inheritance for the descendants of Joseph of old (1 Nephi 13:37; 2 Nephi 10:11–13; 26:29–31; 28:20–24; 3 Nephi 16:16–18).

Evidence suggests that a key moment in LDS Church history in regard to the discovery of the concept of Zion came during Joseph Smith's translation of the King James Bible. By the time Sidney Rigdon joined the Mormon Prophet in December 1830 and became the principal scribe in the Bible translation, particulars concerning the patriarch Enoch and his ancient city of Zion were first made known. A King James text of three verses on Enoch and his people was expanded to over one hundred verses, setting forth knowledge concerning such things as the manner in which an entire society of antediluvians was spiritually awakened and stimulated to transcendent righteousness; the means by which this ancient people, formerly bent upon selfishness and pride, had their souls changed, saw to the needs of the poor, and became "of one heart and one mind"; and how, through the application of such a divine philosophy, they were translated, taken from the earth into the bosom of God (see Moses 7). Enoch's Zion became the pattern, the scriptural prototype for the Latter-day Saints. In the months that followed, several revelations which we now have in the Doctrine and Covenants spoke of the ancient Zion of Enoch, and also provided the broad framework whereby the Latter-day Saints could lay the foundation for a modern society of Zion.

Among the earliest revelations now found in the Doctrine and Covenants was the repeated command, "Now, as you have asked, behold, I say unto you, keep my commandments, and seek to bring forth and establish the cause of Zion" (D&C 6:6; see also 11:6; 12:6; 14:6). Zion thus came to be associated with the restored *Church* and the grander work of the Restoration, and the faithful could take heart in the midst of their troubles, for Zion was the city of God (D&C 97:19). Indeed, in speaking of the sacred spot where the people of God congregated, the Lord said: "Behold, the land of Zion—I, the Lord, hold it in mine own hands" (D&C 63:25). Surely the King of Zion (Moses 7:53) would deal mercifully with his subjects.

The idea that there was a specific location for the city of Zion within North and South America was made known very early. Oliver Cowdery was called in September 1830 to preach among the native Americans (the Lamanites). He was further instructed that the specific location of the city of Zion "is not revealed, and no man knoweth where the city Zion shall be built, but it shall be given hereafter." The Lord then added that the location "shall be on the borders by the Lamanites" (D&C 28:9). It was on 20 July 1831, just as the leaders of the Saints had begun to arrive in Missouri, that the Mormons learned that the land of Missouri was "the land which I have appointed and consecrated for the gathering of the saints. Wherefore, this is the land of promise, and the place for the city of Zion....The place which is now called Independence is the center place" (D&C 57:1–3).

Zion is spoken of in scripture as a banner or *ensign* around which a weary or beleaguered people can rally. It is also a *standard* against which the substance and quality of all things are to be evaluated. The Saints are expected to judge all things by a set of guidelines obtained from a source beyond that of unenlightened man. Note the language of the revelation: "Behold, I, the Lord, have made my church in these last days like unto a judge sitting on a hill, or in a high place, to judge the nations. For it shall come to pass that the inhabitants of Zion shall judge all things pertaining to Zion" (D&C 64:37–38). As an illustration of this principle, Joseph Young, brother of Brigham Young, explained that Joseph Smith the Prophet "recommended the Saints to cultivate as high a state of perfection in their musical harmonies as the standard of the faith which he had brought was superior to sectarian religion. To obtain this, he gave them to understand that the refinement of singing would depend upon the attainment of the Holy Spirit.

"When these graces and refinements and all the kindred attractions are obtained that characterized the ancient Zion of Enoch, then the Zion of the last days will become beautiful, she will be hailed by the Saints from the four winds, who will gather to Zion with songs of everlasting joy."[4]

In addition, Zion was and is to be the focus, the convergence, and the concentration of all that is good, all that is ennobling, all that is instructive and inspirational. In Zion all things are to be gathered together in one in Christ (Ephesians 1:10). In short, according to Brigham Young, "Every accomplishment, every polished grace, every useful attainment in mathematics, music, in all science and art belong to the Saints."[5] The Saints "rapidly collect the intelligence that is bestowed upon the nations," President Young said on another occasion, "for all this intelligence belongs to Zion."[6]

Zion is people, the people of God, those people who have come out of the world of Babylon into the marvelous light of Christ. In this vein the Lord encouraged his little flock: "Verily, thus saith the Lord, let Zion rejoice, for this is Zion—THE PURE IN HEART; therefore, let Zion rejoice, while all the wicked shall mourn" (D&C 97:21). Thus Zion is *a state of being*, a state of purity of heart that entitles one to be known as a member of the household of faith. Brigham Young therefore spoke of the Saints having Zion in their hearts: "Unless the people live before the Lord in the obedience of His commandments," he said, "they cannot have Zion within them." Further, "As to the spirit of Zion, it is in the hearts of the Saints, of those who love and serve the Lord with all their might, mind, and strength."[7] On another occasion President Young affirmed: "Zion will be redeemed and built up, and the saints will rejoice. This is the land of Zion; and who are Zion? The *pure in heart* are Zion; they have Zion within them. Purify yourselves, sanctify the Lord God in your hearts, and have the Zion of God within you."[8] Finally, President Young asked: "Where is Zion? Where the organization of the Church of God is. And may it dwell spiritually in every heart; and may we so live as to always enjoy the Spirit of Zion."[9]

Isaiah the Prophet had spoken some seven hundred years before Christ of the "mountain of the Lord's house" being established in the tops of the mountains (Isaiah 2:2). In July 1840, Joseph Smith declared (in harmony with the teachings in the Book of Mormon—see 3 Nephi 16:16–18) that "the land of Zion consists of all North and South America, but that *any place* where the Saints gather is Zion."[10] The latter part of this statement—that Zion represented more than a place, a single location, but rather any locus of gathering—is significant. It broadens the notion of Zion to include areas around the world where the people of the covenant congregate. This larger vision of Zion is reflected in the following: "Zion shall not be moved out of her place, notwithstanding her children are scattered. They that remain, and are pure in heart, shall return, and come to their inheritances, they and their children, with songs of everlasting joy, to build up the waste places of Zion—and all these things that the prophets might be fulfilled. And behold, there is none other place appointed than that which I have appointed; neither shall there be any other place appointed than that which I have appointed, for the work of the gathering of my saints—until the day cometh that there is found no more room for them; and then I have other places which I will appoint unto them, and they shall be called *stakes*, for the curtains or the strength of Zion" (D&C 101:17–21, emphasis added).

In the dedicatory prayer of the Kirtland, Ohio, Temple, the Prophet pleaded in behalf of the Saints, "that they may come forth to Zion, or to her *stakes*, the places of thine appointment, with songs of everlasting joy" (D&C 109:39, emphasis added). The revelations are explicit in their pronouncement that safety and refuge are to be found in the stakes of Zion. "Arise and shine forth," the Lord implored, "that thy light may be a standard for the nations; and that the gathering together upon the land of Zion, *and upon her stakes*, may be for a defense, and a refuge from the storm, and from wrath when it shall be poured out without mixture upon the whole earth" (D&C 115:5–6, emphasis added).

As to the future of Zion, Bruce R. McConkie has written: "The center place! Let Israel gather to the stakes of Zion in all nations. Let every land be a Zion to those appointed to dwell there. Let the fullness of the gospel be for all the saints in all nations. Let no blessing be denied them. Let temples arise wherein the fullness of the ordinances of the Lord's house may be administered. But still there is a center place, a place where the chief temple shall stand, a place to which the Lord shall come, a place whence the law shall go forth to govern all the earth in that day when the Second David reigns personally upon the earth. And that center place is what men now call Independence in Jackson County, Missouri, but which in a day to come will be the Zion of our God and the City of Holiness of his people. The site is selected; the place is known; the decree has gone forth; and the promised destiny is assured."[11] At the same time that the Church will establish a significant presence in Independence, Missouri, and though Jackson County will become a gathering place, indeed the Center Place, yet there will always be, as suggested above, a need for the stakes of Zion throughout the earth far and wide, a need for the Saints to gather to their own lands and congregate with their own people.

Like the Church, the concept of Zion has grown and expanded over time. Erastus Snow pointed out in 1884 that when the early Saints "first heard the fullness of the Gospel preached by the first Elders, and read the revelations given through the Prophet Joseph Smith, our ideas of Zion were very limited. But as our minds began to grow and expand, why we began to look upon Zion as a great people, and the Stakes of Zion as numerous.... We ceased to set bounds to Zion and her Stakes."[12] Likewise, Joseph Young explained that many Saints of the nineteenth century misconstrued and miscalculated on a number of matters, including the time when the Saints should return to Missouri and redeem Zion. "The Holy Spirit brought many things close to their minds—they appeared right by, and hence many were deceived.... I knew that faith and the Holy Ghost brought the designs of Providence close by, and by that means we were enabled to scan them,...but we had not knowledge enough to digest and fully comprehend those things."[13]

Zion is the City of God, while Babylon is the city of Satan. Both work upon the souls of their municipals. Both seek to build an allegiance and a loyalty among its citizenry. While Zion looks to the Almighty God for strength and direction, Babylon specializes in idolatry: the people of Babylon seek "not the Lord to establish his righteousness, but every man walketh in his own way, and after the image of his own god, whose image is in the likeness of the world, and whose substance is that of an idol, which waxeth old and shall perish in Babylon, even Babylon the great, which shall fall" (D&C 1:16).

While in the end Babylon will produce withered and benighted souls whose chief aim is self-aggrandizement, Zion seeks to reconcile the irreconcilable, to produce both social union and mature and dynamic individualism. Stephen L. Richards, a counselor in the First Presidency, observed that "there is no fence around Zion or the world, but to one of discernment, they [Zion and Babylon] are separated more completely than if each were surrounded with high unscalable walls. Their underlying concepts, philosophies, and purposes are at complete variance one with another. The philosophy of Zion is humility, not servility, but a willing recognition of the sovereignty of God and dependence on his providence."[14]

Zion is a place. Zion is a people. Zion is a holy state of being. In the words of Spencer W. Kimball, Zion is "the highest order of priesthood society."[15] It is the heritage of the Saints. "The building up of Zion," Joseph Smith taught, "is a cause that has interested the people of God in every age; it is a theme upon which prophets, priests, and kings have dwelt with peculiar delight; they have looked forward with joyful anticipation to the day in which we live; and fired with heavenly and joyful anticipations they have sung and written and prophesied of this our day; but they died without the sight; we are the favored people that God has made choice of to bring about the latter glory."[16] This is the destiny of those who endure faithfully to the end. In that sense, as Joseph Smith stated, "We ought to have the building up of Zion as our greatest object."[17]

ENDNOTES

1. Wright, *Simply Christian*, 31.
2. *Discourses of Wilford Woodruff*, 30.
3. Smith, *TPJS*, 366.

4. Joseph Young, "Vocal Music," 14–15.

5. Young, *JD* 10:224.

6. Ibid., 8:279.

7. Ibid., 2:253.

8. Ibid., 8:198.

9. Ibid., 8:205.

10. Smith, *Words of Joseph Smith*, 415.

11. McConkie, *A New Witness for the Articles of Faith*, 595.

12. Snow, *JD* 25:30–31.

13. Joseph Young, *JD* 9:230.

14. Richards, CR, October 1951, 877.

15. Kimball, CR, October 1977, 125.

16. Smith, *TPJS*, 231–32.

17. Ibid., 160.

TWENTY-ONE

Hard Issues

LEST I GIVE THE wrong impression, not everything that Latter-day Saints do is lovely and uplifting and edifying. Not everything that was taught or practiced in the past is easily understood. There are questions to be answered, issues to be addressed, hard topics to be engaged. For example:

Plural Marriage. Because the practice of plural marriage comes up so often in a discussion of Joseph Smith and The Church of Jesus Christ of Latter-day Saints, the following are some brief observations. The Church of Jesus Christ of Latter-day Saints teaches that marriage is more than a civil ordinance. It is, first and foremost, an institution ordained of God. Marriage between one man and one woman is sacred. Further, Latter-day Saints believe that marriage and the family were intended to last forever, to survive death. We teach, therefore, that marriages performed in temples, by the proper authority, are not ended with the death of the marriage partners but rather endure for time and all eternity.

During the ministry of Joseph Smith, and continuing for over fifty years, plural marriage was practiced. Latter-day Saints practiced plural marriage because they believed God had commanded them to do so. Plural marriage was a religious principle, and this is the only valid explanation as to why the practice was maintained in spite of decades of opposition and persecution. Although it was introduced by Joseph Smith on a very selective basis during his administration as president of the Church (1830–44), the principle of plural marriage was first announced publicly in a general conference of the Church in April 1852 during the administration of President Brigham Young.

Latter-day Saints believe that the practice of plural marriage was a part of the "restitution of all things" (Acts 3:21; D&C 132:40, 45), the grand plan of restoration by which principles, doctrines, covenants, and ordinances (sacraments) from ancient times were restored to earth. Church leaders are quick to observe that monogamy is the rule and polygamy is the exception; unauthorized practice of this principle is condemned in the Book of Mormon (Jacob 2:23, 30, 34; 3:5), Doctrine and Covenants (D&C 132:38–39), the sermons of Joseph Smith himself, and teachings of current Church leaders.

Most all of those who became Latter-day Saints during the nineteenth century had been associated with other religious societies before their conversion and had been reared in traditional monogamous homes. The idea of having more than one wife came into sharp contrast with all they had been taught and brought up to believe. Therefore plural marriage was at first extremely difficult for many of the Saints to accept, including Church presidents Joseph Smith, Brigham Young, and John Taylor. President Taylor remarked that "it was the one of the greatest crosses that ever was taken up by any set of men since the world stood."[1] Brigham Young declared: "It was the first time in my life that I had desired the grave, and I could hardly get over it for a long time. When I saw a funeral I felt to envy the corpse its situation and to regret that I was not in the coffin."[2] Latter-day Saints believed that whatever God commanded was right, and that plural marriages, when properly performed by authorized persons, were both legal and acceptable to God. Men and women within a plural marriage family were expected to demonstrate loyalty and devotion to spouse and to observe the highest standards of fidelity and morality.

There is scriptural precedent for plural marriage in the lives of noble and faithful men and women in the Old Testament. For example, Abraham, Jacob, and Moses took additional wives (Genesis 16:1–11; 29:28; 30:4, 9, 26; Exodus 2:21; Numbers 12:1), and there is no indication that God disapproved of their actions in any way. In fact, note the words of Jesus : "I say unto you, That many shall come from the east and west, and shall sit down with Abraham, and Isaac, and Jacob, in the kingdom of heaven" (Matthew 8:11). God did condemn King David's unauthorized relationship with Bathsheba (2 Samuel 11–12) and King Solomon's marriages to foreign women who turned his heart away from the worship of Jehovah (1 Kings 11). As to New Testament times, Elaine Pagels has indicated that authorized plural marriages took place in the days of Jesus.[3]

Only a small percentage of the Church population was involved, and members of the Church who entered into this order of matrimony did so under the direction of the presiding authorities of the Church. Orson Pratt, one of the early Latter-day Saint apostles who was at first opposed to the principle, stated later: "How are these things to be conducted? Are they to be left at random? Is every servant of God at liberty to run here and there, seeking out the daughters of men as wives unto themselves without any restrictions, law, or condition? No. We find these things were restricted in ancient times. Do you not recollect the circumstances of the Prophet Nathan's coming to David? He came to reprove him for certain disobedience.... Nathan the Prophet, in relation to David, was the man that held the keys concerning this matter in ancient days; and it was governed by the strictest laws.

"So in these last days...there is but one man in all the world, at the same time, who can hold the keys of this matter, but one man has power to turn the key to enquire of the Lord, and to say whether I, or these my brethren, or any of the rest of this congregation, or the Saints upon the face of the whole earth, may have this blessing of Abraham conferred upon them; he holds the keys of these matters now, the same as Nathan, in his day."[4]

Faced with a national antipolygamy campaign, many Latter-day Saint women startled their Eastern sisters (who had equated plural marriage with the oppression of women) by publicly demonstrating in favor of their right to live plural marriage as a religious principle. In January 1870 thousands of women met in the Salt Lake Tabernacle in what they called the Great Indignation Meeting; these women gathered to manifest their protest against antipolygamy laws. Nevertheless, public opposition in the United States to the practice of plural marriage grew during the last quarter of the nineteenth century. A number of Church officials were incarcerated, and the government threatened to confiscate Church property, including the temples. In the wake of oppressive laws that had been enacted, President Woodruff issued what has come to be known as the Manifesto, and a constituent assembly of the Latter-day Saints in general conference accepted it in October 1890. The Manifesto brought about a noticeable change in attitude toward the Church, and by 1896 Utah was granted statehood.

President Gordon B. Hinckley explained: "I wish to state categorically that this Church has nothing whatever to do with those practicing polygamy. They are not members of this Church. Most of them have never been members.... If any of our members are found to be practicing plural marriage, they are excommunicated, the most serious penalty the Church can impose.... More than a century ago God clearly revealed ...that the practice of plural marriage should be discontinued, which means that it is now against the law of God."[5]

Latter-day Saints believe in "obeying, honoring, and sustaining the law" (Articles of Faith 1:12). While they stand firmly against the practice of plural marriage today, they leave in the hands of local magistrates the enforcement of the civil law. In speaking of those who continue the practice, President Hinckley said: "They are in violation of the civil law. They know they are in violation of the law. They are subject to its penalties. The Church, of course, has no jurisdiction whatever in this matter."[6]

Blacks and the Priesthood. A second sensitive issue for the Church has to do with the restriction of priesthood blessings maintained by the Church for so long. Sometime late in the 1830s, Joseph Smith established a practice that the blessings of the priesthood should be withheld from black members of The Church of Jesus Christ of Latter-day Saints. This practice continued in the Church through Joseph Smith's successors until the announcement of a revelation received by President Spencer W. Kimball in June 1978. There is no statement directly from Joseph Smith himself offering commentary or doctrinal explanation for such an action, though the scriptural basis for a lineage-based granting or denial of priesthood anciently may be found in the Pearl of Great Price (Moses 7:8, 22; Abraham 1:21–27; see also Genesis 4:1–15; Moses 5:18–41). Leaders of the Church have repeatedly affirmed that the position of the Church in regard to who does and does not bear the priesthood is a matter of revelation from heaven and not simply social or political expediency.

As to the fact that certain individuals or groups of people have not always had access to the full blessings of the gospel or the priesthood, there is also scriptural precedent. From the days of Moses to the coming of Jesus Christ, the Aaronic or Levitical Priesthood was conferred only upon worthy descendants of the tribe of Levi. In the first Christian century, the message of salvation was presented first to the Jews (the "lost sheep of the house of Israel," Matthew 10:5–6; 15:24) and then later, primarily through the labors of the apostle Paul, to the Gentile nations. Ultimately the blessings of the Lord are for all people, "black and white, bond and free, male and female; and he remembereth the heathen; and all are alike unto God, both Jew and Gentile" (2 Nephi 26:33). We do not know why the priesthood was withheld for so long. We do know, however, that God has a plan, a divine timetable by which his purposes are brought to pass in and through his children on earth. He knows the end from the beginning and the times before appointed for specific doings and eventualities (see Acts 17:26). That timetable may not be ignored, slighted, or altered by finite man. The faithful seek to live in harmony with God's will and go forward in life with all patience and faith.

Women and the Priesthood. Latter-day Saint women are not ordained to the priesthood. The leaders of the Church have instructed that men and women have roles in life that are equally important but different. Some roles are best suited to the masculine nature, while women have natural and innate capacities to do some things that are more difficult for men. Because of the sanctity of the family and the home and because of the vital nature of the family in the preservation of society, Latter-day Saints teach that motherhood is the highest and holiest calling a woman can assume. Women should search, study, learn, prepare, and develop in every way possible—socially, intellectually, and spiritually—but no role in society will bring as much fulfillment or contribute more to the good of humankind than motherhood.

There is nothing in the doctrine of Mormonism to suggest that to be a man is preferred in the sight of God, or that the Almighty loves males more than females. Latter-day Saint doctrine condemns unrighteous dominion in any form as well as any type of discrimination because of race, color, or gender. God is no respecter of persons. Women are the daughters of God and entitled to every spiritual gift, every virtue, and every fruit of the Spirit. Priesthood is not maleness, nor should it be equated with male administration. A man who holds the priesthood does not have any advantage over a woman in qualifying for salvation in the highest heaven. Priesthood is divine authority given to worthy men, as a part of God's great plan of happiness. Why it is bestowed upon men and not women is not known. The highest ordinances of the priesthood, received in the temple, are given only to a man and a woman together.

Elder James E. Talmage stated: "In the restored Church of Jesus Christ, the Holy Priesthood is conferred, as an individual bestowal, upon men only, and this in accordance with Divine requirement. It is not given to woman to exercise the authority of the Priesthood independently; nevertheless, in the sacred endowments associated with the ordinances pertaining to the House of the Lord, woman shares with man the blessings of the Priesthood. When the frailities and imperfections of mortality are left behind, in the glorified state of the blessed hereafter, husband and wife will administer in their respective stations, seeing and understanding alike, and co-operating to the full in the government of their family kingdom. Then shall woman be recompensed in rich measure for all the injustice that womanhood has endured in mortality. Then shall woman reign by Divine right, a queen in the resplendent realm of her glorified state, even as exalted man shall stand, priest and king unto the Most High God. Mortal eye cannot see nor mind comprehend the beauty, glory, and majesty of a righteous woman made perfect in the celestial kingdom of God."[7]

Apostates, Dissidents, and a Violent Faith. If one really wants to better understand present-day Mormonism, why study break-off groups, apostates, those who have distorted and perverted the tenets of the faith? Why make repetitive use of the misleading phrase "Mormon fundamentalists" to describe apostates from The Church of Jesus Christ of Latter-day Saints? If anything, the Mother Church in Salt Lake City is the source of Mormon fundamentalism. Fundamentalists are by definition people who hold to the fundamentals of the faith, not those who refuse to change and refuse to adapt to the changes inherent in a living church. Truly one of the most *fundamental* tenets of the Latter-day Saints is the need to follow the living prophet. In short, while the Latter-day Saints admire, respect, and even revere the founding prophet and president, Joseph Smith—and acknowledge that most of the doctrine of the faith came through his instrumentality—they identify theirs is a "living church."

While it has been the craze of some to try to link Joseph Smith and his claims to visions and revelations with necromancy, black magic, and the occult, the evidence for such claims is flimsy and questionable. While it is still the rage for historians to refer to Fawn M. Brodie's psycho-biography of Joseph Smith as the final word, it really is time for serious scholars to move on and acknowledge an entire corpus of literature on the life and work of Joseph Smith that has grown up since the 1940s. Questionable works on Joseph Smith's "magic worldview" represent a disappointing effort to squeeze the Mormon Prophet's actions into a preconceived model, finding at last that it simply isn't a good fit.

As mentioned earlier in this work, during the period known as the Mormon Reformation, individual members and families were encouraged strongly to observe with exactness the standards of the faith and return to the obedience they had enjoyed prior to the exodus to the Great Basin. In addition, a number of sermons were delivered by Church leaders that clearly had the intention of striking fear into the hearts of the members—both condemning their sins and warning them of the dreadful consequences of sin. Like Jonathan Edwards speaking of "sinners in the hands of an angry God," Brigham Young and Jedidiah M. Grant delivered fiery sermons that were far more of revival rhetoric than they were reflections of Mormon doctrine or practice. As far as the Latter-day Saints are concerned, the only blood atonement that has any efficacy, virtue, or force, either in time or eternity, is the blood Atonement of Jesus Christ. His is the only name and His is the only blood by which men and women can be saved. While some of these sermons even threatened peoples' lives if they wandered from the path of righteousness, there is no historical evidence whatsoever that people were put to death for disobedience.

Surely no critique of Mormonism would be complete without some mention of the Mountain Meadows Massacre. Indeed, the massacre is truly one of the black marks on our history, an event that has spawned ill will, guilt, and embarrassment for a century and a half. To be sure, there were many things leading up to the massacre: the fact that Johnston's army was coming to Utah and that the "Utah War" seemed inevitable; the fact that Apostle Parley P. Pratt had recently been brutally assassinated in Arkansas; the fact that some of those who accompanied the Arkansans through the Utah Territory were Missourians who claimed to have had a role in the Hauns Mill Massacre; and the rather incendiary sermons of Church leaders toward those outside the faith who were seeking to disturb the peace. In other words, there was in the air a tension, a stress, a war hysteria that hung over the people—Mormon and non-Mormon alike—like a dark shroud. As a result of these and perhaps other factors that incited the local Mormon leaders and settlers to react, the massacre occurred and 120 people died. There may have been reasons the Latter-day Saints chose to act as they did, but in reality there is no excuse for what took place. It was an act of savage brutality, both uncivilized and un-Christian, a terrible atrocity. The Saints knew better and had been taught to abide by a higher standard.

One of the attacks leveled regularly against Mormon society is that it is patriarchal. It is true that Latter-day Saints are firm believers in the Old Testament and that families today are organized in a patriarchal manner. But for Latter-day Saints the patriarchal order is a family-centered government, a home where husband and wife counsel together and make decisions in conjunction with the family, not a place where the man rules with an iron scepter in dictatorial fashion. The doctrine of the Church is that a man and a woman enter the patriarchal order when they enter into eternal marriage, when they are married in the temple. They then begin a new eternal family unit. The priesthood is neither male nor female, but instead God's divine authority. Why it is conferred upon men and not women is not known, but men who are ordained to the priesthood are expected to lead their families with humility, love, patience, and tenderness, even as Christ leads the Church (Ephesians 5:23).

Church leaders have repeatedly warned the men of the Church that any effort to bully or dominate either their wives or their children is a violation of priesthood principles and results in the loss of God's sustaining Spirit. For example, one Church president, Howard W. Hunter, stated: "A man who holds the priesthood accepts his wife as a partner in the leadership of the home and family with full knowledge of and full participation in all decisions relating thereto.... Presiding in righteousness necessitates a shared responsibility between husband and wife; together you act with knowledge and participation in all family matters. For a man to operate independently of or without regard to the feelings and counsel of his wife in governing the family is to exercise unrighteous dominion."[8]

As to the matter of dissent within the Church, it is a fact that a member of the Church is free to feel how he or she chooses to feel about a given doctrine or practice. Agency is paramount in the Church, and thus no one is forced to believe or observe the principles of the Church. The Church has drawn the line, however, between one's personal dissent and their tendency to publish the same widely. Apostasy consists of continuing in the teaching of false doctrines or the voicing of one's dissent in public forums after having been counseled by Church leaders. There are within the Church disciplinary measures that are occasionally implemented in dealing with apostasy, just as is the case in other religious organizations; Latter-day Saints are not alone in such a stance. Noted Roman Catholic scholars such as Hans Küng and Charles Curran and Evangelical Christian writers such as Clark Pinnock and John Sanders have had firsthand experience with censure following their expression of views at variance with more popular opinions. In short, a person who is dissatisfied with life within Mormonism or uncomfortable with the teachings of the faith is at liberty to ask questions, discuss the issues, and even, sadly, to leave the faith as a final resort. They are not, however, permitted to continue to fight the Church, stir discontent, and sow discord among the members.

In speaking to those Latter-day Saints who have been hurt or embarrassed or taken advantage of by someone bearing LDS Church membership, Boyd K. Packer asked: "Have you ever in your life attended any Church meeting…where any encouragement or authorization was given to be dishonest, to cheat in business, or to take advantage of anyone?...

"Have you read, or do you know of anything in the literature of the Church, in the scriptures themselves, in lesson manuals, in Church magazines or books, in Church publications of any kind, which contains any consent to lie, or to steal, to misrepresent, to defraud, to be immoral or vulgar, to profane, to be brutal, or to abuse any living soul?...

"Have you ever been encouraged in a training session, a leadership meeting, or an interview to transgress or misbehave in any way? Have you ever been encouraged to be extreme or unreasonable or intemperate?...

"You are inside the Church where you can see at close hand the conduct of bishops [pastors] or Relief Society [women's organization] presidents," or other local or general Church leaders. "Could such conduct be described as being typical of them? ...

"You are active and have held positions in the Church. Surely you would have noticed if the Church promoted any of these things in any way....

"Why then," I [ask], "when you hear reports of this kind, should you feel that the Church is to blame?...

"There are those who assume that if someone is depressed, the Church must have caused it. If there is a divorce, somehow the Church is to blame. And on and on."[9]

I suppose that as long as you and I are mortals we will be prone to sin and error and poor judgment. Mormons are under the influence of the same Fall as other people of the earth, and so our perspectives are sometimes myopic and our decisions faulty. Fortunately or unfortunately, when a Latter-day Saint is pronounced guilty of a serious crime, the fact that he or she is a Mormon is almost always mentioned or even dwelt upon at length. I suppose that such a singling out is a bit of a backhanded compliment of sorts: to some extent at least, Mormons are expected to be law-abiding and honorable folks, and the public expects more from them. They have certainly been taught better. But they are, sadly enough, human beings. And human beings make mistakes.

ENDNOTES

1. Taylor, *JD* 11:221.
2. Young, *JD* 3:266.
3. Pagels, *Adam, Eve, and the Serpent*, 11.
4. Pratt, *JD* 1:63–64.
5. Hinckley, CR, October 1998, 92.
6. Ibid.
7. Talmage, "The Eternity of Sex," 602–3.
8. Hunter, CR, October 1994, 68.
9. Packer, *"That All May Be Edified."* 156–57.

TWENTY-TWO

"If a Man Die..."

I SAT BESIDE MY father only a matter of hours before his death in 1988. He knew, and I knew, that a chapter in his eternal journey was coming to a close. There was a yearning in my soul to communicate—no, to commune—about meaningful things, about things that matter most. We spoke at length about home and family and hereafter. We expressed our love to each other and brought to an end, at least for a short season, a sweet association, one that I look forward to resuming, even more than I can say.

I knew then that I would miss him, that our family, especially my mother, would mourn his loss, and that it would be impossible to completely fill the void of his passing. And yet there was no doubt whatsoever, in his heart or mine, that Albert Louis Millet would continue to live, that he was about to be transferred to another field of labor. I was totally at peace during those tender moments, and that consummate assurance continued through his death and funeral. It continues to this day. It is a peace borne of perspective, a peace undergirded by the doctrine of life beyond the grave. It is a peace that derives from that Spirit who confirms that what my father had taught me through the years relative to life after death was indeed true. Since that time I have on several occasions held the hand of those who stared death in the face, those sanctified souls whose lives equipped them to avoid the sting of death and almost seemed to rob the grim reaper of his victory. Doctrine informs. It inspires. It empowers.

It is comforting to know that God our Heavenly Father has a plan and that there is purpose to struggles and suffering, and even death. Our doctrine of a divine plan—including that which deals with heaven and the hereafter—is especially appealing to those who encounter Mormonism. "All men know they must die," Joseph Smith explained to the Latter-day Saints in Nauvoo. "And it is important that we should understand the reasons and causes of our exposure to the vicissitudes of life and of death, and the designs and purposes of God in our coming into the world, our sufferings here, and our departure hence.... It is but reasonable to suppose that God would reveal something in reference to the matter, and it is a subject we ought to study more than any other. We ought to study it day and night, for the world is ignorant in reference to their true condition and relation. If we have any claim on our Heavenly Father for anything, it is for knowledge on this important subject."[1]

Nothing is more common to mortals than death; it is the common lot of all who come into this life to leave it. Every man or woman is born, and every man or woman must die. All are born as helpless infants, and all depart this sphere equally helpless in the face of death. Death is something most of us fear, something from which we hide, something most of us would avoid if we could. Even among those who read by the lamp of gospel understanding, death is frequently viewed with fear and trembling. Wilford Woodruff "referred to a saying of Joseph Smith, which he heard him utter (like this), That if the people knew what was behind the veil, they would try by every means to... get there. *But the Lord in his wisdom had implanted the fear of death in every person that they might cling to life* and thus accomplish the designs of their Creator."[2]

In the purest sense, there is no death and there are no dead. When things die, they do not cease to be; they merely cease to be in this world. Life goes on. Death is a transition, a change in assignment, a transfer to another realm. When we die, the spirit continues to see and act and feel and associate; it is only the physical body that becomes inactive and lifeless for a season. And so it is that we use a term—death—to describe what appears to be from our limited perspective. From an eternal vantage point, however, there is only life. We speak often of a person's "untimely death." Generally we mean that it is untimely for us, for those who remain behind. Though it is true that individuals may hasten their death and thus shorten their day of probation, for the faithful there is nothing untimely about death. Joseph Fielding Smith thus stated: "May I say for the consolation of those who mourn, and for the comfort and guidance of all of us, that no righteous man is ever taken before his time. In the case of the faithful saints, they are simply transferred to other fields of labor. The Lord's work goes on in this life, in the world of spirits, and in the kingdoms of glory where men go after their resurrection."[3]

In a sense, we die as to premortality (our first estate) in order to be born into mortality (our second estate). Likewise, we must die as pertaining to time in order to be born into eternity. The separation of the physical body and the eternal spirit is a necessary part of the plan of God. Truly, death passes upon all men and women to fulfill "the merciful plan of the great Creator" (2 Nephi 9:6). It is merciful in the sense that it delivers us from the toils and agonies of this life. "When men are prepared," Joseph observed, "they are better off to go hence."[4] In speaking of little children who depart this life before they arrive at the age of accountability, he said: "The Lord takes many away even in infancy, that they may escape the envy of man, and the sorrows and evils of this present world; they were too pure, too lovely, to live on earth; therefore, if rightly considered, instead of mourning we have reason to rejoice as they are delivered from evil, and we shall soon have them again."[5]

Death is merciful too because it opens us to a new phase of life, a time wherein the restrictions of this mortal coil are gone and the mind or spirit can soar. Brigham Young, in speaking of the glory of what lies ahead, remarked: "I can say with regard to parting with our friends, and going ourselves, that I have been near enough to understand eternity so that I have had to exercise a great deal more faith to desire to live than I ever exercised in my whole life to live. The brightness and glory of the next apartment is inexpressible. It is not encumbered so that when we advance in years we have to be stubbing along and be careful lest we fall down. We see our youth, even, frequently stubbing their toes and falling down. But yonder, how different! They move with ease and like lightning."[6]

"How do we know," asked Elder Orson Pratt, "when this spirit is freed from this mortal tabernacle, but that all [our] senses will be greatly enlarged?

"Unclothe the spirit, and instead of exposing a small portion of it about the size of a pea to the action of the rays of light, the whole of it would be exposed…. I believe we shall be freed, in the next world, in a great measure, from these narrow, contracted methods of thinking. Instead of thinking in one channel, and following up one certain course of reasoning to find a certain truth, knowledge will rush in from all quarters…, informing the spirit, and giving understanding concerning ten thousand things at the same time; and the mind will be capable of receiving and retaining all."[7]

The severance of family ties through death is of all things most painful, bringing with it an avalanche of emotions, including loneliness and sorrow. Those of the household of faith are not spared such feelings. He who knows all things and has a present view of all time and eternity, even He is aware of such agonies. We weep and we long for a reassociation, but we do not grieve as those who have no hope (1 Thessalonians 4:13), for to do so is to express a lack of faith in the purposes and plan of God and to ignore the promise of reunion and restoration given by our Lord and Savior. Indeed, life's bitter winters may find us walking alone. During these cold and dark seasons of solitude, we wrap ourselves in the protective clothing of faith and its perspective and are warmed by precious memories. Thus we move on, seeking always to view things as God views them. "Precious in the sight of the Lord," the revealed word declares, "is the death of his saints" (Psalm 116:15). As taught in the Doctrine and Covenants "those that die shall rest from all their labors, and their works shall follow them; and they shall receive a crown in the mansions of my Father, which I have prepared for them" (D&C 59:2).

Death is not the end, but instead a significant point along the infinite line of life. Truly, Brother Joseph said, "This life is not all; the voice of reason, the language of inspiration, and the Spirit of the living God, our Creator, teaches us, as we hold the record of truth in our hands, that this is not the case, that this is not so; for, the heavens declare the glory of a God, and the firmament showeth His handiwork."[8] We are born, we die, we are born again, and we die. And thus the cycle of life continues everlastingly. If there were no death, there would be no life. If there were no death, then the growth and development and expansion that lie ahead would be forever withheld from us. There is purpose in life, and there is purpose in death. He who knows all things orchestrates the events of our existence and knows what is best for us. The Mormon Prophet therefore observed: "With respect to the deaths in Zion, we feel to mourn with those that mourn, but remember that the God of all the earth will do right."[9]

Latter-day Saint prophet-leaders have taught that the transition from time into eternity is immediate. As the individual breathes his last breath, his spirit leaves the body and passes directly into the postmortal world of spirits. Joseph Smith taught: "The spirits of the just are exalted to a greater and more glorious work; hence they are blessed in their departure to the world of spirits. Enveloped in flaming fire, *they are not far from us*, and know and understand our thoughts, feelings, and motions, and are often pained therewith."[10] "Is the spirit world here?" Brigham Young asked. "It is not beyond the sun, but is on this earth that was organized for the people that have lived and that do and will live upon it."[11] Parley P. Pratt similarly explained that the spirit world "is here on the very planet where we were born."[12]

At the time of one's entrance into the spirit world, the individual experiences what has been called a "partial judgment." He or she goes either to paradise or to hell (see also 1 Nephi 15:29; 2 Nephi 9:12). Paradise is the abode of the faithful, a state of happiness, "a state of rest, a state of peace, where they shall rest from all their troubles and from all care, and sorrow" (Alma 40:12). Paradise is a place where spirits "expand in wisdom, where they have respite from all their troubles, and where care and sorrow do not annoy."[13] On the other hand, the spirits of the wicked "shall be cast out into outer darkness; there shall be weeping, and wailing, and gnashing of teeth, and this because of their own iniquity, being led captive by the devil" (Alma 40:13).

Though there are divisions of some kind between the righteous and the wicked, all of the spirits of men and women are in one world, just as they are in the flesh. In the postmortal spirit world, the disembodied long for deliverance, seek for relief from their present condition;

they look upon the long absence of their spirits from their bodies as a bondage (D&C 45:17; 138:50; see also 138:15–18, 23). "When our spirits leave these bodies, will they be happy?" Orson Pratt asked. "Not perfectly so," he responded. "Why? Because the spirit is absent from the body; it cannot be perfectly happy while a part of the man is lying in the earth…. You will be happy, you will be at ease in paradise; but still you will be looking for a house where your spirit can enter and act as you did in former times."[14] Joseph Smith explained that "Hades, the Greek, or Sheol, the Hebrew, these two significations mean a world of spirits. Hades, Sheol, paradise, spirits in prison, are all one: it is a world of spirits."[15] In a later chapter we will discuss at some length the manner in which persons are taught the gospel hereafter.

"In this space between death and the resurrection of the body, the two classes of souls remain, in happiness or in misery, until the time which is appointed of God that the dead shall come forth and be reunited both spirit and body."[16] And so the postmortal spirit world is an intermediate stop for all men and women. It is a place of waiting, of repentance and suffering, of peace and rest, and of instruction and preparation. Those who receive and enjoy the blessings of the gospel or who receive the testimony of Jesus will come forth from the spirit world unto the first resurrection (see D&C 76:51, 74, 82). Those who continue to assert their own will and refuse the Savior's offer of enlightenment and renewal will remain in the spirit world until the thousand years are ended. Then in that second or last resurrection they will come forth.

The apostle Paul taught that "if in this life only we have hope in Christ, we are of all men most miserable" (1 Corinthians 15:19). That is to say, if Jesus' greatest accomplishments consisted of his kindness, his generosity, and his sage advice, then our hope for happiness hereafter is unfounded. Like Paul, the Book of Mormon prophet Jacob declared that if Christ did not rise from the dead (as it was predicted that he would do), then we will one and all, at the time of death, be consigned to spiritual ruin and destruction; we will be forevermore subject to the devil. Why? Because if Jesus did not have the power to rise from the dead and thus redeem the body from the grave, then he surely did not have the power to forgive sins and thereby redeem the spirit from hell (2 Nephi 9:7–9; compare 1 Corinthians 15:12–17).

"If the resurrection from the dead be not an important point, or item in our faith," Joseph Smith explained, "we must confess that we know nothing about it; for if there be no resurrection from the dead, then Christ has not risen; and if Christ has not risen He was not the Son of God." On the other hand, "If He has risen from the dead the bands of the temporal death are broken that the grave has no victory. If then, the grave has no victory, those who keep the sayings of Jesus and obey His teachings have not only a promise of a resurrection from the dead, but an assurance of being admitted into His glorious kingdom."[17] Because Jesus Christ has risen from the dead, we also shall rise from the dead. Because he lives, we shall live also, beyond the grave.

The resurrected body is a spiritual body, meaning that it is immortal, not subject to death (1 Corinthians 15:44; Alma 11:45; D&C 88:27). "The soul [meaning, in this instance, the spirit] shall be restored to the body, and the body to the soul; yea, and every limb and joint shall be restored to its body; yea, even a hair of the head shall not be lost; but all things shall be restored to their proper and perfect frame" (Alma 40:23; see also 11:43). In speaking of the righteous who waited anxiously for the Savior's entrance into paradise, Joseph F. Smith wrote: "Their sleeping dust was to be restored unto its perfect frame, bone to his bone, and the sinews and the flesh upon them, the spirit and the body to be united never again to be divided, that they might receive a fulness of joy" (D&C 138:16). Latter-day prophets have instructed that the body comes forth from the grave as it is laid down, "whether old or young; there will not be 'added unto their stature one cubit,' neither taken from it; all will be raised by the power of God, having spirit in their bodies, and not blood."[18] We are not to understand that physical deformities will be a part of the resurrected body, for "deformity will be removed; defects will be eliminated, and men and women shall attain to the perfection of their spirits, to the perfection that God designed in the beginning."[19]

Finally, we have the comforting assurance that even though men and women are refined, renewed, and perfected body and soul in the resurrection, we will maintain our identity. We will know friends and loved ones in and after the resurrection, even as we know them now. In speaking of meeting a departed loved one in the future, Joseph F.

Smith taught: "I expect to be able to recognize her, just as I could recognize her tomorrow, if she were living..., because her identity is fixed and indestructible, just as fixed and indestructible as the identity of God the Father and Jesus Christ the Son. They cannot be any other than themselves. They cannot be changed; they are from everlasting to everlasting, eternally the same; so it will be with us. We will progress and develop and grow in wisdom and understanding, but our identity can never change."[20]

In the Book of Mormon, resurrection and eternal judgment are companion doctrines, just as are the Fall and Atonement. One of the great acts of mercy and grace is that all men and women who took a physical body will be resurrected and thereafter brought to stand before God to be judged of their works. In a sense, therefore, the Atonement overcomes spiritual death for all, at least for a short season wherein men stand once again in the divine presence. "And it shall come to pass that when all men shall have passed from this first death unto life, insomuch as they have become immortal, they must appear before the judgment-seat of the Holy One of Israel; and then cometh the judgment, and then must they be judged according to the holy judgment of God" (2 Nephi 9:15). Jesus "surely must die that salvation may come; yea, it behooveth him and becometh expedient that he dieth, to bring to pass the resurrection of the dead, that thereby men may be brought into the presence of the Lord" (Helaman 14:15; compare 3 Nephi 27:13–16). Finally, "because of Jesus Christ came the redemption of man. And because of the redemption of man, which came by Jesus Christ, they are brought back into the presence of the Lord; yea, *this is wherein all men are redeemed*" (Mormon 9:12–13, emphasis added).

"More painful to me are the thoughts of annihilation than death," Joseph Smith once declared.[21] The testimony of holy writ resounds: In Christ there is peace. In Christ there is hope, hope for deliverance from sin and death. There are no wrongs that will not be righted in time or eternity, no burdens that will not be lifted. Joseph Smith confidently promised: "All your losses will be made up to you in the resurrection, provided you continue faithful. By the vision of the Almighty I have seen it."[22]

No question could be more poignant than that posed by Job: "If a man die, shall he live again?" (Job 14:14). Latter-day Saints believe the scriptures. We believe the doctrine of life after death is neither myth nor metaphor, that the burden of holy writ is that we can exercise a lively hope in what lies ahead. Our identities continue. The resurrected body is a physical, tangible reality. The continuation of families and the resumption of valued associations are real. Jesus is the Christ, the Savior and Redeemer of our souls. He has "abolished death, and hath brought life and immortality to light through the gospel" (2 Timothy 1:10). "As mortals we all must die," President Gordon B. Hinckley explained. "Death is as much a part of eternal life as is birth. Looked at through mortal eyes, without comprehension of the eternal plan of God, death is a bleak, final, and unrelenting experience....

"But our Eternal Father, whose children we are, made possible a far better thing through the sacrifice of His Only Begotten Son, the Lord Jesus Christ. This had to be. Can anyone believe that the Great Creator would provide for life and growth and achievement only to snuff it all into oblivion in the process of death? Reason says no. Justice demands a better answer. The God of heaven has given one. The Lord Jesus Christ provided it."[23]

ENDNOTES

1. Smith, *TPJS*, 324.
2. *Diary of Charles L. Walker*, 1:595–96, emphasis added.
3. Smith, funeral address for Elder Richard L. Evans, 1.
4. Smith, *TPJS*, 326.
5. Ibid., 196–97.
6. Young, *JD* 14:231.
7. Pratt, *JD* 2:243, 246.
8. Smith, *TPJS*, 56.
9. Smith, *History of the Church* 1:341.

10. Smith, *TPJS*, 326, emphasis added.

11. Young, *JD* 3:372.

12. Pratt, *Key to the Science of Theology*, 80.

13. Joseph F. Smith, *Gospel Doctrine*, 448.

14. Pratt, *JD* 1:289–90.

15. Smith, *TPJS*, 310.

16. Joseph F. Smith, *Gospel Doctrine*, 448.

17. Smith, *TPJS*, 62.

18. Ibid., 199–200.

19. Joseph F. Smith, *Gospel Doctrine*, 23.

20. Ibid., 25.

21. Smith, *TPJS*, 296.

22. Ibid.

23. *Teachings of Gordon B. Hinckley*, 152.

TWENTY-THREE

Who Has Heard of Jesus?

SURELY NO QUESTION HAS so plagued the Christian world as the following: What of those who live and die and never hear of Jesus Christ—who he is, what he has done, and why his life and death matter? This has been termed by some as the "soteriological problem of evil." Soteriology is the study of salvation. The soteriological problem of evil might be stated as follows: If Jesus Christ is the only name by which salvation comes to people of all times and places (Acts 4:12), then what of the bulk of humanity who will go to their graves having never even heard his name spoken? What is the fate of the unevangelized?

Some believe that people are saved only if they accept the Lord Jesus Christ here and now, in this life. That includes a worship and practice of the only true God, a union with Christ through full acceptance of his saving grace and Atonement, and a Christian walk that reflects one's membership in the body of Christ. All others will be damned. There is no chance for salvation or receipt of the gospel hereafter. In short, in this view our eternal fate is sealed at death.

On the other end of the theological spectrum, there are those who point out that there is goodness and morality in religions and religious practices throughout the world; Christians do not have a monopoly on ethical decency. The philosopher John Hick has written that "if we define salvation as being forgiven and accepted by God because of Jesus' death on the cross, then it becomes a tautology that Christianity alone knows and is able to preach the source of salvation. But if we define salvation as an actual human change, a gradual transformation from natural self-centeredness (with all the human evils that flow from this) to a radically new orientation centered in God and manifested in the 'fruit of the Spirit,' then it seems clear that salvation is taking place within all of the world religions—and taking place, so far as we can tell, to more or less the same extent." He thus argues "on Christian grounds for a doctrine of universal salvation."[1]

A third approach: Justin Martyr, the early Christian apologist (ca. A.D. 100–165), believed that all are partakers of a general revelation through the universal logos, though in Jesus Christ the logos was revealed in its fullness. Likewise Irenaeus (ca. A.D. 130–200) contended that God has never been completely unknown to any race of people, inasmuch as the universal Spirit of Christ is inherent in the minds of men and women of all times and places. "For it was not merely for those who believed on Him in the time of Tiberius Caesar that Christ came, nor did the Father exercise his providence for the men only who are now alive, but for all men altogether, who from the beginning, according to their capacity, in their generation have both feared and loved God, and practiced justice and piety towards their neighbors, and have earnestly desired to see Christ, and to hear His voice. Wherefore He shall, at His second coming…give them a place in His kingdom."[2]

Beloved Christian writer C. S. Lewis pursued a similar, more inclusive path to this vexing question. Lewis explained that "those who put themselves in [God's] hands will become perfect, as He is perfect—perfect in love, wisdom, joy, beauty, and immortality. The change will not be completed in this life, for death is an important part of the treatment."[3] On another occasion he remarked: "Here is another thing that used to puzzle me. Is it not frightfully unfair that this new life [in Christ] should be confined to people who have heard of Christ and been able to believe in Him? But the truth is God has not told us what His arrangements about the other people are. We do know that no man can be saved except through Christ; we do not know that only those who know Him can be saved through Him."[4]

"There are people (a great many of them)," Lewis observed, "who are slowly ceasing to be Christians but who still call themselves by that name: Some of them are clergymen. There are other people who are slowly becoming Christians though they do not yet call themselves so.

There are people who do not accept the full Christian doctrine about Christ but who are so strongly attracted by Him that they are His in a much deeper sense than they themselves understand. There are people in other religions who are being led by God's secret influence to concentrate on those parts of their religion which are in agreement with Christianity, and who thus belong to Christ without knowing it.... Many of the good Pagans long before Christ's birth may have been in this position." In short, although "all salvation is through Christ, we need not conclude that He cannot save those who have not explicitly accepted Him in this life. And it should (at least in my judgment) be made clear that we are not pronouncing all other religions to be totally false, but rather saying that in Christ whatever is true in all religions is consummated and perfected."[5]

The Roman Catholic document *Lumen Gentium* states: "Those who, through no fault of their own, do not know the Gospel of Christ or his Church, but who nevertheless seek God with a sincere heart, and, moved by grace, try in their actions to do his will as they know it through the dictates of their conscience—those, too, may achieve eternal salvation." Father Richard John Neuhaus comments on these words as follows: "The rule is that God denies nobody, absolutely nobody, the grace necessary for salvation. What they do with that grace is another matter."[6]

A fourth position suggests that all have an opportunity to know of Christ and his salvation, even if that opportunity comes at or near the time of death. Proponents of this view teach that the message may come at the hand of mortals, inspired dreams, angels, or even by open vision or revelation. One view is that Jesus himself appears to each man or woman at the time of death and allows them to affirm or deny the faith. This is known as the "final option" theory. "Proponents of the theory maintain that the moment the soul is being separated from the body is the first time in an individual's existence that he or she has the ability to make a fully free personal act.... The soul is fully awake and aware of the seriousness of the situation. At this moment the soul ceases to act in a changeable way and acts rather with an unchangeable intent toward a particular end. Hence, the decision made at this moment is irreversible. The final distinguishing characteristic is that prior choices we have made deeply influence but do not determine our final decision. We may confirm to choose the way we have lived or we may reject it." Should one not, then, wait until death to decide for or against Christ? No, for "who can assure me that I will wish to change my stand later?"[7]

A fifth position taken by some Christians in regard to the soteriological problem of evil is what has variously been called future probation, second probation, eschatological evangelism, divine perseverance, and postmortem evangelism. According to this view, those who die without a knowledge of the gospel are not damned; they have an opportunity to receive the truth in the world to come. "God is resolute," one advocate of this position has pointed out, "never giving up on getting the Word out. In this world God will give us the power to spread the gospel far and wide. But the Word will also be declared to those we can't reach, even if it takes an eternity."[8] He adds that "God's love is patient and persistent. It outlasts us." Donald Bloesch has explained: "We do not wish to build fences around God's grace, …and we do not preclude the possibility that some in hell might finally be translated into heaven. The gates of the holy city are depicted as being open day and night (Isa. 60:11; Rev. 21:25), and this means that access to the throne of grace is possible continuously. The gates of hell are locked, but they are locked only from within."[9]

Latter-day Saints have taught since the days of Joseph Smith that some time during or just following the mortal ministry of Jesus, the doctrine of salvation for the dead was revealed to the first-century Church. In the fifteenth chapter of his first epistle to the Corinthians, the apostle Paul testifies of the resurrection of the Lord. Paul presents the core of that supernal message known to us as the gospel, or the "glad tidings," that Christ suffered for our sins, died, rose again the third day, and ascended into heaven. Paul showed the necessity for the Savior's rising from the tomb and explained that the physical evidence of the divine Sonship of Christ is the resurrection. If Christ had not risen from the dead, Paul asserted, the preaching of the apostles and the faith of the Saints would be in vain. "If in this life only we have hope in Christ," he said, "we are of all men most miserable" (1 Corinthians 15:19).

After establishing that the Lord has conquered all enemies, including death, Paul added: "And when all things shall be subdued unto him, then shall the Son also himself be subject unto him [the Father] that put all things under him, that God may be all in all. Else *what shall they do which are baptized for the dead,* if the dead rise not at all? why are they then baptized for the dead?" (1 Corinthians 15:28–29; emphasis added.) Verse 29 has spawned a host of interpretations by biblical scholars of various faiths. Many consider the original meaning of the passage to be at best "difficult" or "unclear." One commentator stated that Paul here "alludes to a practice of the Corinthian community as evidence for Christian faith in the resurrection of the dead. It seems that in Corinth some Christians would undergo baptism in the name of their deceased non-Christian relatives and friends, hoping that this vicarious baptism might assure them a share in the redemption of Christ."[10]

New Testament scholar Gordon Fee noted that "it is difficult to imagine any circumstances under which Paul would think it permissible for living Christians to be baptized for the sake of unbelievers in general. Such a view, adopted in part by the Mormons, lies totally outside the NT understanding both of salvation and of baptism."[11] Many non-Latter-day Saint scholars believe that in 1 Corinthians, Paul was denouncing or condemning the practice of baptism for the dead as heretical. This is a strange conclusion, since Paul uses the practice to support the doctrine of the resurrection. In essence, he says, "Why are we performing baptism in behalf of our dead, if, as some propose, there will be no resurrection of the dead? If there is to be no resurrection, would not such baptisms be a waste of time?"

On the subject of baptism for the dead, one non-Latter-day Saint scholar has recently observed: "Paul had no reason to mention baptism for the dead unless he thought it would be an effective argument with the Corinthians, so presumably he introduced what he thought was an inconsistency in the Corinthians' theology. In this case, some at Corinth might have rejected an afterlife but practiced baptism for the dead, not realizing what the rite implied." In addition, "Because his mention [of the practice] could imply his toleration or approval of it, many have tried to distance Paul from baptism for the dead or remove features regarded as offensive from it. Some maintain that Paul was arguing *ad hominem* or *ex concessu* in 1 Corinthians 15:29, so that he neither approved nor disapproved of the practice by referring to it. Yet it would have been unlike Paul to refrain from criticizing a practice he did not at least tolerate."[12] Or as Richard L. Anderson has pointed out: "Paul was most sensitive to blasphemy and false ceremonialism—of all people he would not have argued for the foundation truth of the resurrection with a questionable example. He obviously did not feel that the principle was disharmonious with the gospel."[13]

One of the early Christian documents linking the writings of Peter on Christ's ministry in the spirit world (see 1 Peter 3:18–20; 4:6) with those of Paul on baptism for the dead is the "Shepherd of Hermas," which states that "these apostles and teachers who preached the name of the Son of God, having fallen asleep in the power and faith of the Son of God, preached also to those who had fallen asleep before them, and themselves gave to them the seal of the preaching. They went down therefore with them into the water and came up again, but the latter went down alive and came up alive, while the former, who had fallen asleep before, went down dead but came up alive. Through them, therefore, they were *made alive,* and received the knowledge of the name of the Son of God."[14]

In a modern commentary on 1 Peter, the author observes that 1 Peter 3:19 and 4:6 are the only passages in the New Testament that refer to the ministry of Christ to the postmortal spirit world. "But 1 Peter would not be able," he points out, "to make such brief reference to this idea if it were not already known in the churches as tradition. What 1 Peter says in regard to this tradition is, in comparison with the traditions of the second century, quite 'apostolic.'" Through this means, he points out, "The saving effectiveness of [the Lord's] suffering unto death extends even to those mortals who in earthly life do not come to a conscious encounter with him, even to the most lost among them."[15]

On the afternoon of Tuesday, 8 May 1838, the Prophet Joseph answered a series of questions about the faith and practices of the Latter-day Saints. One of the questions was: "If the Mormon doctrine is true, what has become of all those who died since the days of the Apostles?" His response: "All those who have not had an opportunity of hearing the Gospel, and being administered unto by an inspired man in the flesh, must have it hereafter, before they can be finally judged."[16]

The first public discourse on the subject by Joseph was delivered on 15 August 1840 at the funeral of a man named Seymour Brunson. Simon Baker described the occasion: "I was present at a discourse that the prophet Joseph delivered on baptism for the dead 15 August 1840. He read the greater part of the fifteenth chapter of Corinthians and remarked that the Gospel of Jesus Christ brought glad tidings of great joy, and then remarked that he saw a widow in that congregation that had a son who died without being baptized, and this widow in reading the sayings of Jesus 'except a man be born of water and of the spirit he cannot enter the kingdom of heaven,' and that not one jot nor tittle of the Savior's words should pass away, but all should be fulfilled. He then said that this widow should have glad tidings in that thing. He also said the apostle [Paul] was talking to a people who understood baptism for the dead, for it was practiced among them. He went on to say that people could now act for their friends who had departed this life, and that the plan of salvation was calculated to save all who were willing to obey the requirements of the law of God. He went on and made a very beautiful discourse."[17]

In an epistle to the Twelve dated 19 October 1840, Joseph Smith stated: "I presume the doctrine of 'baptism for the dead' has ere this reached your ears, and may have raised some inquiries in your minds respecting the same.... I would say that it was certainly practiced by the ancient churches." Joseph then quotes from 1 Corinthians 15:29 and continues: "The Saints have the privilege of being baptized for those of their relatives who are dead, whom they believe would have embraced the Gospel, if they had been privileged with hearing it, and who have received the Gospel in the spirit, through the instrumentality of those who have been commissioned to preach to them while in prison."[18]

The good news or glad tidings of salvation in Christ is intended to lift our sights and bring hope to our souls, to "bind up the brokenhearted, to proclaim liberty to the captives, and the opening of the prison to them that are bound" (Isaiah 61:1). That hope in Christ is in the infinite capacity of an infinite Being to save men and women from ignorance, as well as from sin and death. The God of Abraham, Isaac, and Jacob is indeed the God of the living (Matthew 22:32), and his influence and redemptive mercies span the veil of death.

And so what of those who never have the opportunity in this life to know of Christ and his gospel; who never have the opportunity to be baptized for a remission of sins and for entrance into the kingdom of God; who never have the privilege of being bound in marriage and sealed in the family unit? In a world gripped by cynicism and strangled by hopelessness, the Latter-day Saints teach of a God of mercy and vision, of an Omnipotent One whose reach to his children is neither blocked by distance nor dimmed by death. Truly, as Joseph Smith explained, "It is no more incredible that God should save the dead, than that he should raise the dead."[19]

Before we close this discussion, there is a question that might appropriately be asked in regard to salvation for the dead: Why do missionary work? That is, why send our young people and experienced couples into the world to preach the gospel? Why spend so much money and expend so much time and effort when in fact all people will have the opportunity to hear about the gospel eventually in the world to come? First of all, we go into all the world in an effort to reach every creature because our Lord and Savior has commissioned us to do so (Matthew 28:19–20; Mark 16:15–16; D&C 68:8). But there is always a reason behind what the Lord commands, and so it is with missionary work. We have found one pearl of great price, something worth more than all the silver and all the gold of the earth; we simply want to share it with others. We don't want people to miss any blessing, any privilege, any joy that could be theirs through the fullness of the gospel. The doctrine of salvation for the dead, Joseph once declared, "presents in a clear light the wisdom and mercy of God in preparing an ordinance for the salvation of the dead, being baptized by proxy, their names recorded in heaven and they judged according to the deeds done in the body. This doctrine was the burden of the scriptures."[20]

ENDNOTES

1. Hick, "A Pluralist View," in *Four Views of Salvation in a Pluralistic World*, ed. Okholm and Phillips, 39, 43, 45.

2. Irenaeus, *Ante-Nicene Fathers* 1:494.

3. Lewis, *Mere Christianity*, 177.

4. Ibid., 65.

5. Ibid., 178.

6. Neuhaus, *Catholic Matters*, 24.

7. John Sanders, *No Other Name*, 164–65.

8. Gabriel Fackre, in Sanders, ed., *What about Those Who Never Heard?* 73, 78.

9. Bloesch, *Essentials of Evangelical Theology* 2:226–27.

10. Richard Kuegelman, "The First Letter to the Corinthians," in *Jerome Biblical Commentary*, 2:273.

11. Fee, *The First Epistle to the Corinthians*, 767.

12. Richard E. DeMaris, "Corinthian Religion and Baptism for the Dead (1 Corinthians 15:29): Insights from Archaeology and Anthropology," 678, 679.

13. Anderson, *Understanding Paul*, 405.

14. *The Shepherd of Hermas*, similitude 9.16.2–4; cited in Anderson, *Understanding Paul*, 407–8.

15. Leon Hard Goppelt, *A Commentary on First Peter*, 263, 259.

16. Smith, *TPJS*, 121.

17. Baker, in *Words of Joseph Smith*, 49.

18. Smith, *TPJS*, 179.

19. Ibid., 191.

20. Ibid., 193.

TWENTY-FOUR

Never-Ending Relationships

LATTER-DAY SAINTS BELIEVE THE family is the most important unit in time or in eternity. Families, not classes, are saved. Families, not church groups, are saved. "The home is the basis of a righteous life, and no other instrumentality can take its place, nor fulfill its essential functions."[1] Neal A. Maxwell, a modern Church leader, warned the Latter-day Saints that "healthy, traditional families are becoming an endangered species! Perhaps, one day, families may even rank with the threatened spotted owl in effective attention given!" He continued:

"When parents fail to transmit testimony and theology along with decency, those families are only one generation from serious spiritual decline, having lost their savor [see Matthew 5:13]. The law of the harvest [see Galatians 6:7–8] is nowhere more in evidence and nowhere more relentless than in family gardens!

"Society should focus anew on the headwaters—the family—where values can be taught, lived, experienced, and perpetuated. Otherwise, brothers and sisters, we will witness even more widespread flooding downstream, featuring even more corruption and violence (see Genesis 6:11–12; Matthew 24:37).

"As the number of dysfunctional families increases, their failures will spill into already burdened schools and streets. It is not a pretty scene even now.

"Nations in which traditional idealism gives way to modern cynicism will forfeit the blessings of heaven, which they so urgently need, and such nations will also lose legitimacy in the eyes of their citizens."[2]

Anticipating attacks on the family, in the 1960s a general directive from Church headquarters asked that Monday evenings be set aside by all members for Family Home Evening. No Church meetings or group activities were to be scheduled. The Family Home Evening is to be a time for gospel instruction as well as social activity. It is a time for the family to put aside work, school, and everyday pressures and focus on the things that matter most—parents and children, fathers and mothers, brothers and sisters. In addition, parents have been encouraged to read scripture and hold regular family devotionals, pray, and communicate meaningfully with their children. Family togetherness and family religious observance are intended to instill within the children the need for individual involvement with spiritual things.

To be sure, Mormons struggle to hold their families together, just as do people of other faiths. On the whole, however, studies show that LDS young people, especially those who have incorporated the teachings of the Church and the family, those who engage in private religious behavior, are much less prone to delinquency than other youth. The young people studied "appear to have internalized a set of religious values and practices that are related to less frequent participation in delinquent activity in both high and low moral communities. The relationship of religion with delinquency for this population is not entirely a cultural or social phenomenon. The link between religion and delinquency was just as robust in the low-LDS religious climate of the eastern states as it was in the powerful religious environments of Southern California, Idaho, and Utah."[3]

Mormons believe there is a commitment to the marriage union, a commitment to family life, and a commitment to Christian principles that flow from the ennobling concept of the eternal family. Once a man or a woman senses and realizes that their covenant with the spouse and with God are eternal, intended to span the veil of death and transcend time, they can hardly view one another in quite the same way. Small provocations between marriage partners, for example, seldom result in serious discussions about divorce, inasmuch as marriage and family have been exalted beyond the realm of social dynamics to that of an everlasting religious institution. One sociologist commented: "Mormons are more likely than other groups to marry; they are less likely to divorce; if they do divorce, they are more likely to remarry; and they are likely to bear a larger number of children. On each measure [of the study performed], there is a clearly-defined impact associated with one's religious affiliation. Those with no religion are generally least likely to marry, most likely to divorce if they marry, least likely to remarry following a divorce, and most likely to have the smallest family size.... Among Latter-day Saints, differences between temple and nontemple marriages enlarge the differences between frequent and infrequent attenders at religious services. Temple marriages are characterized by lower divorce rates and larger family sizes. Nontemple marriages are almost five times more likely to result in divorce than are temple marriages."[4]

Most of the official meetings of The Church of Jesus Christ of Latter-day Saints take place in church houses. These chapels are found throughout the world and are erected whenever a group of Latter-day Saints in the area is in a position to operate the programs of the Church. Sermons, worship services, religious instruction and study, many Church ordinances or sacraments, and social gatherings either take place in the chapel or are organized there. The chapel is thus an important locus of Church activity. But it does not house all that takes place in Mormonism, especially some of the most important features of the faith. The most sacred and lasting of Church sacraments are administered and received in temples. Like Israel of old, the ritual and religion of the holy temple give broadened meaning to all that is undertaken in that city of holiness we call Zion.

Within the power to perform temple marriage (also called eternal marriage, celestial marriage, and the new and everlasting covenant of marriage) is the power to unite man and woman according to the laws of the land. But also within that power (the "sealing power"), Latter-day Saints affirm, is the right to seal that union through death and into the world to come. This sealing power also binds and seals children to their parents, thus making the parents and children an eternal family. Joseph Smith taught that in the celestial glory there are three heavens or degrees, and that in order to enter into the highest, one must participate in the new and everlasting covenant of marriage (D&C 131:1–4).

Brother Joseph never lived to see the Nauvoo, Illinois, Temple completed and dedicated. The duty of administering the blessings of the temple to thousands of Saints before the exodus across the plains devolved upon Brigham Young and the Quorum of the Twelve Apostles. Before his martyrdom, however, the Prophet and the Twelve met in long and extended sessions in which significant truths and saving powers were delivered. On one occasion he said to the apostles: "I have sealed upon your heads all the keys of the kingdom of God. I have sealed upon you every key, power, [and] principle that the God of heaven has revealed to me. Now, no matter where I may go or what I may do, the kingdom rests upon you. But, ye apostles of the Lamb of God, my brethren, upon your shoulders this kingdom rests; now you have got to round up your shoulders and bear off the kingdom. If you do not do it you will be damned."[5]

It is not uncommon to have a Christian friend ask: "If you sincerely believe in the ransoming power and completed work of Jesus Christ, why do you as a people build and attend temples? Is salvation really in Christ, or must you enter the temple to be saved?" President Gordon B. Hinckley taught that "each temple built by The Church of Jesus Christ of Latter-day Saints stands as an expression of the testimony of this people that God our Eternal Father lives, that He has a plan for the blessing of His sons and daughters of all generations, that His Beloved Son, Jesus the Christ, who was born in Bethlehem of Judea and was crucified on the cross of Golgotha, is the Savior and Redeemer of the world, whose atoning sacrifice makes possible the fulfillment of that plan in the eternal life of each who accepts and lives the gospel."

"These unique and wonderful buildings," he stated on another occasion, "and the ordinances administered therein, represent the ultimate in our worship. These ordinances become the most profound expressions of our theology." Thus the temple is "a statement that we as a people believe in the immortality of the human soul.... It speaks of life here and life beyond the grave."[6]

Like most Christians, Latter-day Saints believe that the ancient tabernacle and temples were types of the Savior. That is, the "placement, the furniture, the clothing—each item was specified by the Lord to bear witness, in typology, symbolism, and similitude of Jesus Christ and his atoning sacrifice."[7] This appears to be the message of Hebrews, chapters 9–10. "Accordingly," one LDS writer has observed, "it should not seem surprising that the Atonement is a focal point of modern temple worship, just as it was in ancient times."[8] The temple and its ordinances are the highest channel of grace, indeed, the culminating channel, the means by which men and women are endowed with power from on high (see Luke 24:49). These ordinances serve as extensions and reminders of the Lord's infinite and eternal Atonement.

Because the ordinances or sacraments are essential—inasmuch as they represent, symbolize, and consummate our covenants with Christ—each son or daughter of God must receive the sacraments in order to gain the highest of eternal rewards. If the opportunity to receive such rites is not possible in mortality, it will be made available in the world to come. Thus temples become the place of covenant, the place of ordinance, for both the living and the dead. A living person may thus enter the temple and be baptized, for example, in behalf of one who has died. "This is a sanctuary of service," President Hinckley pointed out. "Most of the work done in this sacred house is performed vicariously in behalf of those who have passed beyond the veil of death. I know of no other work to compare with it. It more nearly approaches the vicarious sacrifice of the Son of God in behalf of all mankind than any other work of which I am aware.... It is a service of the living in behalf of the dead. It is a service which is of the very essence of selflessness."[9] Salvation is in Christ. We believe the temple to be a house of learning, of communion and inspiration, of covenants and ordinances, of service, and of personal refinement. We believe the temple is the house of the Lord. But it is not the Lord. We look to Christ the Person for salvation.

Consider the following statement by a respected Evangelical Christian pastor-teacher, a view that would reflect much of the sentiment of present-day Christendom:

> The question I'm most often asked about heaven is, "Will I be married to the same spouse in heaven?" Most are saying, "I don't want to lose my relationship with my wife; I can't imagine going to heaven and not being married to her."...

Marriage and other business of this life can sometimes intrude on more important matters of eternal concern. Paul writes, "He that is unmarried careth for the things that belong to the Lord, how he may please the Lord: but he that is married careth for the things that are of the world, how he may please his wife" (1 Corinthians 7:32–33). So if you can remain single, do. Concentrate on the things of the Lord, because marriage is only a temporary provision....

While married couples are heirs together of the grace of *this* life (cf. 1 Peter 3:7), the institution of marriage is passing away. There are higher eternal values.

Jesus Himself taught that marriage is an earthly union only....

In other words, angels don't procreate. Neither will we in heaven. All the reasons for marriage will be gone. Here on earth man needs a helper, woman needs a protector, and God has designed both to produce children. In heaven, man will no longer require a helper because he will be perfect. Woman will no longer need a protector because she will be perfect. And the population of heaven will be fixed. Thus marriage as an institution will be unnecessary....

But what of those of us who are happily married supposed to think of this? I love my wife. She's my best friend and my dearest companion in every area of life. If those are your thoughts about your spouse as well, don't despair! You will enjoy an eternal companionship in heaven that is more perfect than any earthly partnership. The difference is that you will have such a perfect relationship with every other person in heaven as well. If having such a deep relationship with your spouse here is so wonderful, imagine how glorious it will be to enjoy a perfect relationship with every human in the whole expanse of heaven—forever![10]

Now note the contrast in a statement from an early LDS apostle, Parley P. Pratt, who learned of eternal marriage and the perpetuation of the family from Joseph Smith:

It was at this time [in Philadelphia in 1839] that I received from [Joseph Smith] the first idea of eternal family organization, and the eternal union of the sexes in those inexpressibly endearing relation-ships which none but the highly intellectual, the refined and pure in heart, know how to prize, and which are at the very foundation of everything worthy to be called happiness.

Till then I had learned to esteem kindred affections and sym-pathies as appertaining solely to this transitory state, as something from which the heart must be entirely weaned, in order to be fitted for its heavenly state.

It was Joseph Smith who taught me how to prize the endearing relationships of father and mother, husband and wife; of brother and sister, son and daughter.

It was from him that I learned that the wife of my bosom might be secured to me for time and all eternity; and that the refined sympathies and affections which endeared us to each other ema-nated from the fountain of divine eternal love. It was from him that I learned that we might cultivate these affections, and grow and increase in the same to all eternity....

I had loved before, but I knew not why. But now I loved—with a pureness—an intensity of elevated, exalted feeling, which would lift my soul from the transitory things of this groveling sphere and expand it as the ocean. I felt that God was my heavenly Father indeed; that Jesus was my brother, and that the wife of my bosom was an immortal, eternal companion; a kind ministering angel, given to me as a comfort, and a crown of glory for ever and ever. In short, I could now love with the spirit and with the understanding also."[11]

Colleen McDannell and Bernhard Lang have written:

Expressions of the eternal nature of love and the hope for heavenly reunion, persist in contemporary Christianity.

Such sentiments, however, are not situated within a theological structure. Hoping to meet one's family after death is a wish and not a theological argument. While most Christian clergy would not deny that wish, contemporary theologians are not interested in articulat-ing the motif of meeting again in theological terms. The motifs of the

modern heaven—eternal progress, love, and fluidity between earth
and the other world—while acknowledged by pastors in their funeral
sermons, are not fundamental to contemporary Christianity. Priests
and pastors might tell families that they will meet their loved ones in
heaven as a means of consolation, but contemporary thought does
not support that belief as it did in the nineteenth century. There is no
longer a strong theological commitment.

The major exception to this caveat is the teaching of The
Church of Jesus Christ of Latter-day Saints, whose members are
frequently referred to as the Mormons. The modern perspective
on heaven—emphasizing the nearness and similarity of the other
world to our own and arguing for the eternal nature of love, family, progress, and work—finds its greatest proponent in Latter-day
Saints' (LDS) understanding of the afterlife. While most contemporary Christian groups neglect afterlife beliefs, what happens to
people after they die is crucial to LDS teachings and rituals. Heavenly theology is the result not of mere speculation, but of revelation
given to past and present church leaders.[12]

Temples point us back to the beginning; they affirm our lineal and
doctrinal connection to the ancients. Temples point to things in this
life that are of saving worth; they provide a firm but gentle and loving reminder of what matters most. Temples direct us to the world to
come; they focus our minds on the fact that life and love and learning
are forever, that glory and honor and immortality and eternal life await
the faithful. Truly, the course of the Lord is one eternal round (1 Nephi
10:19), for "this same Priesthood, which was in the beginning, shall
be in the end of the world also" (Moses 6:7). Temples are intended to
link the heavens and the earth; time and eternity; the past, present,
and future; husbands to wives and parents to children; and men and
women to Christ and the Father.

For Latter-day Saints salvation is a family affair. Now, lest someone leap to a confusion, we believe that the confession of one's sinfulness, expression of faith, process of repentance, ordinance of baptism,
reception of the Spirit, and the living out of one's profession of faith
in discipleship—all of these things must be an individual decision

and an individual process: We come unto Christ one by one. But the family is the most important unit in time or eternity, and thus family association is linked to the highest and grandest joys of the human soul. Simply stated, and in the words of M. Russell Ballard, a modern apostle, "What matters most is what lasts longest, and our families are for eternity."[13]

I sat with a friend of mine not long ago, a man who is of a different faith but one with whom I have developed a close and dear personal relationship. We were at the time, as we often are, engaged in religious conversation when he mentioned something about the temple and the LDS practice of temple marriage. I asked him: "Bill, we're friends, aren't we?" He nodded. I continued: "We trust one another, don't we?"

"Of course we do," he said.

"Are you willing to open up to me and speak what's in your heart?" I followed up.

"Yes, I am," he replied.

I said to Bill: "I'd like to ask you to take off your Presbyterian hat for just a moment, if you will."

"What do you mean?" he shot right back. "I'd like you to put away your Presbyterian way of thinking for just a matter of seconds and respond to some of my questions, answering from your heart rather than your head."

"I'll do my best," he said.

"You love your wife, Carol, don't you?"

"Of course I love Carol," he said. "You know that."

"You love those three children of yours with all your heart, don't you? There's not a thing in this world that you wouldn't do to demonstrate that love, protect them, and see to their happiness and well being, is there?"

"No," he responded, "there's nothing I wouldn't do, even give my life if necessary, to make sure they are happy and safe."

"Now, Bill, here's the question I want to pose to you," I remarked, "one that will require you to put away your religious training and just listen to your heart." The sobriety in Bill's eyes matched the sober mood that filled the room. Then I pursued my course: "You really do plan to be with Carol and Ted and Elizabeth and Larry after this life, don't you? You really do plan to spend eternity with them, in the presence of God, do you not?"

There was a long pause, followed by a soft but certain answer: "Yes, Bob, I do plan to spend eternity with them as their husband and their father."

I then added: "Well, my dear friend, what you need to understand and appreciate is that all LDS temples do is formalize the very thing you know to be true, deep down in your heart of hearts." Bill nodded.

"There is no union more sacred," Gordon B. Hinckley taught, "or more beautiful than a happily married husband and wife. There is no association that even approximates in the bonds of love, tenderness, and respect a family of parents and children. I ask, Would the God of heaven, who is our divine Father who loves us, fail to provide a means whereby His most precious creation, the human family, could not continue after the curtains of death quietly close? Our Heavenly Father has made provision for this. It is one of the great elements, the crowning element, of all that has come to us through the restoration of the gospel."[14]

ENDNOTES

1. David O. McKay, in *Family Home Evening Manual,* 1965, preface.

2. Maxwell, CR, April 1994, 119–22.

3. Chadwick and Top, "Religiosity and Delinquincy among LDS Adolescents," 51–67; see also Top and Chadwick, "The Power of the Word: Religion, Family, Friends, and Delinquent Behavior of LDS Youth," 293–310.

4. Albrecht, "The Consequential Dimension of Mormon Religiosity," 88, 91.

5. *Discourses of Wilford Woodruff,* 72.

6. *Teachings of Gordon B. Hinckley,* 623, 636, 638.

7. Tad R. Callister, *The Infinite Atonement*, 294.

8. Ibid., 295.

9. *Teachings of Gordon B. Hinckley*, 635.

10. John MacArthur, *The Glory of Heaven*, 135–38.

11. *Autobiography of Parley P. Pratt*, 297–98.

12. McDannell and Lang, *Heaven: A History*, 313, 322.

13. Ballard, CR, October 2005, 46.

14. Hinckley, member meeting, Sacramento, California, temple ground-breaking, 22 August 2004; cited in *Church News*, 3 December 2005, 2.

TWENTY-FIVE

Many Mansions

A T THE LAST SUPPER the Master said: "Let not your heart be troubled: ye believe in God, believe also in me. In my Father's house are many mansions: if it were not so, I would have told you. I go to prepare a place for you" (John 14:1–2.) This is a most intriguing statement. The Savior is saying, in essence: "It should be obvious, self-evident, to anyone that life hereafter consists of more than merely a heaven and a hell; if it were not so, I would have told you otherwise." Reason suggests that not all people are equally good, and thus not all good people deserve the same reward hereafter. Likewise, not all bad people are equally bad, and surely some are so bad that they deserve to sink to the lowest pit in hell.

In June 1830, Joseph Smith began a translation of the King James Bible, a labor to which he felt divinely directed and appointed, a work he considered to be a branch of his calling. The Prophet and his scribes progressed through the Book of Genesis until 7 March 1831, when they turned their attention to the New Testament. On 12 September 1831, Joseph relocated to Hiram, Ohio, to escape persecution. On 16 February 1832, Brother Joseph and his counselor, Sidney Rigdon, had translated much of the fifth chapter of John. In verse 28 the Savior indicates that the time will come when the dead will hear the voice of the Son of God and will come forth from the graves, "they that have done good, unto the resurrection of life; and they that have done evil, unto the resurrection of damnation." The Prophet felt impressed to alter the text as follows: "And shall come forth; they who have done good, *in the resurrection of the just*; and they who have done evil, *in the resurrection of the unjust*" (emphasis added). "Now this caused us to marvel," Joseph stated, "for it was given unto us of the Spirit. And while we meditated upon these things, the Lord touched the eyes of our understandings and they were opened, and the glory of the Lord shone round about" (D&C 76:18–19). What was then recorded is what the Latter-day Saints call the Vision of the Glories, section 76 of the Doctrine and Covenants, an interpretive commentary upon the Savior's words concerning "many mansions" in the world to come.

Philo Dibble, one who was present when the Vision was received, has left us the following fascinating account:

> The vision of the three degrees of glory which is recorded in the Doctrine and Covenants was given at the house of Father Johnson, in Hiram, Ohio, and during the time that Joseph and Sidney were in the Spirit and saw the heavens open there were other men in the room, perhaps twelve, among whom I was one during a part of the time, probably two-thirds of the time. I saw the glory and felt the power, but did not see the vision.
>
> Joseph wore black clothes, but at this time seemed to be dressed in an element of glorious white, and his face shone as if it were transparent, but I did not see the same glory attending Sidney....
>
> Joseph would, at intervals, say: "What do I see?" as one might say while looking out the window and beholding what all in the room could not see. Then he would relate what he had seen or what he was looking at.
>
> Then Sidney replied, "I see the same."
>
> Presently Sidney would say, "What do I see?" and would repeat what he had seen or was seeing.
>
> And Joseph would reply, "I see the same."
>
> This manner of conversation was repeated at short intervals to the end of the vision, and during the whole time not a word was spoken by any other person. Not a sound or motion was made by anyone but Joseph and Sidney, and it seemed to me that they never

moved a joint or limb during the time I was there, which I think was over an hour, and to the end of the vision.

Joseph sat firmly and calmly all the time in the midst of a magnificent glory, but Sidney sat limp and pale, apparently as limber as a rag, observing which, Joseph remarked, smilingly, "Sidney is not used to it as I am."[1]

In fact, the Vision actually consists of six visions, each of which we will now consider briefly. The first vision is brief, but it sets the stage for what follows; it places things in proper perspective in regard to the work of redemption and salvation, namely, that salvation is in Christ and comes through the shedding of his own blood and through his glorious rise to newness of life in the resurrection. The translators thus saw in vision "the glory of the Son, on the right hand of the Father, and received of his fullness; and saw the holy angels, and them who are sanctified before his throne, worshiping God, and the Lamb, who worship him forever and ever" (D&C 76:20–21). Doesn't this sound like what John the Revelator recorded concerning the Redeemer? Ten thousand times ten thousand proclaim: "Worthy is the Lamb that was slain to receive power, and riches, and wisdom, and strength, and honour, and glory and blessing" (Revelation 5:12).

The translators bore witness of the Redeemer in powerful language: "And now, after the many testimonies which have been given of him, this is the testimony, last of all, which we give of him: That he lives! For we saw him, even on the right hand of God; and we heard the voice bearing record that he is the Only Begotten of the Father, that by him, and through him, and of him, the worlds are and were created, and the inhabitants thereof are begotten sons and daughters unto God" (D&C 76:22–24). Truly, the testimony of Jesus is the spirit of prophecy (Revelation 19:10), and all the holy prophets, from the beginning, have testified of the One who called and sent them (see Acts 10:43; Jacob 4:4; 7:11; Mosiah 13:33). This testimony affirms the burden of scripture—that Christ was and is the Creator of worlds without number (Moses 1:33; 7:30; see also Ephesians 3:9; Hebrews 1:1–2).

Having laid the foundation of our faith through a discussion of redemption in Christ, the Prophet and Sidney Rigdon now learned a vital element of the Plan of Salvation: the nature of opposition through Satan and satanic influences. Lucifer is described in the Vision as one "who was in authority in the presence of God," who rebelled against the Father and the Son in the premortal council in heaven, thus becoming known as perdition, meaning ruin or destruction. Because he was indeed a spirit son of God, the heavens wept over his defection. He coveted the throne of the Father and proposed to save all of the sons and daughters of God in a way contrary to the Plan of the Father (Moses 4:1–4). Lucifer becomes thereby an enemy to God and to all righteousness. "Wherefore, he maketh war with the saints of God, and encompasseth them round about" (D&C 76:25–29).

Verses 30–49 describe those who have once known light and truth and the revelations of heaven and who choose knowingly to deny the light and defy God and his work (v. 31). These are the sons of perdition, "vessels of wrath, doomed to suffer the wrath of God, with the devil and his angels in eternity" (v. 33). We are taught elsewhere that "it is impossible for those who were once enlightened, and have tasted of the heavenly gift, and were made partakers of the Holy Ghost, and have tasted the good word of God, and the powers of the world to come, if they shall fall away, to renew them again unto repentance" (compare Hebrews 6:4–6 and 10:26–29).

"What must a man do to commit the unpardonable sin?" Joseph asked. "He must receive the Holy Ghost, have the heavens opened unto him, and know God, and then sin against Him. After a man has sinned against the Holy Ghost, there is no repentance for him. He has got to say that the sun does not shine while he sees it; he has got to deny Jesus Christ when the heavens have been opened unto him, and to deny the plan of salvation with his eyes open to the truth of it; and from that time he begins to be an enemy." He continues: "When a man begins to be an enemy to this work, he hunts me, he seeks to kill me, and never ceases to thirst for my blood. He gets the spirit of the devil, the same spirit that they had who crucified the Lord of Life, the same spirit that sins against the Holy Ghost. You cannot save such persons; you cannot bring them to repentance; they make open war, like the devil, and awful is the consequence."[2]

These are guilty of the unpardonable sin, and for them there is no forgiveness here nor hereafter, "having denied the Holy Spirit after having received it, and having denied the Only Begotten Son of the Father, having crucified him unto themselves and put him to an open shame" (vv. 34–35). They are guilty of "shedding innocent blood," meaning the innocent blood of Christ. "The blasphemy against the Holy Ghost," a later revelation affirms, "which shall not be forgiven in the world nor out of the world, is in that ye commit murder wherein *ye shed innocent blood, and assent unto my death*, after ye have received my new and everlasting covenant, saith the Lord God" (D&C 132:27, emphasis added). From an LDS perspective, the sons of perdition are the only ones who will be subject to the second spiritual death, the final expulsion from the presence of God. These, after being resurrected and standing before God to be judged (2 Nephi 9:15; Helaman 13:15–18), will be consigned to a kingdom of no glory.

Interestingly, it is in the midst of this gloomy scene that the Lord provides one of the most beautiful descriptions of the gospel of Jesus Christ, the "glad tidings," that "he came into the world, even Jesus, to be crucified for the world, and to bear the sins of the world, and to sanctify the world, and to cleanse it from all unrighteousness; that through him all might be saved whom the Father had put into his power and made by him; who glorifies the Father, and saves all the works of his hands, except those sons of perdition who deny the Son after the Father has revealed him" (vv. 40–43).

This third vision comes to an end with a sobering reminder that the particulars of the fate of the sons of perdition have not been revealed (vv. 45–48). In 1833, Joseph explained that "the Lord never authorized [certain individuals] to say that the devil, his angels, or the sons of perdition, should ever be restored; for their state of destiny was not revealed to man, is not revealed, nor ever shall be revealed, save to those who are made partakers thereof: consequently those who teach this doctrine have not received it of the Spirit of the Lord. Truly Brother Oliver [Cowdery] declared it to be the doctrine of devils."[3]

The scene shifts now as the translators are permitted to study and learn by contrast: from perdition to exaltation. They now behold the glories of the highest or celestial kingdom and provide broad descriptions of those who inhabit the same. They behold the inhabitants of the "resurrection of the just," what we call the first resurrection (compare Mosiah 15:21–25), the resurrection of celestial and terrestrial persons. The celestial are those who received the testimony of Jesus and also accepted the terms and conditions of the gospel covenant. They were baptized "after the manner of his burial" and received the gift of the Holy Ghost, thereby becoming "cleansed from all their sins" (vv. 50–52).

Those who inherit a celestial glory are they who "overcome by faith," who "withstand every temptation of the devil, with their faith on the Lord Jesus Christ" (Alma 37:33). They overcome the world in the sense that they have forsaken worldliness and the carnal attractions and given themselves to the Lord and his work. These are "sealed by the Holy Spirit of promise, which the Father sheds forth upon all those who are just and true" (v. 53). The Holy Spirit of Promise is the Holy Ghost, the Holy Spirit promised to the Saints. Since "the Comforter knoweth all things" (D&C 42:17; Moses 6:61), the Spirit is able to search the souls of men and women and to ascertain the degree to which people have truly yielded their hearts unto God, the degree to which they are "just and true" (D&C 76:53). Thus to be sealed by the Holy Spirit of Promise is to have the ratifying approval of the Spirit upon our lives, and upon the ordinances and covenants into which we have entered. It is to have passed the tests of mortality, to have qualified for celestial glory hereafter.

These are the ones who will accompany the Master when he returns in glory, those who, if they have already passed through the veil of death, will come forth from the grave in glorious immortality. The first resurrection that began at the time of Christ's resurrection (see Matthew 27:52–53) will thus resume. These are the ones whose names are written in heaven, in the Lamb's Book of Life (compare D&C 88:2), where God and Christ are the judge of all (D&C 63–65).

And then, lest we should conclude that such persons have attained to this highest degree of glory on their own, through their own merits and mortal accomplishments or without divine assistance, the word attests: "These are they who are *just men made perfect* through Jesus the mediator of the new covenant, who wrought out this perfect atonement through the shedding of his own blood" (v. 69, emphasis added). They are made perfect—whole, complete, fully formed, spiritually mature—through their covenant union with the Savior.

The next vision represents a continuation of the first resurrection or resurrection of the just. The translators witness the final state of those who chose to abide by goodness and equity and decency during their mortal lives but chose also not to receive and incorporate the fullness of that light and power that derive from the receipt of the everlasting gospel. The terrestrial glory is made up of those who did not receive the testimony of Jesus in this life—the testimony that he is the Savior and Redeemer of mankind—but afterward received it, that is, they received that witness in the postmortal spirit world (vv. 73–74). The terrestrial world is inhabited by those also who knew in this life that Jesus was the Christ but who were not valiant enough in that witness to receive the fullness of the gospel when it was presented to them.

Remembering that celestial persons receive the testimony of Jesus and also the gospel covenant, and that terrestrial persons receive the testimony of Jesus but not the gospel covenant, we now learn concerning the inhabitants of the telestial world: "These are they who received not the gospel of Christ, neither the testimony of Jesus" (v. 82; see also v. 101). They "deny not the Holy Spirit" (v. 83). That is, their wickedness is not such as to lead to complete perdition; they do not qualify to become sons of perdition. Instead, they "are thrust down to hell" (v. 84); at the time of their mortal death, they enter into that realm of the postmortal sphere we know as hell and are confronted with their sinfulness. These do not come forth from the grave until the "last resurrection," until the end of the Millennium, "until the Lord, even Christ the Lamb, shall have finished his work" (v. 85).

As is the case with the other kingdoms of glory, there are broad classifications of telestial people. These are they "who are of Paul, and of Apollos, and of Cephas. These are they who say they are some of one and some of another, some of Christ and some of John, and some of Moses, and some of…Isaiah, and some of Enoch; but received not the gospel, neither the testimony of Jesus, neither the prophets, neither the everlasting covenant" (vv. 99–101). Further, the telestial kingdom is the final abode of liars, sorcerers, adulterers and whoremongers, and, as John the Revelator learned, of murderers (v. 103; Revelation 21:8; 22:15).

Finally, the Vision adds the sobering detail that the inhabitants of the telestial world, "as innumerable as the stars in the firmament of heaven, or as the sand upon the seashore," will be "servants of the Most High; but where God and Christ dwell they cannot come, worlds without end" (vv. 109, 112). In short, the celestial body is qualitatively different from the terrestrial or the telestial body. Melvin J. Ballard pointed out that "One who gains possession of the lowest degree of the telestial glory may ultimately arise to the highest degree of that glory, but no provision has been made for promotion from one glory to another.... [T]hose who come forth in the celestial glory with celestial bodies have a body that is more refined. It is different. The very fiber and texture of the celestial body is more pure and holy than a telestial or terrestrial body, and a celestial body alone can endure celestial glory.... When we have a celestial body it will be suited to the celestial conditions, and a telestial body could not endure celestial glory. It would be torment and affliction to them. I have not read in the scripture where there will be another resurrection where we can obtain a celestial body for a terrestrial body. What we receive in the resurrection will be ours forever and ever."[4] As Spencer W. Kimball has written: "After a person has been assigned to his place in the kingdom, either in the telestial, the terrestrial or the celestial, or to his exaltation, he will never advance from his assigned glory to another glory. That is eternal! That is why we must make our decisions early in life and why it is imperative that such decisions be right."[5]

Although the telestial kingdom is the lowest of the kingdoms of glory, the inhabitants of that glory will be "heirs of salvation" in a world that "surpasses all understanding" (vv. 88–89). Generally speaking, the word *salvation* means in scripture exactly the same thing as exaltation or eternal life (see D&C 6:13; 14:7; Alma 11:40). There are those few times in scripture, however, where salvation refers to something less than exaltation (see, for example, D&C 132:17), and this is one of those. In this broad and expansive sense, our Lord seeks to save all of his children with an everlasting salvation. And he does so, in that all but the sons of perdition eventually inherit a kingdom of glory (v. 43). In fact, Charles W. Penrose gave the following insightful observation about the telestial kingdom:

"While there is one soul of this race, willing and able to accept and obey the laws of redemption, no matter where or in what condition it may be found, Christ's work will be incomplete until that being is brought up from death and hell, and placed in a position of progress, upward and onward, in such glory as is possible for its enjoyment and the service of the great God.

"The punishment inflicted will be adequate to the wrongs performed. In one sense the sinner will always suffer its effects. When the debt is paid and justice is satisfied; when obedience is learned through the lessons of sad experience; when the grateful and subdued soul comes forth from the everlasting punishment, thoroughly willing to comply with the laws once rejected; there will be an abiding sense of loss. The fullness of celestial glory in the presence and society of God and the Lamb are beyond the reach of that saved but not perfected soul, forever. The power of increase, wherein are dominion and exaltation and crowns of immeasurable glory, is not for the class of beings who have been thrust down to hell and endured the wrath of God for the period allotted by eternal judgment....

"Those who were cast down to the depths of their sins, who rejected the gospel of Jesus, who persecuted the Saints, who reveled in iniquity, who committed all manner of transgressions except the unpardonable crime, will also come forth in the Lord's time, through the blood of the Lamb and the ministry of His disciples and their own repentance and willing acceptance of divine law, and enter into the various degrees of glory and power and progress and light, according to their different capacities and adaptabilities. They cannot go up into the society of the Father nor receive of the presence of the Son, but will have ministrations of messengers from the terrestrial world, and have joy beyond all expectations and the conception of uninspired mortal minds. They will all bow the knee to Christ and serve God the Father, and have an eternity of usefulness and happiness in harmony with the higher powers. They receive the telestial glory."[6]

"Nothing could be more pleasing to the Saints upon the order of the Kingdom of the Lord," Joseph Smith stated, "than the light which burst upon the world through the foregoing vision. Every law, every commandment, every promise, every truth, and every point touching the destiny of man, from Genesis to Revelation,...witness the fact that the document is a transcript from the records of the eternal world. The sublimity of the ideas; the purity of the language; the scope for action; the continued duration for completion, in order that the heirs of salvation may confess the Lord and bow the knee; the rewards for faithfulness, and the punishments for sins, are so much beyond the narrow-mindedness of men, that every man is constrained to exclaim: 'It came from God.'"[7]

This idea of varying rewards hereafter is not totally foreign to other Christians. In the words of popular writer Bruce Wilkinson, "Although your eternal destination is based on your belief [in Jesus Christ as Lord and Savior], how you spend eternity is based on your behavior while on earth." Thus "The Unbreakable Link" is stated as follows: "Your choices on earth have direct consequences on your life in eternity." Discipleship flows from true conversion. That is, "Doing is a servant's language of devotion." In short, "There will be degrees of reward in heaven."[8]

The great American theologian of the First Great Awakening, Jonathan Edwards, stated that "There are many mansions in God's house because heaven is intended for various degrees of honor and blessedness. Some are designed to sit in higher places there than others; some are designed to be advanced to higher degrees of honor and glory than others are."[9] Similarly, John Wesley, the father of Methodism, spoke of some persons enjoying "higher degrees of glory" hereafter. "There is an inconceivable variety in the degrees of reward in the other world.... In worldly things men are ambitious to get as high as they can. Christians have a far more noble ambition. The difference between the very highest and the lowest state in the world is nothing to the smallest difference between the degrees of glory."[10]

While sitting with a group of religious scholars once, they commented to me that the problem with the LDS conception of heaven is that everyone is saved. I thought of that conversation as I later read the following from a Roman Catholic scholar, Richard John Neuhaus: "The hope that all may be saved...offends some Christians. It is as though salvation were a zero-sum proposition, as though there is only so much to go around, as though God's grace to others will somehow diminish our portion of grace.... If we love others, it seems that we must hope that, in the end, they will be saved. We must hope that all will one day hear the words of Christ, 'Today you will be with me in paradise.' Given the evidence of Scripture and tradition, we cannot deny that hell exists. We can, however, hope that hell is empty. We cannot know that, but we can hope it is the case."[11]

During the next twelve years of his ministry, Joseph Smith would add increments of understanding to the Vision. After April 1836, Joseph introduced the doctrine and practice of eternal marriage. He taught that "in the celestial glory there are three heavens or degrees; and in order to obtain the highest, a man must enter into this order of the priesthood [meaning the new and everlasting covenant of marriage]; and if he does not, he cannot obtain it. He may enter into the other, but that is the end of his kingdom; he cannot have an increase" (D&C 131:1–4.) Or, stated another way, "Except a man and his wife enter into an everlasting covenant and be married for eternity, while in this probation, by the power and authority of the Holy Priesthood, they will cease to increase when they die; that is, they will not have any children after the resurrection. But those who are married by the power and authority of the priesthood in this life, and continue without committing the sin against the Holy Ghost, will continue to increase and have children in the celestial glory."[12]

Truly there are many mansions of the Father (John 14:1–2), and the Holy One of Israel has made provision for his people to attain unto that level of glory hereafter that they are willing to receive. The Prophet quoted the Savior about many mansions and said: "It should be, 'In my Father's kingdom are many kingdoms,' in order that ye may be heirs of God and joint-heirs with me."[13] Mormons view this teaching as a message of hope, a breath of fresh air, a doctrine that manifests the mercy and wisdom of our Divine Redeemer.

ENDNOTES

1. Dibble, cited in Andrus and Andrus, *They Knew the Prophet*, 67–68.
2. Smith, *TPJS*, 358.

3. Ibid., 24.

4. Melvin J. Ballard, *Crusader for Righteousness*, 224–25; see also Joseph Fielding Smith, *Doctrines of Salvation* 2:31–34.

5. Kimball, *The Miracle of Forgiveness*, 243–44.

6. Penrose, "Mormon Doctrine" (1897), 72, 74, 75.

7. Smith, *TPJS*, 11.

8. Wilkinson, *A Life God Rewards*, 23, 25, 73, 98.

9. Edwards, cited in Wilkinson, *A Life God Rewards*, 119.

10. Wesley, cited in Wilkinson, *A Life God Rewards*, 120–21.

11. Neuhaus, *Death on a Friday Afternoon*, 57, 61.

12. Smith, *TPJS*, 300–301.

13. Ibid., 366.

TWENTY-SIX

Acquiring the Divine Nature

I SUPPOSE FEW TEACHINGS found within LDS writings and culture have proven to be more controversial than the concept that men and women have the capacity to become as God is. Critics of this view are quick to point out that such a notion lessens God in the eternal scheme of things. Others, such as Ed Decker, who produced the video, *The Godmakers,* contend that such a grand and unreachable ideal leads to frustration, exasperation, and spiritual burnout among Mormons far and wide. Let me, in this chapter, attempt to respond to some of the objections raised to the doctrine of human deification or *theosis* and suggest what Latter-day Saints know and believe and what they do not.

Jesus Christ is a glorified, exalted, perfected personage. He is also one who yearns to forgive our sins and purify our hearts, one who delights to honor those who serve him in righteousness and in truth to the end (D&C 76:5). That is, he is not possessive of his powers, nor is he hesitant about dispensing spiritual gifts or sharing his divine attributes. In the words of Max Lucado, "God loves you just the way you are, but he refuses to leave you that way. He wants you to be just like Jesus."[1] Dallas Willard likewise noted that "Jesus offers himself as God's doorway into the life that is truly life. Confidence in him leads us today, as in other times, to become his apprentices in eternal living."[2] Joseph Smith taught that all those who keep God's commandments "shall grow up from grace to grace, and become heirs of the heavenly kingdom, and joint heirs with Jesus Christ; possessing the same mind, being transformed into the same image or likeness." In other words,"[3]

N. T. Wright speaks of "two golden rules at the heart of spirituality." First of all, "You become like what you worship. When you gaze in awe, admiration, and wonder at something or someone, you begin to take on something of the character of the object of your worship." The second golden rule is as follows: "Because you were made in God's image, worship makes you more truly human. When you gaze in love and gratitude at the God in whose image you were made, you do indeed grow. You discover more of what it means to be fully alive."[4]

On the one hand, we worship a divine Being with whom we can identify. That is to say, his infinity does not preclude either his immediacy or his intimacy. "In the day that God created man," LDS scripture attests, "in the likeness of God made he him; in the image of his own body, male and female, created he them" (Moses 6:8–9). We believe that God is not simply a spirit influence, a force in the universe, or the Great First Cause; when we pray "Our Father which art in heaven" (Matthew 6:9), we mean what we say. We believe God is comprehendible, knowable, approachable, and, like his Beloved Son, touched with the feeling of our infirmities (Hebrews 4:15). On the other hand, our God is God. There is no knowledge of which the Father is ignorant and no power he does not possess. We feel that scriptural passages which speak of him being the same yesterday, today, and forever clearly have reference to his divine attributes—his love, justice, constancy, and willingness to bless his children.

Eternal life consists in being *with* God; in addition, it entails being *like* God. "People who live long lives together," Max Lucado observed, "eventually begin to sound alike, to talk alike, even to think alike. As we walk with God, we take on his thoughts, his principles, his attitudes. We take on his heart."[5] That is, we begin to be more and more like God. A study of Christian history reveals that the doctrine of the deification of man was taught at least into the fifth century by such notables as Irenaeus, Clement of Alexandria, Justin Martyr, Athanasius, and Augustine. Latter-day Saints might not agree with some of what was taught about deification by such Christian thinkers, but it is clear that the idea was not foreign to the people of the early Church.

Veli-Matti Kärkkäinen at Fuller Theological Seminary has described this doctrine as "the most profound question of human life, namely, what is the way back to God, to live with God, to live in God and share in the divine? Christian theology from the beginning has offered an answer to the world and its followers in the form of the doctrine of deification and/or union with God."[6] One scholar has written: "In the Orthodox understanding Christianity signifies not merely an adherence to certain dogmas, not merely an exterior imitation of Christ through moral effort, but direct union with the living God, the total transformatioin of the human person by divine grace and glory—what the Greek Fathers termed 'deification' or 'divinization.' In the words of St. Basil the Great, man is nothing less than a creature that has received the order to *become god*."[7]

Note the following from early Christian thinkers:[8]

Irenaeus (ca. A.D. 130–200): "Do we cast blame on [God] because we were not made gods from the beginning, but were at first created merely as men, and then later as gods?" Also: "But man receives progression and increase towards God. For as God is always the same, so also man, when found in God, shall always progress toward God."

Clement of Alexandria (ca. 150–215): "If one knows himself, he will know God and knowing God will become like God."

Athanasius, bishop of Alexandria (ca. 296–373): "The word was made flesh in order that we might be enabled to be made gods.... Just as the Lord, putting on the body, became a man, so also we men are both deified through his flesh, and henceforth inherit everlasting life."

Augustine of Hippo (ca. 354–430): "But he himself that justifies also deifies, for by justifying he makes sons of God. 'For he has given them power to become the sons of God' (John 1:12). If then we have been made sons of God, we have also been made gods."

All men and women, like Christ, are made in the image and likeness of God (Genesis 1:27; Moses 2:27), and so we feel it is neither audacity nor heresy for the children of God to aspire to be like God. Consider further the implications of the following scriptural passages:

"Be ye therefore *perfect*, even as your Father which is in heaven is perfect" (Matthew 5:48, emphasis added).

"For as many as are led by the Spirit of God, they are the sons of God. For ye have not received the spirit of bondage again to fear; but ye have received the spirit of adoption, whereby we cry, Abba, Father. The Spirit itself beareth witness with our spirit, that we are the children of God: and *if children, then heirs: heirs of God, and joint-heirs with Christ*; if so be that we suffer with him, that we may be also glorified together" (Romans 8:14–17, emphasis added).

"Grace and peace be multiplied unto you through the knowledge of God, and of Jesus our Lord. According as his divine power hath given unto us all things that pertain unto life and godliness, through the knowledge of him that hath called us to glory and virtue: whereby are given unto us exceeding great and precious promises: that by these *we might be partakers of the divine nature*, having escaped the corruption that is in the world through lust" (2 Peter 1:2–4, emphasis added).

"Behold, what manner of love the Father hath bestowed upon us, that we should be called the [children] of God: therefore the world knoweth us not, because it knew him not. Beloved, now are we the [children] of God, and it doth not yet appear what we shall be: but we know that, *when he shall appear, we shall be like him;* for we shall see him as he is" (1 John 3:1–2, emphasis added).

The idea of the ultimate deification of man has not been completely lost from Christian thinking in our own time. "The Son of God became a man," C. S. Lewis pointed out, "to enable men to become sons of God."[9] Further, Lewis explained: God "said (in the Bible) that we were 'gods' and He is going to make good his words. If we let Him—for we can prevent Him, if we choose—He will make the feeblest and filthiest of us into a god or goddess, dazzling, radiant, immortal creature, pulsating all through with such energy and joy and wisdom and love as we cannot now imagine, a bright stainless mirror which reflects back to God perfectly (though, of course, on a smaller scale) His own boundless power and delight and goodness. The process will be long and in parts very painful; but that is what we are in for. Nothing less. He meant what He said."[10]

Lewis wrote elsewhere: "It may be possible for each to think too much of his own potential glory hereafter; it is hardly possible for him to think too often or too deeply about that of his neighbour. ...It is a serious thing to live in a society of possible gods and goddesses, to remember that the dullest and most uninteresting person you can talk to may one day be a creature which, if you saw it now, you would be strongly tempted to worship. . . . There are no ordinary people."[11]

I honestly don't know what Lewis meant fully (and certainly what he understood or intended) by these statements. The doctrine of the deification of man did not originate with Lewis, nor with the Latter-day Saints; it is to be found throughout Christian history and within Orthodox Christian theology today. Whether Lewis would have agreed fully with the teachings of early Christian leaders on deification—or, for that matter, with what the Latter-day Saints teach—I cannot tell.

While Latter-day Saints certainly accept the teachings of Joseph Smith regarding man becoming like God, we do not fully comprehend all that is entailed by such a bold declaration. Subsequent or even current Church leaders have spoken very little concerning which of God's attributes are communicable and which are incommunicable. While we believe that becoming like God is entailed in eternal life (D&C 132:19–20), we do not believe we will ever, worlds without end, unseat or oust God the Eternal Father or his Only Begotten Son, Jesus Christ; those holy beings are and forever will be the Gods we worship. Even though we believe in the ultimate deification of man, I am unaware of any authoritative statement in LDS literature that suggests that men and women will ever worship any being other than the ones within the present Godhead.

Parley P. Pratt, early Mormon apostle, wrote one of the first LDS theological treatises within Mormonism. In describing those who are glorified and attain eternal life, Parley stated: "The difference between Jesus Christ and another immortal and celestial man is this—the man is subordinate to Jesus Christ, does nothing in and of himself, but does all things in the name of Christ, and by his authority, being of the same mind, and ascribing all the glory to him and his Father."[12] We believe in "one God" in the sense that we love and serve one Godhead, one divine presidency, each of whom possesses all of the attributes of Godhood (Alma 11:44; D&C 20:28). While we do not believe that God and man are of a different species, we readily acknowledge that the chasm between a fallen, mortal being and an immortal, resurrected, and glorified Being is immense, almost infinite (see D&C 20:17; 109:77).

Many critics of Mormonism have been eager to question the couplet of Lorenzo Snow, the fifth president of the Church:

> As man is, God once was.
> As God is, man may become.[13]

As we indicated earlier in this work, we know little or nothing about God's life before he was God; that God is and was once a man was taught by Joseph Smith, to be sure, but is not something that has received much attention (except by critics of the LDS faith) through the years since then. It is not a central, saving doctrine. As to the second issue raised within Brother Snow's words, I ask: What if this couplet read differently?

> As man is, Christ once was.
> As Christ is, man may become.

President Gordon B. Hinckley observed that "the whole design of the gospel is to lead us onward and upward to greater achievement, even, eventually, to godhood. This great possibility was enunciated by the Prophet Joseph Smith in the King Follett sermon and emphasized by President Lorenzo Snow.... Our enemies have criticized us for believing in this. Our reply is that this lofty concept in no way diminishes God the Eternal Father. He is the Almighty. He is the Creator and Governor of the universe. He is the greatest of all and will always be so. But just as any earthly father wishes for his sons and daughters every success in life, so I believe our Father in Heaven wishes for his children that they might approach him in stature and stand beside him resplendent in godly strength and wisdom."[14]

To summarize, Latter-day Saints teach that through the cleansing and transforming power of the blood of Jesus Christ, men and women may over time mature spiritually. That is, according to Joseph Smith, by and through the Savior's blood, we "have a forgiveness of sins, and also a sure reward laid up for [us] in heaven, even that of partaking of the fullness of the Father and the Son through the Spirit. As the Son partakes of the fullness of the Father through the Spirit, so the saints are, by the same Spirit, to be partakers of the same fullness, to enjoy the same glory; for as the Father and the Son are one, so, in like manner, the saints are to be one in them. Through the love of the Father, the mediation of Jesus Christ, and the gift of the Holy Spirit, they are to be heirs of God, and joint heirs with Jesus Christ."[15] Becoming like Deity thus goes well beyond the imitation of Christ or the emulation of the Savior; it requires the transformation of the human soul.

To clarify, Mormons do not believe they can work themselves into glory or godhood. Mormons do not believe they can gain eternal life through human effort. Mormons do not believe that one becomes more and more Christlike through sheer grit and will power. Central to any and all spiritual progress is the Atonement of Jesus Christ, and it is only by and through his righteousness that we may be pronounced righteous. It is only by the power of his precious blood that we may be cleansed and sanctified from the taint and tyranny of sin. And it is only by and through the power of his everlasting life that we receive life—energy, strength, vitality, renewal, enabling power—to accomplish what we could never accomplish on our own.

Just how strange, then, is the LDS doctrine of deification? How unscriptural is it? It's fascinating to read two statements made by Martin Luther. The first, written in his Christmas sermon of 1514, affirms: "Just as the word of God becomes flesh [Jesus becomes man], so it is certainly also necessary that the flesh become word [that man become like Christ]. For the word becomes flesh precisely so that the flesh may become word. In other words: God becomes man so that man may become God. Thus power becomes powerless so that weakness may become powerful."[16] In 1519, Luther wrote: "For it is true that a man helped by grace is more than a man; indeed, the grace of God gives him the form of God and deifies him, so that even the Scriptures call him 'God' and 'God's son.'"[17]

John teaches that one day, through the divine process of glorification, we shall be like God, "for we shall see him as he is." So often you and I do not see things as they really are; we see things *as we are*. Sin and preoccupation with secondary matters and distraction so often prevent us from perceiving the Truth as we ought; the eyes of our understandings are closed to the mysteries of God because we are gazing through the eyes of flesh. As we learn to repent and as we allow the Atonement to have its way in our souls, however, we begin to have the layers of duplicity and superficiality removed from our eyes; we begin to see things as they are, see things as God sees them, see things through the eyes of faith. We begin to gain what Paul called "the mind of Christ" (1 Corinthians 2:16). We become "joint heirs" or co-inheritors with Christ to all the Father has prepared for those who wait for him, who love him (Isaiah 64:4; 1 Corinthians 2:9). We become "partakers of the divine nature" and thereby grow in that mature spiritual union that exists between the Almighty and his covenant people who have come to know him. In short, as Kärkkäinen has written: "The Biblical tradition, both in the Old Testament and the New, approaches the question of salvation from the perspective of the likeness of God's people to God. In other words, to be saved means becoming like God."[18]

ENDNOTES

1. Lucado, *Just Like Jesus*, 3.

2. Willard, *The Divine Conspiracy*, 12.

3. Smith, *Lectures on Faith* 5:2.

4. Wright, *Simply Christian*, 148.

5. Lucado, *Just Like Jesus*, 61.

6. Kärkkäinen, *One with God*, 1.

7. Bishop Kallistos of Diokleia; in Ibid., 17.

8. The following four statements are cited in Stephen Robinson, *Are Mormons Christians?* 60–61.

9. Lewis, *Mere Christianity*, 155.

10. Ibid., 176.

11. Lewis, *The Weight of Glory*, 39.

12. Pratt, *Key to the Science of Theology*, 21–22.

13. *Teachings of Lorenzo Snow*, 1.

14. Hinckley, CR, October 1994, 64.

15. Smith, *Lectures on Faith* 5:3.

16. Luther, cited in Kärkkäienen, *One with God*, 47.

17. Ibid.

18. Kärkkäienen, *One with God*, 123.

TWENTY-SEVEN

A Foretaste of Heaven

MANY A MORMON MISSIONARY or member of the LDS Church has sought to share their faith with friends, only to hear the following response: "Thank you, but I'm a saved Christian." We recoil, space out, or, I suppose in some cases, even try to argue with them about what they mean. Or we may respond as my father did so many times: "Yes, of course, you are saved; you are saved from the grave." But that's obviously not what they intended. In like fashion, when a Protestant asks us: "Are you a saved Christian?" we as Latter-day Saints may well stumble over our words and wonder how to respond. Generally, even if we do not voice our feelings, we believe that one is not fully saved until he or she endures to the end of their mortal life.

Over the years as I have spoken openly with friends or colleagues from other faiths, I have come to appreciate a little better what they have in mind. Some mean that they have received in their heart a witness that Jesus is the Christ; that the Savior has forgiven their sins and they are now willing to turn their lives over to him; and that they are now in a saved condition in regard to happiness here and eternal reward hereafter. For them, to be converted to Christ is to be saved, to have the assurance of eternal life.

I have no reason to doubt their sincerity or the reality of their witness of Christ; the influence of the Holy Spirit is real, available, and the source of the testimony of Jesus. I know there are people out there who feel that once they profess Jesus with their lips they are saved forevermore and that what they do thereafter with their lives in terms of goodness and morality is immaterial. Yes, there are such people, but I don't know many of them. Most of those Protestants that I grew up with and most of the ministers and theologians I have encountered since then, really do see a very close tie between their saved condition and a righteous, God-fearing life. Those who are serious students of the New Testament understand the central message of the second chapter of James—that good works flow from the regenerate heart, that righteousness evidences true faith.

So let's turn our attention to the matter of being saved. In the words of Joseph Smith, to be saved is to be placed beyond the power of our enemies. "Salvation consists in the glory, authority, majesty, power and dominion which Jehovah possesses and in nothing else; and no being can possess it but himself or one like him."[1] To be saved is to be conformed into the image of Christ, to become like unto the Prototype of all saved beings. There is obviously what might be called a limited dimension to salvation—meaning, salvation from the grave, salvation from physical death. All mortals will be resurrected and thus enjoy this aspect of salvation. With but few exceptions, however, when the prophets speak of salvation they are referring to the highest of eternal rewards hereafter. Salvation is redemption, exaltation, eternal life; each of these words mean the same thing, but each lays stress on a particular aspect of the saved condition. And so in the ultimate meaning, to be saved is to qualify for life in the highest heaven, what the Latter-day Saints would call the celestial kingdom—to be endowed with a fulness of the glory of the Father and to enjoy a continuation of the family unit into eternity (D&C 132:19).

But now to the question: Do Latter-day Saints believe that men and women may only enjoy the benefits of salvation in the world to come? Is there no sense in which we may be saved in the present, in the here and now? Though I quickly acknowledge that most scriptural references to salvation seem to point toward that which comes in the next life, we do have within our theology principles and doctrines that suggest a form of salvation in this life. That same Holy Spirit of Promise who searches the hearts of men and women, who ratifies and approves and seals ordinances and lives, that same Holy Spirit serves, as Paul indicates, as the "earnest of our inheritance" (Ephesians 1:14). The

Lord's "earnest money" on us, his down payment, his indication to us that he will save us, is the Holy Spirit. We know we are on course when the Spirit is with us. We know our lives are approved of God when the Spirit is with us. We know we are in Christ, in covenant, when the Spirit is with us. And we know, I suggest, that we are saved when the Spirit is with us. If we maintain the gift and gifts of the Spirit, then we are in the line of our duty; we are approved of the heavens, and if we were to die suddenly, we would go into paradise and eventually into the celestial kingdom. N. T. Wright speaks of Paul's characterization as "the *guarantee* or the *downpayment* of what is to come. The Greek word…means *an engagement ring,* a sign in the present of what is to come in the future."[2] In other words, the Spirit works in the present to focus our hearts on what lies ahead. "So what does it mean to say that this future has begun to arrive in the present?" Wright follows up. "What Paul means is that those who follow Jesus, those who find themselves believing that he is the world's true Lord, that he rose from the dead—these people are given the Spirit as a foretaste of what that new world will be like."[3]

The King James Version of 1 John 3:9 states: "Whosoever is born of God doth not commit sin." The problem is that those who have been born again are not free from sin. But they repent quickly (D&C 109:21). They move rapidly from the darkness back into the light. The God-fearing live always in a state of repentance. Brigham Young made this important explanation: "I do not recollect that I have seen five minutes since I was baptized that I have not been ready to preach a funeral sermon, lay hands on the sick, or to pray in private or in public. I will tell you the secret of this. In all your business transactions, words, and communications, *if you commit an overt act,* repent of that immediately, and call upon God to deliver you from evil and give you the light of His Spirit…. *If I commit an overt act,* the Lord knows the integrity of my heart, and, through sincere repentance, He forgives me."[4]

I remember coming home from work after a very long day. It seemed that everything that could have gone wrong went wrong. I was physically exhausted and emotionally spent. I sat in my recliner and began to doze off. My wife Shauna came into the room in what seemed to me a mood that was much too happy for what I had experienced in the last twelve hours. She asked how my day had gone, and without catching myself I sat up in my chair and sarcastically responded that she wouldn't understand if I took the time to explain. I immediately saw the pain in her eyes as she quickly made her way into another part of the house. I was disgusted with myself. I sensed that she was trying to be friendly, to be helpful, to lift my spirits. I grieved over my indiscretion against charity and found myself thinking: "I'm gonna deal with this right now." I hopped out of the chair, went into the bedroom, and said to her: "It's been a miserable day. The walls have been crashing down all day long. But that's no reason to react meanly to you. I'm sorry. Will you forgive me?" She of course quickly nodded and hugged me. I went back to my chair, silently asked the Lord to forgive me, and immediately felt the peace of the Spirit return. I was back in the light.

Obviously, more serious sins require more time, deeper repentance, and a period of appropriate godly sorrow. But if we are honest, truly honest with ourselves and with the Lord, we quickly acknowledge that most of our sins are inadvertent sins against charity. "When men truly and heartily repent," President Young taught, "and make manifest to the heavens that their repentance is genuine by obedience to the requirements made known to them through the laws of the gospel, then are they entitled to the administration of salvation, and no power can withhold the good spirit from them."[5] The Joseph Smith Translation of 1 John 3:9 reads as follows: "Whosoever is born of God *doth not continue in sin;* for the Spirit of God remaineth in him; and he cannot continue in sin, because he is born of God, having received that Holy Spirit of promise" (emphasis added).

A revelation in the Doctrine and Covenants attests: "But learn that he who doeth the works of righteousness shall receive his reward, even peace in this world, and eternal life in the world to come" (D&C 59:23). On another occasion: "If you desire a further witness, cast your mind upon the night that you cried unto me in your heart, that you might know concerning the truth of these things. Did I not speak *peace* to your mind? What greater witness can you have than from God?" (D&C 6:22–23, emphasis added). Another way of making my point is to state that we are living in a saved condition to the extent that we are living in the light, living according to our spiritual privileges, living in harmony with the knowledge and the blessings we have received to that point.

Peace is what it's all about in the gospel sense. Although most people know what peace is, peace has not yet been given its day in court; that is, we have not fully appreciated what a remarkable fruit of the Spirit (Galatians 5:22) and what a transcendent manifestation of the new birth, peace is. Peace is a priceless gift in a world that is at war with itself. Disciples look to Him who is the Prince of Peace for their succor and their support. They know that peace is not only a cherished commodity in the here and now but also a harbinger of glorious things yet to be. Peace is a sure and solid sign from God that the heavens are pleased.

While sin and neglect of duty result in disunity of the soul and strife and confusion, repentance and forgiveness and rebirth bring quiet and rest and peace. While sin results in disorder, the Holy Spirit is an organizing principle that brings order and congruence. The world and the worldly cannot bring peace. They cannot settle the soul (see D&C 101:36). "Peace, peace to him that is far off, and to him that is near, saith the Lord; and I will heal him. But the wicked are like the troubled sea, when it cannot rest, whose waters cast up mire and dirt. There is no peace, saith my God, to the wicked" (Isaiah 57:19–21).

Hope in Christ, which is a natural result of our saving faith in Christ, comes through spiritual reawakening. We sense our place in the royal family and are warmed by the sweet family association. And what is our indication that we are on course? How do we know we are in the gospel harness? "Hereby know we that we dwell in him, and he in us, *because he hath given us of his Spirit*" (1 John 4:13, emphasis added). The presence of God's Spirit is the attestation, the divine assurance that we are headed in the right direction. It is God's seal, his anointing, his unction (1 John 2:20) to us that our lives are in order.

The following is an intriguing statement from Brigham Young: "It is *present salvation* and the present influence of the Holy Ghost that we need every day to keep us on saving ground.... . I want present salvation. I preach, comparatively, but little about the eternities and Gods, and their wonderful works in eternity; and do not tell who first made them, nor how they were made; for I know nothing about that. Life is for us, and it for us to *receive it today,* and not wait for the Millennium. Let us take a course to be saved today, and, when evening comes, review the acts of the day, repent of our sins, if we have any to repent of, and say our prayers; then we can lie down and sleep in peace until the morning, arise with gratitude to God, commence the labors of another day, and strive to live the whole day to God and nobody else."[6]

"I am in the hands of the Lord," President Young pointed out, "and never trouble myself about my salvation, or what the Lord will do with me hereafter."[7] As he said on another occasion, our work "is a work of the present. *The salvation we are seeking is for the present,* and sought correctly, *it can be obtained,* and be continually enjoyed. If it continues today, it is upon the same principle that it will continue tomorrow, the next day, the next week, or the next year, and, we might say, the next eternity."[8]

"Salvation is a big and comprehensive word," John Stott emphasized. "It embraces the totality of God's saving work, from beginning to end. In fact, salvation has three tenses, past, present, and future.... I have been saved (in the past) from the penalty of sin by a crucified Saviour. I am being saved (in the present) from the power of sin by a living Saviour. And I shall be saved (in the future) from the very presence of sin by a coming Saviour....

"If therefore you were to ask me. 'Are you saved?' there is only one correct biblical answer which I could give you: 'yes and no.' Yes, in the sense that by the sheer grace and mercy of God through the death of Jesus Christ my Saviour he has forgiven my sins, justified me and reconciled me to himself. But no, in the sense that I still have a fallen nature and live in a fallen world and have a corruptible body, and I am longing for my salvation to be brought to its triumphant completion."[9]

Though we must guard against all forms of pride or self-assurance, we must also avoid the kind of false modesty or doubt that is antithetical to faith; Joseph Smith taught that doubt—certainly including a constant worry as to our standing before God or our capacity to go where Christ is—doubt cannot coexist with saving faith. Fear and doubt preclude the possibility of growing in saving faith. If, as Joseph Smith taught, "Happiness is the object and design of our existence,"[10] then happiness is something to be enjoyed in the present, in the here and now, not something reserved for the distant there and then. "*If we are saved,*" Brother Brigham declared, "*we are happy,* we are filled with light, glory, intelligence, and we pursue a course to enjoy the blessings that the Lord has in store for us. If we continue to pursue that course, it produces just the thing we want, that is, to be saved at this present moment. And that will lay the foundation to be saved forever and forever, which will amount to an *eternal salvation.*"[11]

Living in a state of salvation does not entail an inordinate self-confidence, but rather a hope in Christ. To hope in our modern world is to wish, to worry, to fret about some particular outcome. In the scriptures, however, hope is expectation, anticipation, and assurance. Faith in Christ, true faith, always gives rise to hope in Christ. "And what is it that ye shall hope for? Behold I say unto you that ye shall have hope through the atonement of Christ and the power of his resurrection, to be raised unto life eternal" (Moroni 7:41). To have faith in Christ is to know that as we rely wholly upon his merits and mercy and trust in his redeeming grace, we will make it (2 Nephi 31:19; Moroni 6:4). He will not only bridge the chasm between the ideal and the real and thus provide that final spiritual boost into eternal life, but he will also extend to us that marvelous enabling power so essential to daily living, a power that enables us to conquer weakness and acquire the divine nature. In short, living in a state of salvation is living in the quiet assurance that God is in his heaven, Christ is the Lord, and that the plan of redemption is real and in active operation in our personal lives. It is not to be totally free of weakness, but to proceed confidently in the Savior's promise that in him we will find strength to overcome, as well as rest and peace, here and hereafter.

ENDNOTES

1. Joseph Smith, *Lectures on Faith* 7:9.
2. Wright, *Simply Christian*, 125, emphasis added.
3. Ibid., 126.

4. Young, *JD* 12:103, emphasis added.

5. Ibid., 10:18.

6. Ibid., JD 8:124–25, emphasis added.

7. Ibid., 6:276.

8. Ibid., 1:131, emphasis added.

9. Stott, *Authentic Christianity from the Writings of John Stott*, 168.

10. Smith, *TPJS*, 255–56.

11. Young, *JD* 1:131, emphasis added.

TWENTY-EIGHT

What of Joseph Smith?

I HAVE HAD THE opportunity of being involved in hundreds of hours of conversation with persons of other faiths, and I acknowledge it to be a consummate privilege to be able to build bridges, build friendships, and build understanding and mutual respect. I have worked as a religious educator now for over thirty years, and I would have to admit that the last decade—the time in which I have been heavily immersed in outreach and interfaith activities—has been the most personally and professionally fulfilling time of my academic life. I have learned a ton about other Christian faiths in particular, but I've learned half a ton about Mormonism. There's nothing quite like being asked new questions, hard questions, probing questions to cause one to rethink, reevaluate, reassess, and restate one's perspective. I have not viewed my colleagues' inquiries as challenges to my personal faith, nor have they been. While I confess to being more committed to the LDS faith now than I have ever been, I also confess that I am more liberal—in the best sense of that term, meaning "open" and "receptive"—than ever before. I see the hand of God working in human lives throughout the earth in mysterious but magnificent ways.

Most of the people I have met and conversed with are men and women of faith, believers, for example, in the reality of God and in the divinity of Jesus Christ. And yet even from such persons I have occasionally been asked, most sincerely, how I can in good conscience be a Latter-day Saint. I remember very well the time just prior to the Southern Baptist Convention holding their meetings in Salt Lake City in June 1998. Religious leaders and journalists conducted scores of interviews with me on the radio, television, in local and national magazines, and in local and national newspapers. In one of the TV interviews in Salt Lake City, I was asked to meet with a local Baptist pastor and discuss similarities and differences between Latter-day Saints and Baptists. In spite of the talk show host's efforts to stir up a bit of controversy, the Baptist fellow was pleasant, soft-spoken, and easy to chat with. I found the interview to be a delightful experience. The next day I received a phone call from another Baptist minister in the Provo area who felt the other guy "didn't know his stuff" and was simply too nice to me. He asked if he could meet soon to "straighten me out" on some things that he felt needed resolution. I agreed. In fact, I invited him to my office (I was serving as the dean of religious education at the time) for lunch. I asked if he would mind if one of my associate deans, Brent Top, joined our conversation, and he consented.

Our meeting was most interesting. He was quite a young man, explained that he had responsibility for working with college age young people, and indicated that he had many, many questions to raise. We encouraged him to proceed. He then raised one anti-Mormon issue after another, old and worn out matters that have been answered hundreds of times before, both in print and in verbal conversations. We responded in each case, until about 30 to 45 minutes had passed. I interrupted the inquisition with this question: "Pastor, are these the kinds of things you really would like to ask? I mean, I rather doubt that you're going to come up with a question we have never heard before; you see, we do this for a living." He then stuttered a bit and agreed to pursue a different course. "I'd ask you some questions about LDS interpretations of the Bible, but you folks don't know anything about the Bible."

Brent and I looked at each other quizzically, and then Brent responded: "What do you mean? We love the Bible. We teach and study the Bible. We have both been to the Holy Land many times and taught the Old and New Testaments on site." I followed up: "Yes, what would you like to discuss? Would you like to start with Paul's epistle to the Romans? That's one of my favorite sections of scripture."

After about half an hour discussing the nature of fallen humanity, the Atonement, and justification by faith, our Baptist friend went quiet for about a minute. He then looked up, and in a voice filled with stunned surprise, said: "I don't understand this. You two seem to be decent, God-fearing men who know your way around theology quite well. I don't mean to offend you, but how in the world can you understand the things we've been discussing and still be Mormons?" I have encountered one form or another of that question more times than I can remember. Another rendition of the query might go something like this: "How could you receive doctoral training in religious studies, know the issues, be aware of where most scholars come down on the issues, and still be a believing, practicing Latter-day Saint?"

When I push the matter farther down the road, the questioner will frequently say something like: "Well, what I really mean is: How can you accept the truthfulness of the Bible, the divinity of Jesus, and his substitutionary atonement and resurrection, and still believe in Joseph Smith—you know, the whole ball of wax: visions and revelations and golden plates and angels?" I find that those who raise this concern usually fall into one of two groups. The first group is made up of men and women who do indeed believe in the supernatural, in the possibility that God *could have* come to Joseph Smith, but who feel that modern prophets and modern revelation are unnecessary because of the sufficiency of the biblical record. In order to get at the heart of the second group's concerns, I must push harder. And eventually I discover that their refusal to even consider the possibility of a Joseph Smith or a modern revelation is inextricably linked to their refusal to accept supernatural events of that magnitude in our modern times. They believe in signs and wonders and miracles and divine appearances as set forth in antiquity, to be sure, but …today? Or the nineteenth century? No way!

We find ourselves, in other words, in an age filled with facts but a little weak on the faith factor, at least when faith is required to believe in the supernatural in our naturalistic age. In speaking of how the announcement of the Incarnation might be received in our time, Malcolm Muggeridge observed: "In humanistic times like ours, a contemporary virgin—assuming there are any such—would regard a message from the Angel Gabriel that she might expect to give birth to a son to be called the Son of the Highest as ill-tidings of great sorrow and a slur on the local family-planning centre. It is, in point of fact, extremely

improbable, under existing conditions, that Jesus would have been permitted to be born at all. Mary's pregnancy, in poor circumstances, and
with the father unknown, would have been an obvious case for abortion; and her talk of having conceived as a result of the intervention of
the Holy Ghost would have pointed to the need for psychiatric treatment, and made the case for terminating her pregnancy even stronger. Thus our generation, needing a Saviour more, perhaps, than any
that has ever existed, would be too humane to allow one to be born;
too enlightened to permit the Light of the World to shine in a darkness that grows ever more oppressive.... Are we, then, to suppose that
our forebears who believed implicitly in the Virgin Birth were gullible
fools, whereas we, who would no more believe in such notions than we
would that the world is flat, have put aside childish things and become
mature? Is our skepticism one more manifestation of our having—in
[Dietrich] Bonhoeffer's unhappy phrase—come of age?"[1]

I recall listening to a popular talk show some years back when a
woman called in with a rather unusual comment. She indicated that she
was a religious woman, that she and her family attended church regularly, that she was very involved in community affairs; in other words,
she was trying to make the point that she was a "good" person. She then
blurted out: "But why do people like me have to put up with fanatics
knocking on their doors to try to convert them to another faith?" The
host asked who the door knockers were, and the woman responded: "It's
the Mormons, and I don't want to have anything to do with them."

"Why is that," the host asked.

"Because they are so weird. They believe in strange stuff."

"What kinds of strange stuff?" was the retort.

"Oh, you know, God and angels appearing, modern revelations,
new scripture; stuff like that."

The host paused for a moment and responded in a most interesting
manner: "Let me see now. You're upset because these strange people
who believe in supernatural things want to share what they believe. Is
that correct?"

"Yeah, that's it," the caller came right back.

Then the host added: "God appearing, angels coming, golden
plates, new scripture. Yes, accepting those things would be like believing in a burning bush that doesn't go out, or crossing the Red Sea on

dry ground, or walking on water, or feeding five thousand people with five loaves of bread and two fish, wouldn't it?"

The fact is, it's pretty tough to respect Mormonism on the one hand and anathamatize Joseph Smith on the other. President Gordon B. Hinckley wrote: "An acquaintance said to me one day: 'I admire your church very much. I think I could accept everything about it—except Joseph Smith.' To which I responded: 'That statement is a contradiction. If you accept the revelation, you must accept the revelator.'

"It is a constantly recurring mystery to me how some people speak with admiration for the Church and its work while at the same time disdaining him through whom, as a servant of the Lord, came the framework of all that the Church is, of all that it teaches, and of all that it stands for. They would pluck the fruit from the tree while cutting off the root from which it grows."[2]

Well, of course Joseph Smith's claims are fantastic! So were those of prophets of old. So were those of Jesus himself. I think that's the nature of divine intervention in human affairs, isn't it? Then how *should* persons of other faiths look upon Joseph Smith?

Or, as Harold Bloom wrote: "I am in no position to judge Joseph Smith as a revelator, but as a student of the American imagination I observe that his achievement as national prophet and seer is clearly unique in our history. Ralph Waldo Emerson and Walt Whitman were great writers, Jonathan Edwards and Horace Bushnell major theologians, William James a superb psychologist, and all these are crucial figures in the spiritual history of our country. Joseph Smith did not excel as a writer or as a theologian, let alone as psychologist and philosopher. But he was an authentic religious genius, and surpassed all Americans, before or since, in the possession and expression of what could be called the religion-making imagination. Even the force of Brigham Young's genius for leadership and the heroic intensity of the early Mormon people could not have assured the survival of the new religion. There had to be an immense power of the myth-making imagination at work to sustain so astonishing an innovation. That power when it appears, invariably manifests itself in the phenomenon Max Weber taught us to call charisma." Bloom went on to point out that Joseph Smith was martyred, "not so much for having offended American democracy or our national sexual morality, but for having been rather too dangerously charismatic."[5]

Nor need one accept all of the faith statements put forward by the Latter-day Saints to appreciate the possibility that God may have been working through Joseph Smith in some unusual way. "Do I personally believe?" historian Robert Remini asked. "No. [Joseph] may have believed that he did [see God]. But whether he saw, I have no evidence for that. And since I'm not a Mormon who by an act of faith believes it, even though it can't be proved, I have to then make a judgment on the basis of the evidence. However, you can say, look what he did. Is one human being capable of doing this? Without divine help and intervention?"[6] Remini wrote in a recent biography: "The Prophet, Joseph Smith Jr., is unquestionably the most important reformer and innovator in American religious history, and he needs to be understood if we want to have a clearer idea about what this country was like in the Jacksonian era, just prior to the Civil War."[7]

At the least, I have encouraged those who are fascinated with our doctrine or inspired by our humanitarian efforts or appreciative of our moral stand, but who at the same time cannot accept Joseph Smith as a modern prophet, to see him as a religious leader who sought (1) to correct what he believed to be the flaws of current Christianity, much as John Hus, Martin Luther, John Calvin, John Wesley, Roger Williams, or Alexander Campbell sought to do; and (2) to restore primitive Christianity, to recover "the ancient order of things." The work he set in motion is growing rapidly, and so no informed person, especially in the United States, should be ignorant of who he was, what he claimed, and the fruits of his endeavors.

By way of conclusion, let me add that while the Latter-day Saints look to Joseph Smith with love and admiration as the prophet of the Restoration and the head of what they call the dispensation of the fullness of times, they do not live in the past, nor do they suppose that once the foundation was laid the building was complete. One newspaper article written just after the murder of Joseph and Hyrum Smith in Carthage, Illinois, in late June 1844, described the events of the lynching and ended on this note: "Thus ends Mormonism." Well, not exactly. While Mormons look to their past and their forebears with fond appreciation, they are for the most part a forward-looking people. "I can imagine," Bruce McConkie stated, "that when the Prophet Joseph Smith was taken from this life the Saints felt themselves in the depths of despair. To think that a leader of such spiritual magnitude had been taken from them! ... And yet when he was taken the Lord had Brigham Young. Brigham Young stepped forth and wore the mantle of leadership. With all respect and admiration and every accolade of praise resting upon the Prophet Joseph, still Brigham Young came forward and did things that then had to be done in a better way than the Prophet Joseph could have done them."[8]

In a similar vein, Spencer W. Kimball, twelfth president of the Church, attested to the continuation of the spirit of revelation associated with the prophetic and apostolic succession since the time of Joseph Smith. "Expecting the spectacular, one may not be alerted to the constant flow of revealed communication. I say, in the deepest of humility, but also by the power and force of a burning testimony in my soul, that from the prophet of the Restoration [Joseph Smith] to the prophet of our own year, the communication line is unbroken, the authority is continuous, a light, brilliant and penetrating, continues to shine. The sound of the voice of the Lord is a continuous melody and a thunderous appeal. For [over] a century and a half there has been no interruption."[9]

ENDNOTES

1. Muggeridge, *Jesus, The Man Who Lives*, 19–20.

2. Hinckley, "Joseph Smith, Jr.: Prophet of God, Mighty Servant," 2.

3. Bushman, cited in Heidi Swinton, *American Prophet*, 128.

4. Hatch, *The Democratization of American Christianity*, 115.

5. Bloom, *The American Religion*, 96–97.

6. Remini, cited in Swinton, *American Prophet*, 46.

7. Remini, *Joseph Smith*, ix.

8. McConkie, "Succession in the Presidency," 24.

9. Kimball, CR, April 1977, 115.

CONCLUSION

Into the Mainstream?

I
T IS PROBABLY A GOOD idea, before the book is finished, to suggest what I had in mind by the subtitle of this work, "Pressing the Boundaries of Christianity." For one thing, Mormonism makes some people really nervous. While they admire our way of life, appreciate our moral stand on controversial issues, and welcome our participation in community crises, they simply don't know what to do with us. They don't know where to put us. They don't know where or whether, on the chart of Christian churches, they should stick the Latter-day Saints. We just don't fit!

Some years ago I responded to a call for papers to an academic conference to be held at an Evangelical Christian institution, and my proposal was accepted (to my complete surprise). I made the presentation, had a ton of questions, and stayed for quite a while after the session to chat with other participants, students, and faculty in attendance. Now that the pressure was off, I was able to enjoy the rest of the conference. The next day I was sitting in a large room waiting for a session to start. A very prominent scholar walked in (I recognized him right away from his picture in numerous magazines and newspaper articles) and made his way to the row directly in front of me, where he sat with a colleague. He had been out of town the previous day and simply asked his friend: "How's the conference gone?"

"Quite well," the man responded. Then came a follow-up question, one that sharpened my eavesdropping skills: "How did the Millet paper go yesterday? You know, the talk by the Mormon."

His friend said: "Well, I thought the content was pretty good. But it's clear that he is trying to convince us that Mormons are Christian."

"Well," the scholar said, "I've been to Salt Lake City and Provo, had some pretty serious conversations with LDS thinkers, and you know what? There's a lot of Christianity there."

Now I rather doubt that the majority of his academic friends would agree with his assessment. A number of men and women I have gotten to know well—persons who have spent long hours in doctrinal dialogue, extended vexations of the soul where we have prayed and thought and wrestled and asked and answered and have come away changed by the exchange. More than once I have asked my friends who hesitate to call me a Christian: "Do you believe that every person in your home congregation is Christian? Has every man and woman in your church been born again? Have they made Jesus Christ the Lord of their life?" My friends have to acknowledge that they do not know or even believe that all of those who frequent their houses of worship are in fact Christian.

Mormonism is pressing the boundaries of Christianity because we are a growing organization, one that is becoming more and more an object of historical and religious interest, one whose influence in the world is beginning to be felt. Consequently it becomes tougher to ignore LDS perspectives and exclude LDS voices from the moral and religious conversation. I'm perfectly happy if a person wants to speak of Latter-day Saints as being "Christian but different" or "Christians with a difference." I have no problem when someone refers to me and my tradition as not being part of "traditional Christianity." I take no offense when someone notes that Mormons are not part of "Orthodox Christianity." Recently when I was in New York City, I visited with Richard John Neuhaus, a respected Roman Catholic thinker. He made the observation that the time was long overdue for serious interfaith dialogue between "Latter-day Saint Christians" and "Nicene Christians." That's a distinction with which I am perfectly happy.

In a 1997 teleconference with religion writers, former president Jimmy Carter, a Southern Baptist himself, called upon others within Christianity to exercise a greater measure of Christian charity and tolerance when it comes to dealing with persons of other faiths. He chastised the leaders of the Southern Baptist Convention for characterizing

Mormons as non-Christian. "Too many leaders now, I think, in the Southern Baptist Convention and in other conventions, are trying to act as the Pharisees did, who were condemned by Christ, in trying to define who can and who cannot be considered an acceptable person in the eyes of God. In other words, they're making judgments on behalf of God. I think that's wrong."

President Carter added that "among the worst things we can do, as believers in Christ, is to spend our time condemning others, who profess faith in Christ and try to have a very narrow definition of who is and who is not an acceptable believer and a child of God.

"I think this is one of the main reasons that Christ not only said once, but repeated on other occasions, that we should not judge others, we should let God be the judge of the sincerity of a human mind or a human heart, and let us spend our time trying to alleviate suffering, opening our hearts to others, learning about the needs of others, being generous, being compassionate and so forth."

The former president reminded us that the Great Commission—to take the gospel of Jesus Christ to all the world (Matthew 28:19–20; Mark 16:15–16)—is "a mandate that has guided Baptists as well as members of The Church of Jesus Christ of Latter-day Saints and others all down through the centuries. I think that…part of my own life commitment is to tell others about Christ, and to offer them, at least, the word of God, and to let the Holy Spirit decide, or ordain the results of those intercessions."[1]

We began this brief tour of Mormonism by suggesting that there are certain ideas, concepts, doctrines, and practices that might be labeled as "Mere Mormonism," inasmuch as they set forth the foundational, well-understood, and established tenets of the faith. Let me now, by way of summary, indicate first what I perceive to be those doctrinal matters that in many ways parallel the teachings of more traditional Christianity and then highlight what seem to be the doctrinal distinctives of The Church of Jesus Christ of Latter-day Saints.

Jesus Christ is the central figure in the doctrine and practice of The Church of Jesus Christ of Latter-day Saints. Joseph Smith explained that "the fundamental principles of our religion are the testimony of the Apostles and Prophets concerning Jesus Christ, that He died, was buried and rose again the third day, and ascended into heaven; and all other things which pertain to our religion are only appendages to it."[3] Latter-day Saints believe that complete salvation is possible only through the life, teachings, example, sufferings, substitutionary Atonement, death, and resurrection of Jesus Christ and in no other way.

From my perspective, the following would represent points that we have in common with more traditional Christians:

1. There is a purpose to life and we are not here by chance.

2. There is a God who lives, hears, and answers our prayers.

3. God is omnipotent, omniscient, and omnipresent; he possesses every Godly attribute in perfection. Further, there are absolute truths, absolute values that cannot be altered by society.

4. Jesus Christ is the Son of God, the Savior and Redeemer of all humankind.

5. The accounts contained in the New Testament of his divinity, his timeless teachings, his miracles, and his matchless life are historical, accurate, and true.

6. Through the Atonement of Christ we may be justified by faith in Jesus Christ, through a total trust, complete confidence and ready reliance upon his merits, mercy, and grace.

7. Jesus suffered and died on the cross as a substitutionary offering and rose from the dead to glorious immortality. Because he rose from the dead, all men and women will likewise be resurrected.

8. The Holy Spirit is a revelator, teacher, and comforter. In addition, through the Holy Spirit, we may be sanctified; in other words, we may be cleansed and purified in our actions, motives, and desires.

9. Our unreserved acceptance of Christ as Savior and Lord should be reflected in how we live our lives. Our lives should

begin to manifest the "fruit of the Spirit." In short, true faith always results in faithfulness.

10. While the Holy Spirit brings to us the "earnest of our inheritance" (Ephesians 1:13–14; 2 Corinthians 1:21–22; 5:5) and thus the assurance of salvation here, the full degree of salvation and glorification come hereafter.

11. The Church of Jesus Christ exists for the perfection of the Saints, for the work of the ministry, and for the edification of the body of Christ (Ephesians 4:11–12). It provides a means for group study and enlightenment, worship, organized sacrifice, and charitable giving.

12. One day Jesus Christ will come again to reign on this earth as King of kings and Lord of lords. For a thousand years Satan will be bound and goodness and righteousness will prevail.

Areas in which Latter-day Saints might differ from more traditional Christian churches in their views of Jesus Christ and the Plan of Salvation would include:

1. We are now living in the second stage of a three-part plan. We lived before we were born as spirit children of God.

2. God our Father, who possesses all godly attributes, is an exalted Man of Holiness who has a body of flesh and bones.

3. The Father, Son, and Holy Spirit are three distinct personages and three Gods. At the same time, Latter-day Saints do not consider themselves to be polytheistic. We believe there is one Godhead, thoroughly and completely united in mind, purpose, attributes, and love, called simply in scripture "God."

4. The gospel of Jesus Christ has been on the earth from the beginning. We believe in various dispensations or periods of time when the gospel or plan of salvation was on earth in its

fullness. Adam was the head of the first dispensation, and thus Adam and Eve were earth's first Christians.

5. Although the fall of Adam and Eve brought dramatic changes to life on earth, resulting in a need for an Atonement, on the whole the Fall "had a twofold direction—downward, yet forward. It brought man into the world and set his feet on progression's highway."

6. The Savior's suffering in the Garden of Gethsemane (as described in the New Testament) was redemptive in nature and thus part of the overall Atonement. What began in Gethsemane was completed on the Cross of Calvary.

7. The gospel of Jesus Christ is a gospel covenant, a two-way promise. God does for us what we could never do for ourselves, and we agree to do what we can do—all as extensions of our faith. Thus our good works are a *necessary* but *insufficient* condition for salvation.

8. There are certain ordinances or sacraments necessary for salvation. These are channels of divine power and grace, the outward expressions of inward covenants. The ordinances of themselves do not save us (Christ does), but they symbolize and reflect our full acceptance of the Master and his gospel covenant.

9. Some time after the first century of the Christian era, an apostasy or falling away took place, resulting in a loss of certain sacred truths and divine authority. This apostasy necessitated more than a Reformation, but instead a complete Restoration, which began with a call of a modern prophet, Joseph Smith, in the spring of 1820.

10. Subsequent heavenly messengers and divine communication (modern revelation) led to the reestablishment of the primitive Church, the delivery of additional scripture, an unfolding of doctrines and truths not found elsewhere in the

religious world, and priesthood or divine authority to act in the name of God.

11. Following his mortal death, Jesus Christ entered into a post-mortal spirit world where he preached the gospel, organized his servants in that realm, and commissioned them to make available the message of salvation to all the dead who would receive it.

12. Following death, men and women enter this postmortal spirit world, there to grow, expand in understanding, repent, and prepare for the resurrection.

13. All who have taken a physical body will eventually be resurrected—their spirits will be reunited with their bodies in an inseparable union. Following the resurrection, all men and women will be judged and inherit one of three kingdoms of glory hereafter (in descending order): celestial, terrestrial, and telestial.

14. Every person is entitled to be taught the gospel of Jesus Christ, either in this life or the next. Those who receive the gospel in the postmortal spirit world may then receive the requisite sacraments or ordinances by those mortal men and women who act as proxy for them in temples.

15. The family is the most important unit in time and eternity. The Church and all its organizations exist to bless individuals and families. Marriages performed in LDS temples are performed "for time and all eternity." Those who are true to their gospel covenant have the assurance that marriage and family will continue into eternity. This is one of the principal blessings of eternal life or salvation.

Some have suggested that The Church of Jesus Christ of Latter-day Saints seems to be moving into the mainstream of Christianity, or at least attempting to do so. What of this claim? For one thing, Latter-day Saint leaders *have* encouraged members of the Church to get to know their neighbors better, be more involved in community and civic and political affairs, show greater love, acceptance, and tolerance for those of other faiths, and in general help the world to know that we are not, strictly speaking, a weird bunch. Second, the Church is seeking to be better understood, to teach their doctrine in a manner that would (a) allow others to see clearly where we stand on important issues, and (b) eliminate misperceptions and misrepresentations. While there is, as we have suggested more than once in this book, a greater stress in the present Church upon the divine Sonship of Christ, the nature of his atoning sacrifice, and the vital place of his redeeming mercy and grace, these matters have been in LDS scripture since the days of Joseph Smith; what has changed is the emphasis, not the content.

While I mean no offense to anyone of another faith, it would be foolish for Latter-day Saints to stray from their moorings and seek to blend in with everyone else. People are joining The Church of Jesus Christ of Latter-day Saints in ever-increasing numbers, not because we are just like the Roman Catholics or the Orthodox or the Baptists or the Methodists or the Presbyterians down the street; they choose to leave their former faith and be baptized as Latter-day Saints because of the LDS distinctives. Our strength lies in our distinctive teachings and lifestyle. In that spirit, Gordon B. Hinckley, fifteenth president of the Church, said: "Our membership has grown. I believe it has grown in faithfulness.... Those who observe us say that we are moving into the mainstream of religion. We are not changing. The world's perception of us is changing. We teach the same doctrine. We have the same organization. We labor to perform the same good works. But the old hatred is disappearing; the old persecution is dying. People are better informed. They are coming to realize what we stand for and what we do."[4]

Latter-day Saints center their worship on, and direct their prayers to, God the Eternal Father. This, as with all things—sermons, testimonies, prayers, and sacraments or ordinances—they do in the name of Jesus Christ. The Latter-day Saints also worship Christ the Son as they acknowledge him as the source of truth and redemption, as the way to the Father. They look to him for deliverance and seek to emulate him, to be like him. David O. McKay, observed that "no man can sincerely resolve to apply to his daily life the teachings of Jesus of Nazareth without sensing a change in his own nature."[5]

This has, in fact, been my own experience. The more I come to know God and to know his Beloved Son, the more I look with love and compassion and interest and respect upon my brothers and sisters of all walks of life. My own feelings vibrate in harmony with the following reflections of Douglas John Hall: "I can say without any doubt at all that I am far more open to Jews and Muslims and Sikhs and humanists and all kinds of other human beings, including self-declared atheists, *because* of Jesus than I should ever have been *apart* from him. Precisely part of what I, for one, would have to mean by 'salvation' is being saved from the seemingly 'natural' but ultimately very destructive tendency of human beings to distrust and exclude others, especially those who are obviously 'other.'"[6]

Mormonism is here to stay. Joseph Smith knew opposition and bitterness and hostility from the time he announced that he had seen the Father and the Son in 1820 until his blood was shed in Carthage, Illinois in 1844. "And as for the perils which I am called to pass through," he wrote to the Saints, "they seem but a small thing to me, as the envy and wrath of man have been my common lot all the days of my life;…Deep water is what I am wont to swim in. It all has become a second nature to me; and I feel, like Paul, to glory in tribulation" (D&C 127:2).

In 1841, Joseph Smith spoke words that seem even more applicable to our own day than his. They bespeak, again, an optimism concerning the future of the Church, as well as the hope for tolerance on the part of those who believe differently. "The time was," he pointed out, "when we were looked upon as deceivers, and that 'Mormonism' would soon pass away, come to naught, and be forgotten. But the time is gone by when it is looked upon as a transient matter, or a bubble on the wave, and it is now taking a deep hold in the hearts and affections of all those, who are noble-minded enough to lay aside the prejudice of education and investigate the subject with candor and honesty. The truth, like the sturdy oak, has stood unhurt among the contending elements, which have beat upon it with tremendous force. The floods have rolled, wave after wave, in quick succession, and have not swallowed it up…nor have the flames of persecution, with all the influence of mobs, been able to destroy it; but like Moses' bush, it has stood unconsumed, and now at this moment presents an important spectacle both to men and angels… Stand fast, ye Saints of God, hold on a little while longer and the storm of life will be past, and you will be rewarded by that God whose servants you are, and who will duly appreciate all your toils and afflictions for Christ's sake and the Gospel's."[7]

ENDNOTES

1. Reported in *Deseret News*, 15 November 1997; see also *The Personal Beliefs of Jimmy Carter*, 185–99.

2. Young, *JD* 13:56.

3. Smith, *TPJS*, 121.

4. Hinckley, CR, October 2001, 3–4.

5. McKay, CR, April 1962, 7.

6. Hall, *Why Christian?* 34, emphasis in original.

7. Smith, *TPJS*, 184–85.

Bibliography

Ahlstrom, Sydney E., ed. *Theology in America*. Indianapolis: Bobbs-Merrill, 1967.

Albrecht, Stan L. "The Consequential Dimension to Mormon Religiosity." *Brigham Young University Studies*, vol. 29, no. 2, 1989.

Albrecht, Stan L. and Tim B. Heaton. "Secularization, Higher Education, and Religiosity." *Review of Religious Research*, vol. 26, no. 1, 1984.

Anderson, Richard Lloyd. *Understanding Paul*. Salt Lake City: Deseret Book, 1983.

Andrus, Hyrum L. and Helen Mae, eds. *They Knew the Prophet*. Salt Lake City: Bookcraft, 1974.

The Ante-Nicene Fathers, 10 vols. Ed. Alexander Roberts and James Donaldson. Grand Rapids, MI: Eerdmans, 1951.

Backman, Milton V., Jr. *American Religions and the Rise of Mormonism*. Salt Lake City: Deseret Book, 1965.

———. *Christian Churches in America: Origins and Beliefs*, rev. ed. New York: Charles Scribner's Sons, 1983.

Ballard, M. Russell. "What Matters Most Is What Lasts Longest." *Ensign*, November 2005.

Ballard, Melvin J. *Melvin J. Ballard: Crusader for Righteousness*. Salt Lake City: Bookcraft, 1966.

Balmer, Randall. *Growing Pains: Learning to Love My Father's Faith*. Grand Rapids, MI: Brazos Press, 2001.

Bangerter, William Grant. "It's a Two-Way Street." *1984–85 Brigham Young University Speeches of the Year*. Provo, UT: Brigham Young University Publications, 1985.

Benson, Ezra Taft. *The Teachings of Ezra Taft Benson*. Salt Lake City: Bookcraft, 1988.

————. *A Witness and a Warning*. Salt Lake City: Deseret Book, 1988.

Bercot, David W., ed. *A Dictionary of Early Christian Beliefs*. Peabody, MA: Hendrickson Publishers, 1998.

Bloesch, Donald. *Essentials of Evangelical Theology*. 2 vols. San Francisco: Harper, 1978.

Blomberg, Craig L. and Stephen E. Robinson. *How Wide the Divide? A Mormon and An Evangelical in Conversation*. Downers Grove, IL: InterVarsity Press, 1997.

Bloom, Harold. *The American Religion*. New York: Simon & Schuster, 1992.

Boyd, Gregory A. *God of the Possible*. Grand Rapids, MI: Baker Books, 2000.

Brown, Raymond E. *The Gospel and Epistles of John*. Collegeville, MN: Liturgical Press, 1988.

Bushman, Richard Lyman. *Believing History*. New York: Columbia University Press, 2004.

————. *Joseph Smith and the Beginnings of Mormonism*. Urbana: University of Illinois Press, 1984.

————. *Joseph Smith: Rough Stone Rolling*. New York: Alfred A. Knopf, 2005.

Callister, Tad R. *The Inevitable Apostasy and the Promised Restoration*. Salt Lake City: Deseret Book, 2006.

————. *The Infinite Atonement*. Salt Lake City: Deseret Book, 2000.

Campbell, Alexander. *The Christian Baptist*, 7 vols., 13th ed. revised. Ed. D. S. Burnet. Bethany, WV: H. S. Bosworth, 1861.

Carter, Jimmy. *The Personal Beliefs of Jimmy Carter*. New York: Three Rivers Press, 1997.

Carter, Stephen L. *The Culture of Disbelief: How American Law and Politics Trivialize Religious Devotion*. New York: HarperCollins, 1993.

Chadwick, Bruce R. and Brent L. Top, "Religiosity and Delinquency among LDS Adolescents." *Journal for the Scientific Study of Religion*, vol. 32, no. 1, 1993.

Chesterton, G. K. *St. Thomas Aquinas*. New York: Sheed & Ward, 1954.

Church News. Salt Lake City: The Church of Jesus Christ of Latter-day Saints, 28 February 1953; 3 June 2000; 3 December 2005.

Conference Report. Salt Lake City: The Church of Jesus Christ of Latter-day Saints, April 1906; April 1907; October 1912; April 1928; October 1936; October 1951; April 1962; April 1968; April 1971; April 1972; April 1973; April 1977; October 1977; October 1979; October 1981; October 1983; October 1984; October 1986; April 1992; April 1994; October 1994; April 1995; October 1995; April 1998; October 1998; April 1999; October 1999; April 2000; October 2001; October 2004; April 2005; October 2005.

Cowley and Whitney on Doctrine. Compiled by Forace Green. Salt Lake City: Bookcraft, 1963.

Davies, Paul. *God and the New Physics*. New York: Simon & Schuster, 1983.

DeMaris, Richard E. "Corinthian Religion and Baptism for the Dead (1 Corinthians 15:29): Insights from Archaeology and Anthropology." *Journal of Biblical Literature* 114/4, 1995.

Diary of Charles L. Walker, 2 vols. Ed. by A. Karl and Katherine Miles Larsen. Logan, UT: Utah State University Press, 1980.

Duke, James T. *Latter-day Saint Social Life: Social Research on the LDS Church and its Members*. Provo, UT: Brigham Young University Religious Studies Center, 1998.

Ehrman, Bart D. *Misquoting Jesus*. San Francisco: HarperSanFrancisco, 2005.

Erickson, Millard. *Making Sense of the Trinity*. Grand Rapids, MI: Baker, 2000.

Eusebius. *The History of the Church*. Tr. by G. A. Williamson. Revised and edited with a new introduction by Andrew Louth. New York: Penguin Books, 1965.

Family Home Evening Manual. Salt Lake City: The Church of Jesus Christ of Latter-day Saints, 1965.

Faust, James E. *Finding Light in a Dark World.* Salt Lake City: Deseret Book, 1995.

Fee, Gordon D. *The First Epistle to the Corinthians.* Grand Rapids, MI: Eerdmans, 1987.

Fortman, Edward J. *The Triune God: A Historical Study of the Doctrine of the Trinity.* Philadelphia: Westminster Press, 1972.

Four Views on Salvation in a Pluralistic World. Ed. Dennis L. Okholm and Timothy R. Phillips. Grand Rapids, MI: Zondervan, 1996.

Frankl, Victor. *Man's Search for Meaning.* New York: Washington Square Press, 1985.

Goppelt, Leonhard. *A Commentary on 1 Peter.* Ed. Ferdinand Hahn. Tr. John E. Alsup. Grand Rapids, MI: Eerdmans, 1993.

Hafen, Bruce C. *The Broken Heart.* Salt Lake City: Deseret Book, 1989.

Hafen, Bruce C. and Marie K. Hafen. *The Belonging Heart.* Salt Lake City: Deseret Book, 1994.

Hahn, Scott and Kimberly. *Rome Sweet Home.* San Francisco: Ignatius Press, 1993.

Hall, Douglas John. *Why Christian? For Those on the Edge of Faith.* Minneapolis: Fortress Press, 1998.

Harper's Bible Dictionary. Ed. by Paul J. Achtemeier. San Francisco: Harper & Row, 1985.

Hatch, Edwin. *The Influence of Greek Ideas on Christianity.* Gloucester, MA: Peter Smith Publishers, 1970.

Hatch, Nathan. *The Democratization of American Christianity.* New Haven: Yale University Press, 1989.

Hinckley, Gordon B. "Excerpts from Recent Addresses of President Gordon B. Hinckley." *Ensign,* February 1998.

————. *Faith, The Essence of True Religion.* Salt Lake City: Deseret Book, 1989.

————. "Joseph Smith Jr., Prophet of God, Mighty Servant." *Ensign,* December 2005.

————. *Teachings of Gordon B. Hinckley.* Salt Lake City: Deseret Book, 1997.

————. "The Continuous Pursuit of Truth." *Ensign,* April 1986.

History of The Church of Jesus Christ of Latter-day Saints, 7 vols., ed. B. H. Roberts. Salt Lake City: Deseret Book, 1957.

Hymns of The Church of Jesus Christ of Latter-day Saints. Salt Lake City: The Church of Jesus Christ of Latter-day Saints, 1985.

Ice, Jackson Lee and John J. Carey, eds. *The Death of God Debate.* Philadelphia: Westminster Press, 1967.

Jackson, Kent P. "Latter-day Saints: A Dynamic Scriptural Process," in *The Holy Book in Comparative Perspective.* Ed. Frederick M. Denny and Rodney L. Taylor. Columbia, SC: University of South Carolina Press, 1985.

Jeffress, Robert. *Grace Gone Wild.* Colorado Springs, CO: Water Brook Press, 2005.

The Jerome Biblical Commentary. Ed. Raymond E. Brown, Joseph A. Fitzmeyer, and Roland E. Murphy. Englewood Cliffs, NJ: Prentice Hall, 1968.

Journal of Discourses. 26 vols. Liverpool: F. D. Richards & Sons, 1851–86.

Kärkkäinen, Veli-matti. *One with God: Salvation as Deification and Justification.* Collegeville, Minnesota: Liturgical Press, 2004.

Kimball, Spencer W. *Faith Precedes the Miracle.* Salt Lake City: Deseret Book, 1974.

————. *The Miracle of Forgiveness.* Salt Lake City: Bookcraft, 1969.

Kreeft, Peter. *Back to Virtue: Traditional Moral Wisdom for Modern Moral Confusion.* San Francisco: Ignatius Press, 1992.

Kugel, James L. *The God of Old: Inside the Lost World of the Bible.* New York: Free Press, 2003.

Kugelman, Richard. "The First Letter to the Corinthians." In *The Jerome Biblical Commentary*. 2 vols. Ed. Raymond E. Brown, Joseph A. Fitzmyer, and Roland E. Murphy. Englewood Cliffs, New Jersey: Prentice-Hall, 1968.

Lee, Harold B. "Be Loyal to the Royal Within You," *1973 Brigham Young University Speeches of the Year.* Provo, UT: Brigham Young University Publications, 1974.

———. *Stand Ye in Holy Places.* Salt Lake City: Deseret Book, 1974.

———. *The Teachings of Harold B. Lee.* Ed. Clyde J. Williams. Salt Lake City: Bookcraft, 1996.

Lewis, C. S. *Christian Reflections.* San Francisco: HarperCollins, 1967.

———. *Mere Christianity.* New York: Touchstone, 1996.

———. *Miracles.* New York: Touchstone, 1996.

———. *The Problem of Pain.* New York: Touchstone, 1996.

———. *The Weight of Glory and Other Addresses.* New York: Touchstone, 1996.

Lucado, Max. *Just Like Jesus.* Dallas: W Publishing Group, 2003.

Lundwall, N. B., compiler. *The Vision.* Salt Lake City: Bookcraft, n.d.

MacArthur, John F. *The Glory of Heaven: The Truth about Heaven, Angels, and Eternal Life.* Wheaton, IL: Crossway Books, 1996.

———. *The Vanishing Conscience: Drawing the Line in a No-fault Guilt-free World.* Dallas: Word Publishing, 1994.

———. *Why One Way?* Nashville: W Publishing, 2002.

The MacArthur Study Bible. Ed. John MacArthur. Nashville: Word, 1997.

Madsen, Truman G. *Eternal Man.* Salt Lake City: Deseret Book, 1970.

———. "The Latter-day Saint View of Human Nature," in *On Human Nature: The Jerusalem Center Symposium.* Ed. Truman G. Madsen, David Noel Freedman, and Pam Fox Kuhlken. Ann Arbor, MI: Pryor Pettengill Publishers, 2004.

Martin, Walter. *The New Cults*. Ventura, CA: Regal Books, 1980.

Matthews, Robert J. "Using the Scriptures." *Brigham Young University Fireside and Devotional Speeches*. Provo, UT: Brigham Young University Publications, 1981.

Maxwell, Neal A. *One More Strain of Praise*. Salt Lake City: Bookcraft, 1999.

———. *Plain and Precious Things*. Salt Lake City: Deseret Book, 1983.

———. *That My Family Should Partake*. Salt Lake City: Deseret Book, 1974.

———. *Things as They Really Are*. Salt Lake City: Deseret Book Co., 1978.

———. "This Is a Special Institution." *Profile Magazine*. Brigham Young University-Hawaii, December 1994.

McConkie, Bruce R. *A New Witness for the Articles of Faith*. Salt Lake City: Deseret Book, 1985.

———. *Doctrines of the Restoration: Sermons and Writings of Bruce R. McConkie*. Ed. Mark L. McConkie. Salt Lake City: Bookcraft, 1989.

———. *The Mortal Messiah*, 4 books. Salt Lake City: Deseret Book, 1979–81.

———. "Succession in the Presidency." *1974 Brigham Young University Speeches of the Year*. Provo, UT: Brigham Young University Publications, 1975.

———. "What Think Ye of Salvation By Grace?" *1983–84 Brigham Young University Speeches of the Year*. Provo, UT: Brigham Young University Publications, 1984.

McConkie, Joseph F. "The Principle of Revelation." *Studies in Scripture*, 8 vols. Ed. Kent P. Jackson and Robert L. Millet. Salt Lake City: Deseret Book, 1985–89.

———. *Sons and Daughters of God*. Salt Lake City: Bookcraft, 1994.

McDannell, Colleen and Bernhard Lange. *Heaven: A History*. New Haven: Yale University Press, 1988.

McDermott, Gerald R. *Jonathan Edwards Confronts the Gods*. New York: Oxford University Press, 2000.

McDonald, Lee M. *The Formation of the Christian Biblical Canon*, rev. ed. Peabody, MA: Hendrickson Publishers, 1995.

McDowell, *Right from Wrong: What You Need to Know to Help Youth Make Right Choices*. Dallas: Word Publishing, 1994.

McKay, David O. *Gospel Ideals*. Salt Lake City: *Improvement Era*, 1953.

Messages of the First Presidency, 6 vols. Ed. James R. Clark. Salt Lake City: Bookcraft, 1965–75.

Millet, Robert L. *A Different Jesus? The Christ of the Latter-day Saints*. Grand Rapids, MI: Eerdmans, 2005.

———. *Are We There Yet?* Salt Lake City: Deseret Book, 2005.

———. *Getting at the Truth: Responding to Difficult Questions about LDS Beliefs*. Salt Lake City: Deseret Book, 2004.

———. *Grace Works*. Salt Lake City: Deseret Book, 2003.

Millet, Robert L. and Kent P. Jackson, eds. *Studies in Scripture, Volume 1: The Doctrine and Covenants*. Salt Lake City: Deseret Book, 1989.

Montgomery, John Warwick. *History and Christianity*. San Bernadino, CA: Here's Life Publishers, 1983.

Morris, Leon. *The Gospel According to John*. Grand Rapids, MI: Eerdmans, 1971.

Morrison, Alexander B. *Turning from Truth: A New Look at the Great Apostasy*. Salt Lake City: Deseret Book, 2005.

Mouw, Richard J. *Calvinism in the Las Vegas Airport: Making Connections in Today's World*. Grand Rapids, MI: Zondervan, 2004.

———. Uncommon *Decency: Christian Civility in an Uncivil World*. Downers Grove, IL: InterVarsity Press, 1992.

Muggeridge, Malcolm. *Jesus: The Man Who Lives*. New York: Harper & Row, 1975.

Neuhaus, Richard John. *Catholic Matters: Confusion, Controversy, and the Splendor of Truth*. New York: Basic Books, 2006.

———. *Death on a Friday Afternoon*. New York: Basic Books, 2000.

The New Shorter Oxford English Dictionary, 2 vols. Oxford: Oxford University Press, 1993.

Nibley, Hugh. *The World and the Prophets*. Salt Lake City: F.A.R.M.S. and Deseret Book, 1987.

Oaks, Dallin H. *The Lord's Way*. Salt Lake City: Deseret Book, 1991.

Oaks, Dallin H. and Lance B. Wickman, "The Missionary Work of The Church of Jesus Christ of Latter-day Saints," *Sharing the Book: Religious Perspectives on the Rights and Wrongs of Proselytism*. Ed. John Witte Jr. and Richard C. Martin. Maryknoll, NY: Orbis Books, 1999.

Ostling, Richard N. and Joan K. Ostling, *Mormon America*. San Francisco: Harper, 1999.

Outler, Albert C. and Richard P. Heitzenrater, eds. *John Wesley's Sermons: An Anthology*. Nashville: Abington Press, 1991.

Packer, Boyd K. *That All May Be Edified*. Salt Lake City: Bookcraft, 1982.

———. "The Great Plan of Happiness." Seventeenth Annual Church Educational System Religious Educators' Symposium, 10 August 1993.

———. "The Light of Christ." *Ensign*, April 2005.

Packer, J. I. and Thomas C. Oden, eds. *One Faith: The Evangelical Consensus*. Downers Grove, IL: InterVarsity Press, 2004.

Pagels, Elaine. *Adam, Eve, and the Serpent*. New York: Random House, 1988.

Paulsen, David L. "The Doctrine of Divine Embodiment: Restoration, Judeo-Christian, and Philosophical Perspectives." *Brigham Young University Studies*, vol. 35, no. 4, 1996.

Penrose, Charles W. *Mormon Doctrine*. Salt Lake City: George Q. Cannon & Sons, 1897.

Philips, J. B. *The Young Church in Action*. London: Collins, 1955.

———. *Your God Is Too Small*. New York: Touchstone, 1997.

Pinnock, Clark H. *Most Moved Mover: A Theology of God's Openness*. Grand Rapids, MI: Baker Books, 2001.

Pinnock, Clark, Richard Rice, John Sanders, William Hasker, and David Basinger. *The Openness of God: A Biblical Challenge to the Traditional Understanding of God*. Downers Grove, IL: InterVarsity Press, 1994.

Plantinga, Cornelius. *Not the Way It's Supposed to Be: A Breviary of Sin*. Grand Rapids, MI: Eerdmans, 1995.

Pratt, Orson. *Masterful Discourses and Writings of Orson Pratt*. Salt Lake City: Bookcraft, 1962.

Pratt, Parley P. *Autobiography of Parley P. Pratt*. Salt Lake City: Deseret Book, 1976.

————. *Key to the Science of Theology*. Salt Lake City: Deseret Book, 1978.

Proust, Marcel. In Gabriel Marcel, *Homo Viator*. New York: Harper & Row, 1963.

Rahner, Karl. *The Trinity*. New York: Herder and Herder, 1970.

Remini, Robert. *Joseph Smith*. New York: Lipper/Viking, 2002.

Richards, LeGrand. *A Marvelous Work and a Wonder*. Salt Lake City: Deseret Book, 1950.

Roberts, B. H. *The Gospel: An Exposition of Its First Principles and Man's Relationship to Deity*. Salt Lake City: Deseret Book, 1966.

Robinson, Stephen E. *Are Mormons Christians?* Salt Lake City: Bookcraft, 1991.

Romney, Marion G. *Learning for the Eternities*. Salt Lake City: Deseret Book, 1977.

Rowe, David L. *I Love Mormons: A New Way to Share Christ with Latter-day Saints*. Grand Rapids, MI: Baker Books, 2005.

Sanders, John. *No Other Name*. Grand Rapids, MI: Eerdmans, 1992.

————, ed. *What about Those Who Have Never Heard?* Downers Grove, IL: InterVarsity Press, 1995.

Shipps, Jan. *Mormonism: The Story of a New Religious Tradition*. Urbana, IL: University of Illinois Press, 1985.

Shoemaker, Donald P. "Why Your Neighbor Joined the Mormon Church." *Christianity Today*, 11 October 1974.

Sider, Ronald J. *The Scandal of the Evangelical Conscience: Why Are Christians Living Just Like the Rest of the World?* Grand Rapids, MI: Baker Books, 2005.

Smith, Joseph. *Lectures on Faith*. Salt Lake City: Deseret Book, 1985.

———. *The Personal Writings of Joseph Smith*, rev. ed. Ed. Dean C. Jessee. Salt Lake City: Deseret Book, 2002.

———. *Teachings of the Prophet Joseph Smith*. Selected by Joseph Fielding Smith. Salt Lake City: Deseret Book, 1976.

———. *The Words of Joseph Smith: The Contemporary Accounts of the Nauvoo Discourses of the Prophet Joseph*. Ed. Andrew F. Ehat and Lyndon W. Cook. Provo, UT: Brigham Young University Religious Studies Center, 1980.

Smith, Joseph F. *Gospel Doctrine*. Salt Lake City: Deseret Book, 1971.

Smith, Joseph Fielding. Address given at the funeral of Richard L. Evans, 4 November 1971, transcript.

———. *Doctrines of Salvation*. 3 vols. Compiled by Bruce R. McConkie. Salt Lake City: Bookcraft, 1954–56.

Snow, Lorenzo. *The Teachings of Lorenzo Snow*. Ed. Clyde J. Williams. Salt Lake City: Bookcraft, 1996.

Stackhouse, John G. Jr. *Evangelical Landscapes: Facing Critical Issues of the Day*. Grand Rapids, MI: Baker Books, 2002.

———. *Humble Apologetics: Defending the Faith Today*. New York: Oxford University Press, 2002.

Stanley, Charles. *The Blessings of Brokenness: Why God Allows Us to Go Through Hard Times*. Grand Rapids, MI: Zondervan, 1997.

Stark, Rodney L. "The Rise of a New World Faith." *Review of Religious Research*, vol. 26, no. 1, 1984.

Steinfels, Peter. "Despite Growth, Mormons Find New Hurdles." *New York Times*, 15 September 1991.

Stott, John. *Authentic Christianity from the Writings of John Stott*. Ed. Timothy Dudley-Smith. Downers Grove, IL: InterVarsity Press, 1995.

———. *Life in Christ*. Wheaton, IL: Tyndale House Publishers, 1991.

———. *Why I Am a Christian*. Downers Grove, IL: InterVarsity Press, 2003.

Strobel, Lee. *The Case for Christ*. Grand Rapids, MI: Zondervan, 1988.

Swinburne, Richard. *Is There a God?* New York: Oxford University Press, 1996.

Swinton, Heidi. *American Prophet*. Salt Lake City: Shadow Mountain, 1999.

Talmage, James E. *The Articles of Faith*. Salt Lake City: The Church of Jesus Christ of Latter-day Saints, 1975.

———. "The Eternity of Sex." *Young Woman's Journal*, vol. 25, October 1914.

Taylor, Barbara Brown. *Speaking of Sin: The Lost Language of Salvation*. Cambridge, MA: Cowley Publications, 2000.

The New International Version Study Bible. Ed. Kenneth Barker. Grand Rapids, MI: Zondervan, 1985.

Top, Brent L. and Bruce R. Chadwick, "The Power of the Word: Religion, Family, Friends, and Delinquent Behavior of LDS Youth," *Brigham Young University Studies*, vol. 33, no. 2, 1993.

Webster, Noah. *American Dictionary of the English Language, 1828*, 4th ed. San Francisco: Foundation for American Christian Education, 1985.

Whitney, Orson F. *Life of Heber C. Kimball*. Salt Lake City: Bookcraft, 1978.

Wilkinson, Bruce. *A Life God Rewards*. Sisters, OR: Multnomah Publishers, 2002.

Willard, Dallas. *The Divine Conspiracy: Rediscovering Our Hidden Life in God*. San Francisco: HarperSanFrancisco, 1998.

Williams, Rowan. *Christ on Trial: How the Gospel Unsettles Our Judgment*. Grand Rapids, MI: Eerdmans, 2000.

Wilson, James. *The Moral Sense*. New York: MacMillan, 1993.

Woodruff, Wilford. *The Discourses of Wilford Woodruff*. Ed. G. Homer Durham. Salt Lake City: Bookcraft, 1969.

Wordsworth, William. "Ode: Intimations of Immortality from Recollections of Early Childhood." *English Romantic Poetry and Prose*. Ed. Alfred Noyes. New York: Oxford University Press, 1956.

Wright, N. T. *The Last Word: Beyond the Bible Wars to a New Understanding of the Authority of Scripture*. San Francisco: HarperSanFrancisco, 2005.

———. *Simply Christian: Why Christianity Makes Sense*. San Francisco: HarperSanFrancisco, 2006.

Yancey, Philip. *The Jesus I Never Knew*. Grand Rapids, MI: Zondervan, 1995.

Young, Joseph. "Vocal Music." *History of the Organization of the Seventies*. Salt Lake City: Deseret News Steam Printing Establishment, 1878.

Index